Easy Sewing With Knits

Easy Sewing With Knits

Judy Lawrence

COUNTRYSIDE PRESS

a division of Farm Journal, Inc., Philadelphia

Distributed to the trade by Doubleday & Company, Inc., Garden City, New York

Drawings: Judy Lawrence
Fashion illustrations: Carol Edgecomb
Cover and book design: Ben Feder, Inc.

Published by Countryside Press, a division of Farm Journal, Inc.
Distributed to the trade by Doubleday & Company, Inc.

Library of Congress Catalog Card Number 72-77659

Contents

Knits—A Whole New Way to Sew

Home sewing is booming all over the country—and knit fabrics are helping it happen. Sewing with stretchable knits is easy, but they do handle differently from the familiar woven fabrics. You just can't follow some of the old rules.

This book, "Easy Sewing with Knits," has the new sewing techniques that will help you make, in less time, garments that fit well. In this one volume, Judy Lawrence gives you both a reference book and a home-study course. It's backed by her experience in teaching women and girls how to sew with knits. As consultant for The Singer Company, Mrs. Lawrence worked with the Singer Educational Department to develop their basic knit sewing course. Questions and problems of home sewing enthusiasts all over the country have helped her write this book.

It will tell you how to sew stretch into seams—with *any* sewing machine . . . how to fit and adjust any pattern for knits. You can save money and time by using a few basic patterns for your complete wardrobe—change the style lines of patterns and use a variety of trims and finishes for individual-looking outfits.

No doubt everybody in your family has discovered the comfort and practicality of wearing knits. Now discover the reward of sewing with knits. You'll find that it's fun—and easy.

JEAN GILLIES
Associate Editor
Farm Journal

1

What You Need To Know About Knit Fabrics

Knit fabrics are comfortable to wear, simple to care for and easy to sew. As their popularity grows, so does your choice of knits for home sewing—in both natural and synthetic fibers. All over the country, you'll find fabric stores specializing in knits, along with trims and elastics to go with them. You can choose from delicate acrylic laces for party dresses, lightweight cotton knits for tops, firm polyesters for suits, heavy-duty nylon for sportswear and wool sweater knits for sweaters and dresses.

TYPES OF KNITS

Some knit fabrics can be fashioned into almost anything, while others are limited in their use. As you handle knits, you'll soon recognize what weight and firmness to choose for a shirt, a skirt or a suit. Also, the general characteristics of each knit type, which are described here, can help guide you.

Doubleknits

Firm doubleknits hold their shape well and are a delight to sew and wear. They are made on machines with two beds of needles; so, the fabrics actually are two single layers knitted together. Doubleknits appear to be the same on both sides unless a texture or pattern is knit into them.

WHAT TO SEW FROM DOUBLEKNITS: Look for patterns with simple lines. Doubleknits are thick; so, they do not adapt well to gathered styles. Seam shaping, darts, eased fullness and soft pleats are suitable. You can have beautiful pocket, collar and banding details; topstitching also is attractive. Use doubleknits for dresses, suits, pants, shirts, skirts, vests, lightweight coats, children's garments and menswear.

Single knits

Single knits are lightweight fabrics, made on machines with only one set of needles. They have definite right and wrong sides, and you often find single knits in tube form. Since they do not keep their shape as well as doubleknits, these fabrics are not suitable for pants or straight skirts.

WHAT TO SEW FROM SINGLE KNITS: This type of fabric adapts well to the skinny look and to soft lines with eased fullness, gathers or draping. Use them for sporty, casual or dressy garments, depending on the particular fabric. You should interface collars, cuffs and other sharp details to add body. Single knits can be made into tops, gathered skirts, dresses, men's shirts and children's wear.

Warp knits for outerwear

The two main types of warp knits are tricot and raschel, and they take their names from the machines that knit them. In tricot knits, you'll see vertical rows of loops on the right side and horizontal rows of loops on the wrong side. For years, "tricot" meant fabrics for lingerie and bonding. Today, tricot warp knits are turning up in outerwear fabrics, and they are especially important in menswear. Warp knits generally are more firm than doubleknits, and they are less likely to snag.

Raschel knits are made on special machines that produce a wide variety of knits, including lacy, openwork designs.

WHAT TO SEW FROM WARP KNITS: Firm, tricot warp knits for outerwear adapt well to almost any pattern. Use them for dresses, tops, pants, vests and skirts. Raschel knits generally have so much surface detail that you will want to select patterns with simple lines.

Lingerie knits

Tricot warp knits for lingerie generally are made from nylon yarns and come in sheer, medium and heavy weights. The greatest stretch is across the width of the fabric, and you may find these knits up to 108" wide.

WHAT TO SEW FROM LINGERIE TRICOT: You can make slips, panties, sleepwear, scarfs and boutique items, such as slippers and curler bonnets.

Sweater knits

Sweater knits look and act like hand knits. They stretch freely in both directions and shape to the body; many times they have a loose, bulky look. You will find sweater knits with a ribbed, textured or flat surface; they are sold by the yard.

Sweater bodies are tubes of sweater knit that have a ribbed bottom edge. They come in various widths and lengths, and you may need more than one tube to make a complete sweater. The sweater bodies are treated in the manufacturing process so they will not ravel when cut. You often can buy matching strips of ribbing to use as neck trims.

WHAT TO SEW FROM SWEATER KNITS: Use patterns designed for knits. You will need little or no ease in the finished garment. Look for straight-cut styles with no darts. You can use sweater knits for dresses, tops, vests and pants.

Ribbing

Ribbing is a special knit trim for the neck and arm openings on knit tops, shirts and dresses. It has a great deal of stretch and bounces back to its original size. Most ribbing comes on a bolt, and you buy it as regular yardage. With this, you can make a trim any width you choose. Other ribbing is knitted to a finished width and sold in the same manner as braid or ribbon.

NOTE: Do not confuse special ribbing with regular knit fabric that has a rib design, such as the knit used in poor-boy shirts. Do not preshrink ribbing.

Power net

Even though power net is lightweight, it has great strength and stretch. It is used for undergarments.

WHAT TO SEW FROM POWER NET: Look for special patterns designed for girdles and bras to be made from power net.

FIBERS FOR KNITS

The most common fibers used in knitted fabrics are listed here alphabetically—by their generic names. You will find some trademarks for the synthetic fibers, although the list is not all-inclusive. You'll also find care suggestions for each fiber.

Acetate

Acetate, a cellulose fiber, takes a wide range of colors and has a luxurious feel.

CARE: You should dry-clean most acetate knits. Occasionally, you will find one marked "washable," but take care to avoid setting wrinkles. Use mild lukewarm suds, and gently squeeze them through the fabric; rinse in lukewarm water. Shake the garment out, and let it drip-dry. Press the garment on the wrong side while it is still damp, using the lowest setting on the iron. Remember that perfume and fingernail polish remover will damage acetate.

TRADEMARKS INCLUDE: Avisco, Estron.

Acrylic

Acrylic, a man-made fiber, can be knit into a variety of textures and weights. The fabrics go into pants, tops, dresses, suits and sweaters.

CARE: Wash delicate acrylic garments by hand in warm water. Rinse thoroughly, and use a fabric softener in the final rinse. You can wash and dry other garments by machine. Use a low temperature setting for the dryer, and remove garments as soon as the tumbling stops. Turn all acrylic garments inside out before washing; this helps prevent fuzz balls from forming on the right side, because of friction.

TRADEMARKS INCLUDE: Acrilan, Creslan, Orlon

Alpaca

Alpaca is a natural fiber and comes from an animal by that name in South America. It is knit into fabric and sold by the yard for sweaters and dresses (usually two-piece). Fabric of pure alpaca or alpaca-wool blend is not available in all areas; it is found most often in knit fabric stores. (Alpaca is sometimes classified as wool.)

CARE: Alpaca knits should be dry-cleaned for best results. It is not necessary to preshrink alpaca. However, you should place the fabric on a flat surface and allow it to relax overnight before you cut it.

Cotton

Cotton makes an easy-care and comfortable knit fabric. The fibers absorb body moisture; it's cool to wear in summer. Cotton is ideal for babies because of its absorption and also because it is non-allergenic.

Cotton is used in single, double and other types of knits, with either a flat or textured surface. Some single knit cottons tend to roll at the edges after you preshrink them. You can control this rolling by spraying the edges with fabric finish, then pressing lightly.

Most cottons are knit in a tube or are sewn into a tube after knitting. Open the tube after you preshrink the fabric.

When processed in the mill, cottons are pressed with much heat and pressure; permanent creases are formed. Avoid these creases when you cut your garment.

Cotton knit does not adapt well to women's dresses or pants because it will bag in the seat and knee areas. It is acceptable for children's dresses and pants.

Cotton velour is a luxurious, but machine-washable knit. Velour has a nap just like velvet; you must place your pattern pieces on the fabric so they all run in the same direction. It is beautiful for tops and robes. You also see it in dresses and pants, but these tend to bag in the seat and knee areas.

Cotton stretch terry has a looped surface. It also has a nap; so, take care when you place your pattern on the fabric. Stretch terry makes beautiful baby clothes and knit tops for the whole family.

CARE: Cotton can be washed and dried by machine, using a warm or hot temperature. Some bulky cottons (including stretch terry) come in tubes and will twist in the washing and drying processes. To preserve the straight of grain, stitch across the open ends of the tube to close them before preshrinking.

Metallic

Metallic fibers may be metal, plastic-coated metal, metal-coated plastic or a core covered by metal. Metallic fibers are used in fabrics and trims for dressy evening wear.

CARE: Follow the bolt-end instructions for washing or cleaning.

Nylon

Nylon is a man-made fiber that is strong, elastic and very resistant to abrasion. It is easy to wash and dry; so, it's ideal for children's clothes and sportswear. Nylon is made into a variety of fabrics—from heavy knits for swim wear to lightweight knits for lingerie. Helenca and Ban-Lon are texturizing processes often used on nylon yarns.

CARE: Wash delicate nylon garments in warm water by hand or on the delicate cycle in your automatic washer. You can wash and dry other garments by machine. Add a fabric softener to the final rinse, and remove garments from the dryer as soon as the machine stops. Press with a warm iron.

Separate colors when you wash nylon; white nylon picks up any stray color in the wash water.

TRADEMARKS INCLUDE: Antron, Caprolan, Enkalure

Polyester

Polyester is a man-made fiber widely used for knit fabrics. It is wrinkle-resistant, easy to wash and dry and takes dye beautifully. It goes into a variety of knit fabrics, and it's the traveler's best friend.

CARE: Wash delicate garments by hand or on the delicate cycle in your washer; add fabric softener to the final rinse. Other garments can be washed and dried by machine. Always use a warm iron for pressing, and avoid placing the iron on the right side of the fabric without a press cloth.

You can remove most stains if you rub liquid detergent into the stain before you wash the garment.

TRADEMARKS INCLUDE: Dacron, Encron, Fortrel, Kodel, Trevira

Polyester/cotton blend

Fabric of polyester/cotton blend is used for sportswear; shape retention is better than with all-cotton. It washes and dries easily and is wrinkle-resistant.

CARE: Give special attention to oil-based stains. Treat stains with liquid detergent before washing.

Polyester/wool blend

The fabric usually is composed of 70 percent polyester and 30 percent wool. It has the look and feel of wool, but you can wash it in your machine.

CARE: Machine-wash fabric in warm water, and machine-dry it at a low temperature. Remove it from the dryer immediately after the tumbling action stops.

Rayon

Rayon, a cellulose fiber, works best for garments that do not get hard wear.

CARE: Dry-clean rayon knits for best results.

TRADEMARKS INCLUDE: Avril, Zantrel

Spandex

Spandex is man-made, has great elasticity, is stronger and more durable than rubber. It is used alone in power net for foundation garments, or it is mixed with other fibers to produce stretch fabrics for swimsuits.

CARE: All-spandex foundation garments or other apparel can be washed by machine or by hand in lukewarm water. If bleach is needed, use oxygen or sodium perborate instead of chlorine bleach. You can machine-dry garments at a low temperature, but they will wear better if you let them drip-dry. Any clothing made of spandex mixed with other fibers should be handled as recommended for the other fiber.

TRADEMARK: Lycra

Triacetate

Triacetate is another cellulose fiber used in many knits. It resists shrinking, wrinkling and fading. Often, triacetate is permanently pleated for skirts and hostess pants.

CARE: Triacetate washes easily. Hand-launder pleated garments for best results. Use the automatic washer and dryer for most other triacetate knits. You can use a higher ironing temperature for triacetate than for acetate.

TRADEMARK: Arnel

Wool

Wool is one of the most popular fibers for knits because it is warm to wear and easy to handle. You'll find it in single knit jerseys, sweater knits and the popular doubleknits. Wool is used in almost every type of garment; it tends to keep its shape without sagging or bagging.

CARE: Dry-clean wool for best results, unless care directions tell you otherwise. You should preshrink wool before you cut it. The easiest method for the home sewer is to put the *dry* wool yardage in the automatic dryer with some damp clothes. Let the fabric and clothes tumble together about 15 minutes; moisture from the damp clothes and the heat of the dryer will do the job. Do not use damp clothes that will put lint on the wool fabric.

Press wool on the wrong side, always using a press cloth. When you press garments, use steam generously in the seam areas.

PRESHRINK YOUR FABRIC

You should preshrink all knits, except alpaca and ribbing for trim, before you cut them. Most knits, especially cotton, will shrink. You must understand this if you are to have good results in sewing with knits. Usually you will buy the popular cotton knit top one or two sizes too large because you expect it to shrink in the wash. When you make it yourself, you can get rid of that shrinkage before you cut your garment. Then you won't have to wonder whether washing or dry cleaning will alter the fit.

To preshrink a fabric, follow the same method you will use later to clean the garment. Most knits are washable, but a few, such as wool and some acetate, must be dry-cleaned. Check the bolt ends for the fiber content when you buy, and refer to "Fibers for knits" in the preceding section for care and cleaning recommendations.

NOTE: Allow extra fabric for shrinkage when you shop. Cotton needs an additional 4″ to 5″ for each yard your pattern requires. Most other fabrics shrink very little, but sometimes this is enough to make a great difference in fit. Allow an extra 2″ to 3″ per yard for knits other than cotton.

BUYING TIPS

Check both sides of the fabric carefully to make sure there are no flaws. This is more important when you are buying mill-end knit fabrics.

Occasionally, you will find some patterned or striped knit fabric that has been pulled out of shape. The design looks crooked. This happens in the finishing process when the knit is given a final press. Avoid this kind of fabric because it is almost impossible to straighten the design. You will have problems matching the design at the seams.

2

How to Choose and Fit Patterns for Knits

Simple styles with few seams are best for most knits. You'll find a large choice of patterns available, with many designed especially for knit fabrics. You can use conventional patterns, of course, but you may have to alter some of them to insure a good fit in knits. This chapter explains the various types of patterns on the market. It also gives you a "Fit and ease guide" for checking patterns, along with helps for laying out the pattern and for cutting your fabric.

PATTERNS FROM COUNTER CATALOGS

You'll find three types of patterns offered by large companies (like Butterick, McCall's, Simplicity and Vogue). There are the regular conventional patterns, plus two newer groups —those "for stretchable knits only" and those "recommended for knits."

Conventional patterns

You buy a conventional pattern for fabrics that do not stretch; the pattern includes ease needed for movement. If you use a conventional pattern for a stretchy knit fabric, you may end up with a garment that's too big. To compensate, you can alter the pattern, take deeper seam allowances or buy the pattern one size smaller than your body measurements indicate.

Patterns for stretchable knits only

Patterns designed for unbonded knits that stretch have less ease than you find in conventional patterns. That's because knit fabrics have built-in ease. The garment can be close-fitting, but the fabric will stretch and move with you. Do not use a pattern "for stretchable knits only" to cut non-stretch fabrics, or your garment will be too small.

Patterns recommended for knits

Some patterns are double-duty. They are designed for non-stretch fabrics. However, the styles lend themselves to knits, so they are "recommended for knits." On some of these patterns, you find two seamlines—one for non-stretch fabrics and one for stretchable knits. If the seamline for stretchables is not included, you may have to take deeper seams or go to a size smaller pattern.

PATTERNS FROM SPECIALTY COMPANIES

Some small companies produce only patterns for knits. The patterns are simple, basic designs and usually are found in fabric stores specializing in knits. More than one size is printed on these pattern sheets, so you can use them for more than one person. This feature also is helpful when you need a smaller size for a very stretchy knit.

Because of this special feature, you should not cut these master patterns. Instead, trace the size you need on a large piece of special pattern paper, tissue paper or butcher paper. You can even use shelf paper for narrow pattern pieces.

NOTE: Special pattern paper, found in most knit fabric stores, is 45" wide; it is marked both lengthwise and crosswise at 1" intervals. You can place this paper over patterns for tracing; use it also for changing style lines and for altering patterns.

Special patterns for knits usually have very little detail printed on them, so study them carefully before you cut the fabric. Note the seam allowances; many allow only ¼".

FIT AND EASE GUIDE (for tops, shirts, dresses)

Check the measurements of each pattern when you first use it. It's easier to change a pattern than to alter the garment itself.

Patterns vary

Every pattern company has its own idea of how much ease to allow. You should decide how much ease you like in your clothes, then measure and adjust each pattern to get that amount.

When in doubt about how you want a garment to fit, make up an experimental model. Or measure a knit garment you find comfortable to see how much ease has been allowed.

When you use a special, multi-size pattern for knits, measure the bust or chest portion of the various sizes until you find one that gives you the desired ease. (Do not include seam allowances.) When you find the proper size, don't be surprised if it is not what you think you should wear. Trust your measurements and go ahead. If you are still in doubt, cut the pattern a bit larger. You can always take in seams, but it is difficult to add ease after you have cut the fabric.

Fabric stretch varies

Some knits are very stretchy, while others have almost no stretch. Degree of stretch in your fabric will influence the pattern size and ease you need. The measurements here are for average single knit and doubleknit fabrics. If you select a very stretchy type of knit, you may find that a pattern one size smaller than you normally use will give you a better-fitting garment.

Check the pattern—and adjust

You should check a pattern for fit before you cut any fabric—woven or knitted. This will save you from making major garment alterations later.

NOTE: These guides are for knit tops, shirts and dresses. Skirts and pants are covered in later chapters.

CHEST OR BUST: Buy your pattern to fit the bust or chest measurement. Generally, 1″ or 2″ of ease is adequate for a knit fabric. For a loose, casual fit, allow 3″.

SHOULDER WIDTH: The paper pattern should measure the same as your shoulder width. Measure the distance from the base of your neck to the bone at the edge of your shoulder. (FIG. 1)

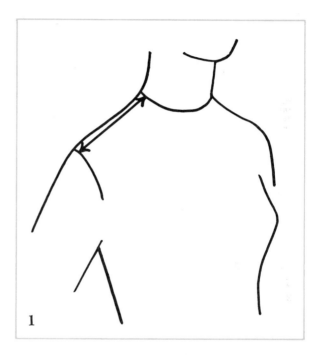

1

Measure the shoulder seam on the pattern; do not include seam allowances. (FIG. 2)

To add width, slash the pattern down from the shoulder and out to the arm edge. (FIG. 3) Do not cut the pattern apart at the arm edge. Spread the pattern until you have added the required width. Fill in the gap with a piece of pattern paper, and tape it in place. Redraw the shoulder line so that it is straight.

To subtract width, slash the pattern along the same lines, and overlap pattern edges the desired amount. Tape together and redraw the shoulder line. (FIG. 4)

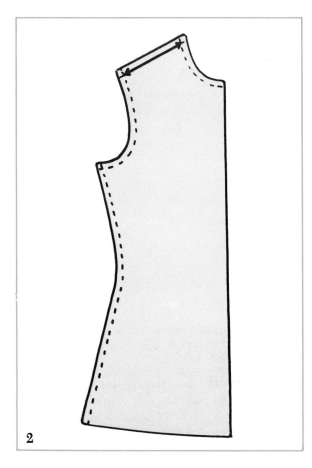

2

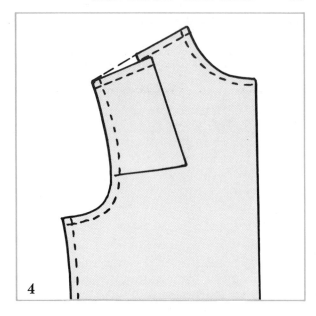

4

HIP WIDTH: The pattern should be 1″ to 2″ larger than your hip measurement. Tie a string around your waist to check this. Measure the fullest part of your hips, then note how far down from the waistline this measurement is taken. (FIG. 5)

Record this hip measurement on your pattern in the same location. Do this by measuring down from the waistline mark on both front and back pattern pieces. If your pat-

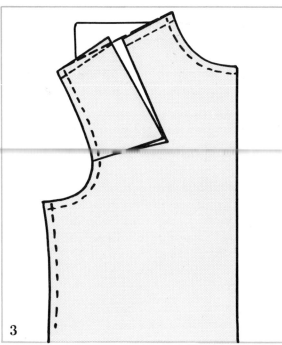

3

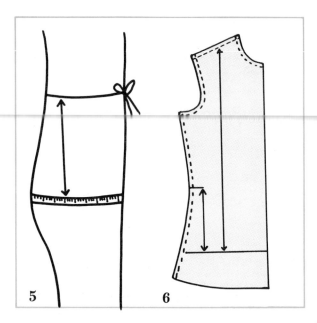

5   6

tern does not have a waistline mark, measure the distance from the middle of your shoulder, over the bust, down to hipline on your body. Then check the measurement on your pattern. (**FIG. 6**)

To add width, make a vertical slash from the bottom edge of the pattern into the waistline area. (**FIG. 7**) Spread the pattern apart the desired amount, and tape in a piece of pattern paper to fill the gap.

To subtract width, trim the side seams the desired amount. (**FIG. 8**)

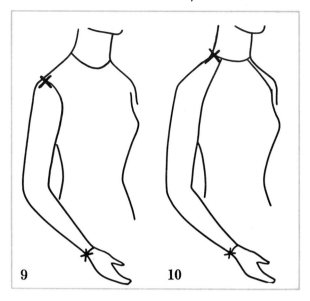

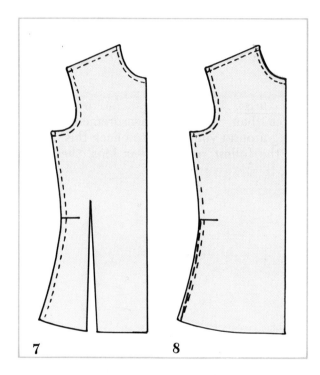

NOTE: A raglan sleeve does not have the conventional sleeve cap. It has diagonal seams that run from neck to underarm.

To add length, cut the pattern apart and spread it the needed amount. Tape it together with an extra piece of paper. (**FIG. 11**)

SLEEVE LENGTH: Allow an extra 1¼″ if you plan to hem the sleeve. Do not allow extra length if you wish to finish the sleeve with a band of ribbing.

For a long set-in sleeve, begin measuring at the point of your shoulder. Run the tape down over your elbow (slightly bent) to the wristbone. (**FIG. 9**)

For a long raglan sleeve, begin measuring at the base of your neck. Run the tape over your shoulder point, past the elbow (slightly bent) to the wristbone. (**FIG. 10**)

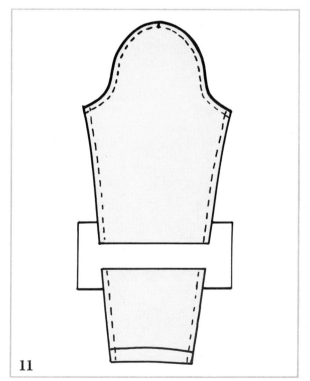

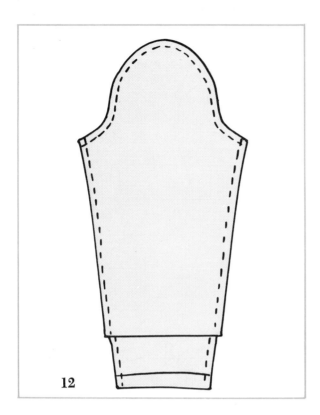

12

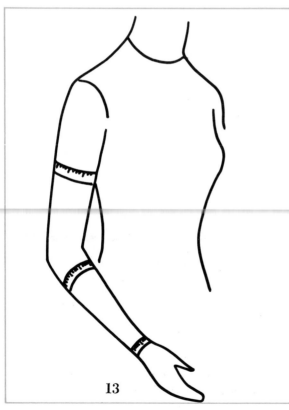

13

To subtract length, make a fold across the width of the pattern (FIG. 12); width of the fold should be one half the amount you want to remove.

SLEEVE WIDTH: The pattern should be 1″ to 2″ wider than your arm at all points. Allow 2″ if you have a full arm or are using a firm knit.

Measure your upper arm, forearm, and wrist. (FIG. 13) Check these measurements against the paper pattern; alter if necessary.

To widen, add an equal amount to both seam allowances. (FIG. 14)

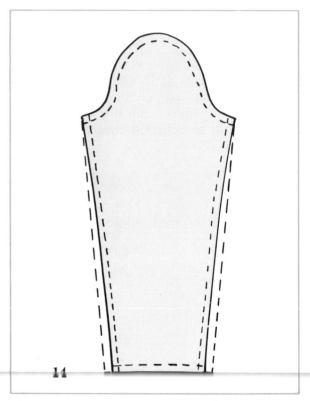

14

If you need fullness in the extreme upper-arm area, you can slash the pattern from the bottom to the top edge. (FIG. 15) Spread the pattern the desired amount—up to 1″—and tape in an extra piece of paper to fill the gap. This extra fullness in the sleeve cap usually can be eased into the armhole.

To subtract width, taper both edges of the sleeve the desired amount. (FIG. 16)

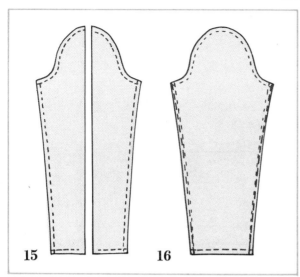

15   16

SLEEVE CAP: This rounded portion at the top of a set-in sleeve should measure only 1" to 2" larger than the arm opening. It is difficult to get a smooth sleeve cap if you work with more than this amount; the stretch of the knit will provide additional ease.

On most conventional patterns, and those recommended for knits, you will find too much ease in the sleeve cap. Alter the sleeve before you sew it into the arm opening.

To remove ease, trim the curve on each side of the sleeve cap. Remove the same amount from each side. (FIG. 17)

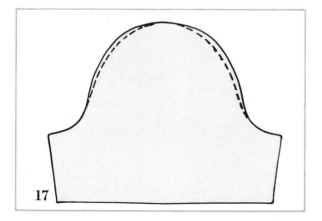

17

TOP, SHIRT OR DRESS LENGTH: Measure in the front, beginning at the middle of the shoulder. Run the tape down over the bust or chest

to the desired length. (FIGS. 18 and 19) Add about 1½" for the hem on a top or shirt; add 2" for the hem on a dress.

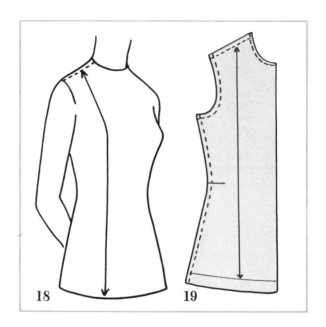

18   19

BUST DART LOCATION: If a top, shirt or dress pattern has an underarm bust dart, make sure the dart is directed toward the high point

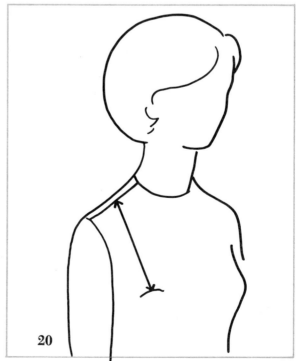

20

of your bust. If the dart is too high or too low, correct the pattern.

To check the dart, determine the "drop" of your bust by measuring from the middle of your shoulder seam (or top of your shoulder) to the high point of your bust. (FIG. 20) Place a dot on your pattern to correspond with this measurement.

Determine the separation of your bust by measuring between the high points. (FIG. 21) Use one half of this measurement, and locate it with a second dot on your pattern; measure in from the center front line.

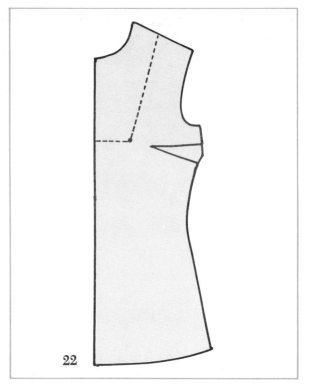

22

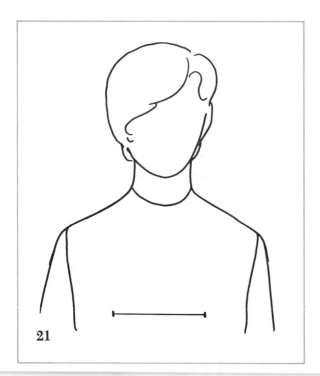

21

If the two dots are not in the same place, move the bust "drop" dot until it is directly above or below the separation dot. The new "drop" point marks the location of the high point of your bust. (FIG. 22)

On your pattern, check the direction of the dart. Place the edge of a ruler along the fold line of the dart, and let the ruler extend beyond the dart. (FIG. 23) If the dart is directed toward the bust dot, your pattern is correct for you. If the dart is directed above or below

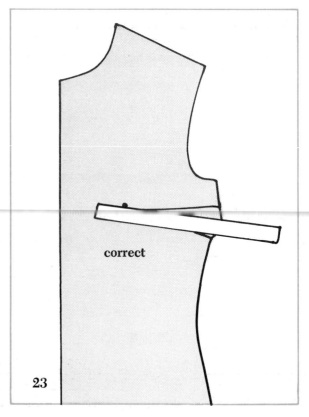

correct

23

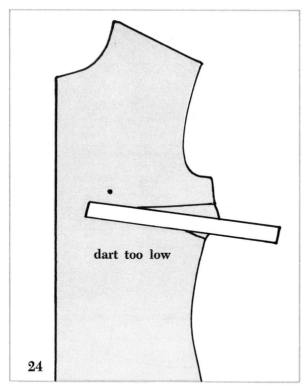

dart too low

24

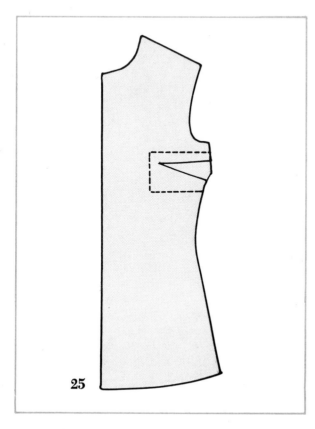

25

the bust dot, you should alter the pattern. (FIG. 24)

To shift the bust dart, cut a box around the dart (FIG. 25); raise or lower the whole section as needed. Tape the dart in the proper place, and fill in the gap with an extra piece of pattern paper.

BUST DART LENGTH: The underarm dart should be sewn short of the bust high point. On size 14 and smaller patterns, end the dart about 1″ short of the high point. For larger sizes, end the dart 1½″ short of the high point.

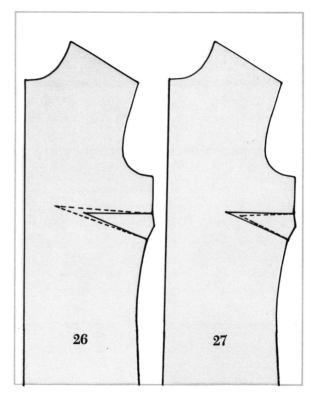

26   27

Check the dart length on your pattern. If the dart stitching lines are not printed, draw them in. Lengthen or shorten the darts as needed; use illustrations as guides. (FIGS. 26 and 27)

NOTE: It is a good idea to check the bust darts on all your patterns. When taking measurements, wear the same bra that you will wear under the finished garment. Changing from an old to a new bra, or changing bra styles, often affects the location of the bust high point.

PATTERN TO FABRIC

Here are some special hints for dealing with knits that you might not find on your pattern envelope or instruction sheet.

Yardage requirements

Check the pattern envelope for yardage requirements; all patterns from large companies include this information. You will not always find it on the patterns for knits produced by small companies. In this case, you can lay the pattern pieces on newspapers that are folded to the fabric width. Measure the length required, and add the extra inches you need for shrinkage in your particular fabric (see Chapter 1).

Generally, if you buy a body length and a sleeve length, plus extra for shrinkage, you will have plenty of fabric. Some knit fabrics are wide enough to accommodate both body and sleeve pattern pieces side by side; children's patterns usually can be cut this way.

Until you become familiar with yardage requirements for various garments, it's a good idea to take your pattern to the store with you. Most stores will let you take time to place pattern pieces on the fabric so you can buy just the right amount.

The expanded pattern

When you must match stripes, it is easier to work with a complete pattern piece (the whole front, for instance) instead of half a pattern piece. You can pin the expanded pattern to a single layer of fabric. (Directions for expanding a pattern follow later.)

Many striped knit fabrics are made on circular knitting machines; this produces a stripe that spirals around the piece of fabric. It is almost impossible to handle two layers of this fabric and have the stripes line up for cutting. You can push, pat and pin the stripes into position, but this is time-consuming and not always accurate. It is easier and quicker to work with a single layer of fabric and an expanded pattern. You can see where the stripes fall on both sides of the pattern pieces, and you can make sure the stripes run straight across the pattern.

Some large pattern companies use expanded patterns in their "for stretchable knits only" series. Most of the small companies use only the half pattern, so you should learn how to expand a pattern yourself.

To make an expanded pattern, take a large sheet of special pattern paper, tracing paper or tissue paper. Have the paper as long as your pattern and twice as wide. Fold the paper in half lengthwise and place it on top of the front pattern piece. The folded edge should be along the center front. (FIG. 28) Trace the pattern, noting all notches, circles and any other markings. Label the new piece as to size, pattern number and section; cut around the tracing lines while the paper is still folded. You now have an expanded front pattern piece, ready to use with striped fabric. (FIG. 29)

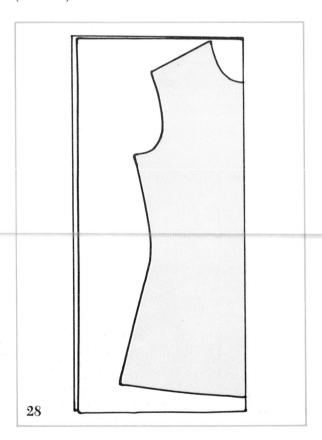

28

29

Follow this same procedure for the back pattern piece. If the pattern has a center back seam allowance, fold it out of the way or trim it off; the fold of the paper should run along the center back line of the pattern. If you are planning a zipper opening in the garment, you can put it in a slash instead of a seam.

Pattern layout

Treat knits as napped fabrics, with the tops of all pattern pieces facing the same end of the fabric. Knits are made with rows of interconnected loops, and the tops of the loops reflect light differently than the bottoms of the loops. If all loops do not run in the same direction, you may notice a color change at the seamline.

Generally, the greatest stretch in a knit is across the width of the fabric; cut your pattern so the greatest amount of stretch goes around the body. If a knit stretches about the

same in both directions, you can cut the pattern either way.

Do not let a knit fabric hang over the table edge when you cut. This will stretch the fabric and cause construction and fitting problems.

A knit fabric often has a permanent crease along the center fold. You should try to avoid this when you pin your pattern to the fabric. However, it is sometimes possible to use this crease down the center of a sleeve without detracting from the appearance of the garment.

For a solid-color fabric, refold the fabric, as illustrated, to avoid the permanent crease. (**FIG. 30**) You will have two folded edges instead of just one. Be sure each fold runs along a lengthwise rib of the knit.

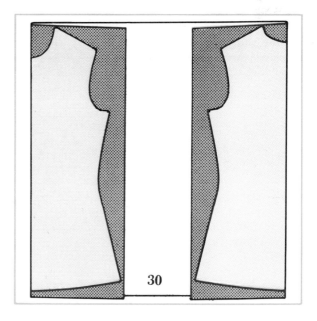

30

Pin the back and front pattern pieces in place with pattern tops facing in the same direction. Sleeves can be cut from the center section or below the body pieces. Place the sleeve top so it runs in the same direction as the body pieces; be sure you cut a left sleeve and a right sleeve.

With a striped fabric, work with a single layer of fabric. Horizontal stripes are cut with the

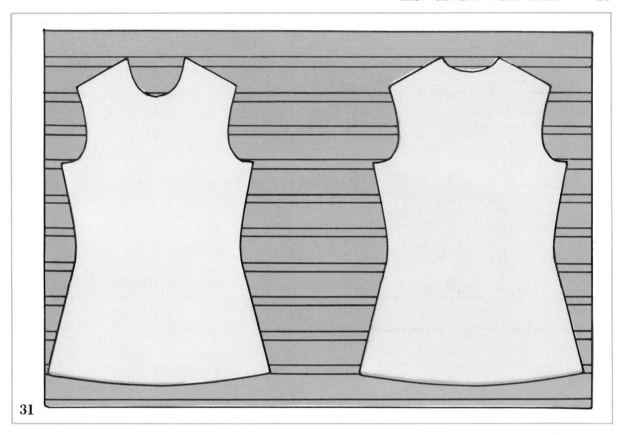

31

pattern grain line at right angles to a stripe. Vertical stripes are cut with the pattern grain line parallel to a stripe. For special effects, you can cut a stripe on the bias.

If the pattern does not have a bust dart, match stripes at the lower corners of the pattern, at the underarm points and at the shoulder points. Match these points on both front and back pattern pieces. (FIG. 31)

If the pattern has a bust dart, place the front and back pattern pieces so the lower corners match. Stripes will match at the side seams up to the dart. They probably will not match above the dart, but it will not be noticeable in this underarm area.

Cut sleeves from the center section or from the area below the body pieces. Match the underarm point of the sleeve with the underarm point of the garment front. To get a right and a left sleeve, cut one sleeve with the printed side of the pattern up. Turn the pattern over and cut another sleeve with the printed side of the pattern down.

NOTE: Sometimes a striped knit has crooked edges and seems to be twisted out of shape after it has been preshrunk. Don't take time to pull it back into shape; work with the knit as it is. As long as your expanded pattern pieces are straight on the stripes, do not worry. Matching stripes at the seamlines is the important thing.

3

Techniques for Sewing on Knits

You use slightly different techniques for sewing knits than for sewing woven fabrics. Eventually, you may find that you prefer working with knits because you can eliminate some steps and save time. For instance, knits do not fray; so, you don't need to add special seam finishes.

The doubleknits you will use for dresses, skirts and pants have enough bounce to keep their shape; so, you don't need to underline them. Linings, if any, are confined to jackets and coats. Many neckline and armhole finishes do not even require facings.

This chapter on techniques covers equipment, stitching on knit fabrics, pressing, using interfacings and stays, and finishing hems.

EQUIPMENT

You may want some new needles and pins, but don't think you must have a lot of expensive new equipment. Most of your regular sewing tools will be fine for sewing knit fabrics.

Sewing machine

Any sewing machine—an old treadle or a fancy new one—will sew knits. The secret to easy sewing is a well-oiled, clean machine. Knit fabrics produce a lot of lint; so, clean your machine often. If your machine has a top-loading bobbin, brush out the bobbin area before every sewing session. Take care of your sewing machine, and it will give you few problems.

Tension on the threads should be balanced so that stitches lock in the middle of the fabric. You need this balance for stitching on knits as well as on woven fabrics. Adjust the tension control, if necessary.

Machine needles

Choose a sharp and fairly fine needle for your sewing machine. A dull needle breaks fabric threads as it goes through, causing holes or runs in your garment. A dull needle, or one of improper size, also can cause your machine to skip stitches.

Size 11 needle is a good choice for most knit fabrics. You may need a smaller needle for

very sheer lingerie fabrics, and a larger size for heavy knits.

A ball-point machine needle is now on the market. The rounded tip is designed to push aside fabric yarns, rather than pierce them, so the chance of holes or runs is reduced. You might like to try this type of needle.

Pins

Fine, sharp pins with large glass or plastic heads are handier than regular pins. The larger heads are easier to find in bulky knit fabrics. You can use corsage pins for heavy fabric.

Don't sew over pins. Pull pins out of the fabric just before you come to them. Lightly hitting a pin with your machine needle can take off the needle point and cause a run or hole in your fabric.

Shears

Knit fabrics require sharp shears. Dull shears chew the fabric and tire your hands at the same time. Do not use pinking shears; these cause many knits to fray.

Thread

New threads suggested for knits generally are all-polyester or a polyester core wrapped with cotton. These threads are strong and have some stretch.

You can use cotton mercerized thread with all knits without any problems if you put stretch into the seams. However, polyester thread is stronger and is recommended for swim wear and action garments.

STITCHING AND SEAM ALLOWANCES

The key to sewing with knits is making a good knit seam—one that stretches. The particular knit you have will determine the type of seam you make, as well as the seam allowance you can use. There also are special stitching techniques, such as stitching in the groove, that will help you to successful sewing with knits.

The knit seam

Because knit fabrics have built-in stretch, you must put stretch into the seams you sew. Seams then move with the fabric when stress is placed on a garment. Otherwise, threads break, and you spend a lot of time repairing them.

DO-IT-YOURSELF METHOD: You can make a knit seam with any sewing machine. Use a straight stitch, and add the stretch manually by stretching the fabric as you sew.

Adjust the machine for 9 to 10 stitches per inch. Anchor the fabric with one hand behind the presser foot, and stretch the fabric in front of the needle as you stitch. Stitches will be slightly loose after you complete the seam. This slack will let the seam stretch without breaking threads.

Stretching the fabric as you stitch isn't difficult, but it takes practice. Use scraps of knit fabric and make sample seams until you master the technique.

You will notice that the width of the seam allowance becomes slightly less when you stretch the fabric. If you sew what looks like a ⅝″ seam allowance on stretched fabric, you end up with a seam closer to ¾″ wide after the fabric is relaxed. Keep this in mind as you stitch. Make the stretched seam about ½″

wide, and it will end up close to ⅝″ when relaxed.

THE AUTOMATIC WAY: Many new machines can be adjusted to make straight-stretch stitches automatically; these combine forward and backward stitches. Some machines also combine this straight-stretch stitch with a side-to-side stitch to give you an over-edge stretch stitch—you get a straight-stretch stitch plus an edge finish, all at once.

These automatic stitches put stretch into seams—with no help from you. Follow directions that come with your machine for using these stitches.

NOTE: Use automatic stretch stitches only after you are sure that a seam will be final. They are convenient to use and make strong seams, but they are difficult to take out if you make a mistake or have a fitting adjustment.

Seam allowances

Examine various ready-made knit garments and you will notice that not all seams are the same width. Some garments have ⅝″ seams that are pressed open. Others have very narrow seams with overcast edges. The type of knit fabric and, sometimes, the type of garment determine the seam allowance to use.

THE WIDE SEAM: With most doubleknits, you can use ⅝″ seam allowances. (FIG. 32) Press seams open; no finish is required. (FIG. 33) When possible, use this type of seam for skirts and slacks to give a smooth line over the hips.

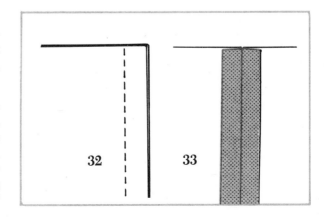

THE NARROW KNIT SEAM: Some knits will not take a press; seam allowances will not stay open and flat. The fabric is so soft that the edges roll up and make ridges along the seamline. Solve this problem by trimming seam allowances to ¼″ and stitching the seam edges together.

You'll find narrow seams (with a second stitching) on most knit shirts and tops and on children's clothes, regardless of the type of knit. The extra stitching makes the strong seams needed for these garments.

Some patterns designed for knits allow only ¼″ seam allowances. If you are working with a pattern that has ⅝″ seam allowances, trim them to ¼″ when narrow knit seams are needed.

You can stitch and finish a narrow knit seam by three different methods, depending on your sewing machine.

1. *With a straight-stitch machine:* Do a row of straight stitching along the seamline, stretching the fabric as you sew.

If you have cut a ¼″ seam allowance, close the seam edges with another row of straight stitching along the edge; stretch as you stitch. (FIG. 34) If you have a ⅝″ seam allowance, make a second row of straight stitches ¼″ to the right of the seamline; stretch as you stitch. Trim away the excess seam allowance.

2. *With a zigzag machine:* Make one row of straight stitching along the seamline, stretching as you sew.

With a ¼″ seam allowance, close the seam edges with a wide zigzag stitch. (FIG. 35) If you have a ⅝″ seam allowance, do the zigzag stitch close to the first line of stitching, then trim away the excess seam allowance.

NOTE: When you use a zigzag stitch, it generally is not necessary to stretch the knit fabric. However, some lightweight knits, especially lingerie knits, need extra support when they are zigzagged; they are easier to stitch if you hold the fabric taut as it goes under the presser foot. This prevents the fabric from being pulled down through the throat plate and helps eliminate skipped stitches.

3. *With an automatic stretch-stitch machine:* If your machine does a straight-stretch stitch, use it along the seamline. Then, finish the seam edges with a wide zigzag stitch; follow directions given for the zigzag machine in the preceding paragraphs.

If your machine has an over-edge stretch stitch (a straight-stretch stitch, plus an over-edge stitch), you can use it along the seamline. (FIG. 36) This closes the seam and finishes the edges in one operation. If you have a ⅝″ seam allowance, trim away excess fabric after you stitch the seam.

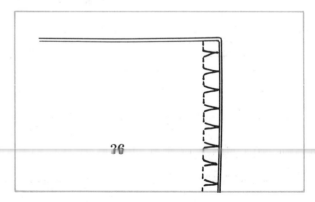

Handling lingerie fabrics

Use a small, sharp needle (size 11 or 9) or a fine ball-point needle when stitching lingerie tricot. Use either nylon or polyester thread.

The best seam for lingerie is a zigzag stitch. Set your machine for 12 stitches to the inch and for a medium width. Let the zigzag go

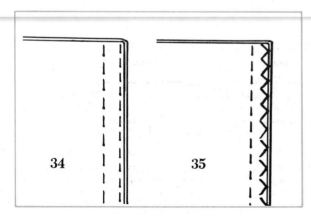

right along the very edge of the fabric; this makes a nice neat finish.

Hold your fabric taut as you stitch to prevent puckering and to reduce the chance of skipped stitches. Whenever you start a seam, hold onto your machine threads; otherwise, the fabric may be pulled through the throat plate.

You also can make seams with a straight stitch, if you stretch the fabric slightly as you stitch. For this seam, make two rows of stitching, about ⅛" apart, along the edge of the fabric.

Darts

Begin stitching at the wide end of a dart, and taper to nothing at the narrow end; stretch as you stitch. (FIG. 37) If you continue stitching a bit after you run off the edge of the fabric, you knot the threads; or you can tie the thread ends. Never backstitch at the end of a dart.

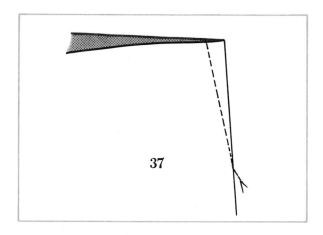

37

Handling "ease"

When one garment piece must be eased to fit another, as with a set-in sleeve, usually there is no need to baste. Divide each seam edge into four equal sections. Pin seam edges together, matching the divisions. With the shorter length on top, begin stitching; stretch the shorter length to fit the longer length. In addition, you must stretch both sections to make a knit (stretch) seam. Do this manually if you sew with a regular straight stitch.

Matching stripes

Pin stripes carefully so they match at the seamlines. It is easier to keep stripes in place if you are not stitching and stretching the fabric at the same time. When your garment calls for a narrow knit seam, first do a row of zigzag stitching to the right of the seamline. Then stitch along the seamline, stretching as you sew.

Some machines have an even-feed mechanism, which reduces matching problems. Follow the machine directions for using this. Also on the market is a special even-feed foot that fits some existing machines.

Curved underarm seams

Do not clip into the curve at the underarm of a garment as you would do with a woven fabric. Instead, trim the seam allowance in the curved area to ¼". Stretch the seam as you stitch; it will be strong enough without reinforcement.

Stitching in the groove

Use the stitch-in-the-groove technique to catch down trims and waistbands. Guide your machine needle down the groove formed where two pieces of fabric are joined. (FIG. 38) If the seam must have stretch, as in the waistband of a pull-on skirt, make a knit seam with 9 stitches to the inch. If the seam does not have to stretch, as in the neckline with a zipper, use shorter stitches—about 18 to 20 per inch. The shorter length helps bury the stitches in the groove, and they are less noticeable.

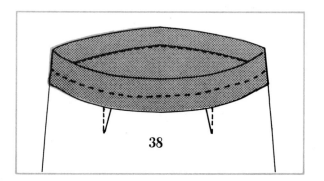

38

Understitching

Use understitching to hold facings inside a garment so they won't show. After you stitch a facing in place, fold it away from the garment with right side of facing up. Pull the seam allowances of both garment and facing away from the garment so they are under the facing. Stitch along the facing, about ⅛" from the seamline (FIG. 39); set machine for 9 stitches to the inch. This understitching catches the seam allowances to the facing and will hold the facing in place.

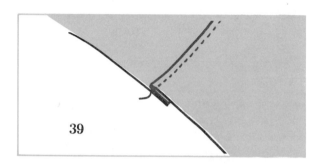

39

Grading seams

You should grade (or layer) seam allowances when there are many stacked in one place. Trim the various seam allowances to different widths; the seam allowance directly against the garment should be the widest.

PRESSING

Pressing is the secret to professional looking garments in either knit or woven fabrics. Your pressing techniques are especially important when you work with knits, because some knits are quite resistant to pressing and seam flattening. However, with a little patience and work, the results are most rewarding. Remember to press as you sew. Do not leave all the pressing until the end.

A good steam iron is your most important tool for pressing knits. Let the steam do the work; don't use too much pressure. An up-and-down motion is better than a back-and-forth motion. Always press with the lengthwise rib of the knit fabric, using a light touch and lots of moisture.

When you have ⅝" seam allowances that will be pressed open, first press the stitched seam in the closed position. This embeds the stitches. Then open the seam and press it flat.

NOTE: Always use a press cloth when you work on the right side of a knit fabric. Moisten the cloth if your steam iron does not provide enough moisture.

INTERFACINGS AND STAYS

You need an interfacing or stay fabric when you are handling design details in knits. This gives support and keeps the knit from stretching as you work. You will not use complete underlinings, however (a woven underlining prevents the knit from stretching and this defeats one of the reasons you select a knit in the first place).

Interfacings

To add support to a neckline, collar or lapel edge, use a woven interfacing fabric, cut on the bias. This gives firmness, but preserves some of the fabric stretch. For small details, such as pocket flaps, a press-on, nonwoven interfacing fabric works well. This is bonded to the knit; so, it's easy to handle.

Lingerie tricot fabric also can add firmness. If you bond the tricot to the wrong side of the knit fabric, you can handle the two layers of fabric as one. Use an iron-on bonding product available at fabric stores, and follow instructions carefully. The secret of a good bond is plenty of steam; use a moist press cloth if your steam iron isn't up to par.

To interface buttonholes, use a firm, woven fabric that is cut on the straight grain. Slip the interfacing between the two layers of knit; stitch or bond it in place before you make the buttonholes.

If you stitch an interfacing to a knit, work with the interfacing side up. This keeps the knit fabric from stretching out of shape as you stitch.

Stays

A stay adds support to detail areas and keeps the knit from stretching; it works much like an interfacing. You will use a stay when you insert a zipper in a slash, for instance. Use a firm, lightweight woven fabric, such as cotton or cotton-blend underlining fabric, and cut it on the straight grain. Since the stay will not be seen, the color is not important.

NOTE: Preshrink all interfacing and stay fabrics before you use them.

HEMS

You can sew stretch into hems of knit garments just as you do with the seams, so they will give with the fabric. Do this by hand or machine.

It is not necessary to turn under the raw edge of a knit hem as you do on lightweight woven fabrics. Knits are too bulky, and a ridge would show on the right side. Also, the cut edge of a knit will not ravel; so, it does not have to be protected in this way.

The hem looks nice if you do a zigzag stitch over the edge before hemming. Seam binding generally is not recommended for knit hems; it does not allow stretch in the hem area, and many times it will cause a ridge to show on the right side.

To reduce bulk in a hem, trim seam allowances in the section that is turned up. After you have established the hemline, narrow the seam allowances from hem fold to hem edge.

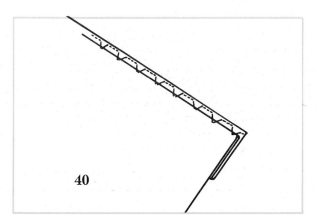

40

Machine hem

You can use the blind hem stitch on your machine to hem casual knit garments. This provides enough stretch because a zigzag stitch is part of the blind hem pattern. (**FIG. 40**) A machine hem is not recommended for your better knit garments, however. Stitches tend to show a bit on the right side, and you want invisible hems.

The knit hem

This hand-finished hem works well on most knits.

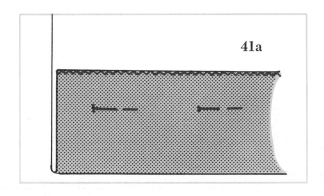

41a

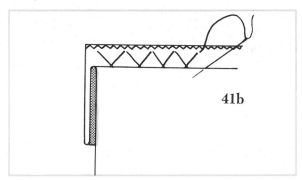

41b

Stitch around the edge of the hem with either a straight or zigzag stitch. Pin the hem in place. (**FIG. 41a**) Fold the hem back as illustrated. Use a double thread, and do a catch stitch between the hem edge and the garment. (**FIG. 41b**) Catch just one thread of the fabric on each side with your needle, and do not pull the hemming threads tight. If you are right-handed, you will put the needle into the fabric from right to left, and you will be hemming toward the right. If you are left-handed, your needle will go into the fabric from left to right, and you will be hemming toward the left.

Press the edge of the hem carefully from the wrong side, but avoid pressing the top edge of the hem. You should have a beautiful hem that will not show on the right side of the garment.

The catch stitch also can be used over the raw edge of a hem if the fabric is loosely knit. (FIG. 42) Hemming threads help control the edge of the fabric. If hand stitches are loose enough, the hem will show very little

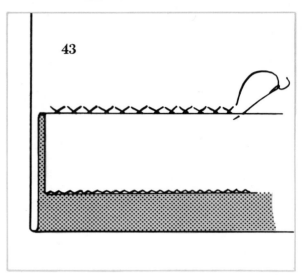

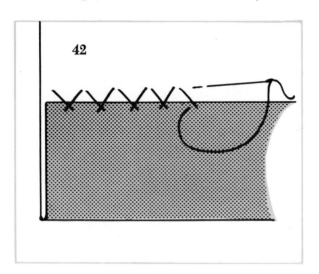

from the right side. This hemming stitch works well on sweater knits.

The double hem for knits

Some bulky and heavy knit fabrics need extra support in the hem. Otherwise, the weight of the fabric pulls on the hem stitches and causes them to show.

Make one row of catch stitches halfway between bottom and top edge of the hem. (FIG. 43) Then make a regular knit hem at the top edge.

A. Casual shirt with crew neck
B. The shell
C. The tank top

4

How to Fit and Sew
Basic Knit Tops

You can take one or two basic patterns and make a whole wardrobe of tops or shirts. The trick is to use different neck, sleeve and hem finishes, so that each top has an individual look. In this chapter, you'll find guides for making casual tops, shells and tank tops.

CASUAL TOP OR SHIRT

This pullover top or shirt is one of the easiest knit garments to make; so, it's a good choice for your first project. It can have a crew neck, a turtleneck or a mock turtleneck finish, and you can use the same techniques on tops for everyone in the family.

Pick a pattern

Look for a pattern with a high, round neckline and set-in sleeves. The pattern may have an underarm dart. However, for an easy-to-make top, you may want a pattern with no darts.

NOTE: You can make a casual shirt with raglan sleeves; but, this chapter gives you directions for set-in sleeves.

Choose a neckline—adjust the pattern

The crew neckline ends at the base of the neck. (**FIG. 44**)

A turtleneck (**FIG. 45**) and mock turtleneck (**FIG. 46**) begin at the base of the neck and go up the neck about 2″; the turtleneck is wider so it can fold back on itself.

Many special patterns for knits have two necklines indicated—a high neckline for turtlenecks and mock turtlenecks, and a lower neckline for crew necks. If your pattern does not have these neckline markings, you can add them yourself.

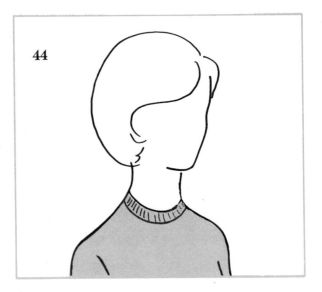

44

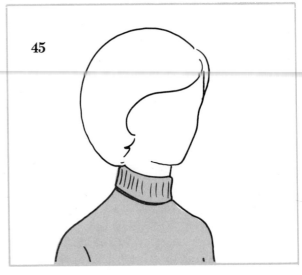

45

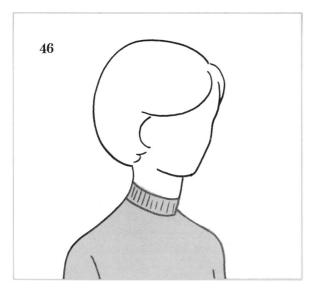

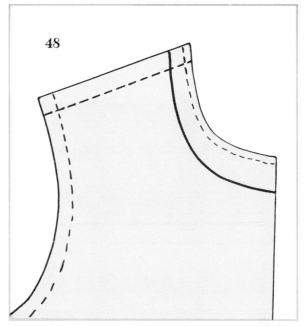

For a turtleneck or mock turtleneck, use the high round neckline with a ¼″ seam allowance. Trim the pattern seam allowance, if necessary. (**FIG. 47**)

For a crew neck, draw a lower neckline on the pattern, both back and front pieces, by following the illustration. (**FIG. 48**) Cut away 1″ at the center front; gradually taper this to ½″ at the shoulder. Cut away ¾″ at the center back; gradually taper this to ½″ at the shoulder. The new line is your cutting line; you still have a ¼″ seam allowance below it.

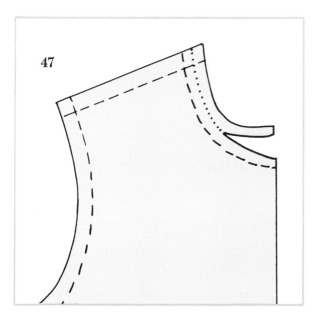

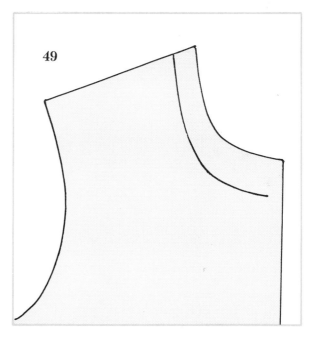

NOTE: You can prepare a pattern so that it can be used for both crew neck and turtleneck. First, adjust the pattern for a turtleneck. (**FIG. 49**) Then, cut along the seam allowance for the lower, crew neckline to within ½″ of the center front and center back. Keep the small section in place for a high neckline; fold it down, out of the way for a crew neckline. (**FIG. 50**)

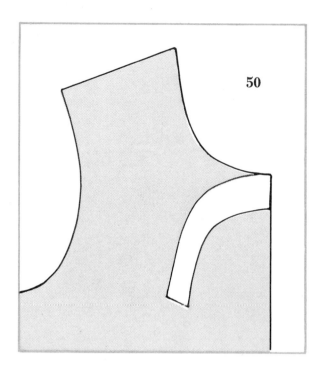

50

Check the pattern for fit

Take your measurements and compare them with the pattern to make sure you have the recommended amount of ease (see Chapter 2). Make any necessary adjustments.

Cut the fabric

See Chapter 2 for pattern layout guides. Remember to expand your pattern (also explained in Chapter 2) if you are working with a striped fabric.

Do you need a zipper?

If you use special ribbing fabric for the neck finish, you won't need a zipper. The ribbing has enough stretch to slip over your head and snap back to fit snugly against your neck.

If ribbing is not available, you can sometimes substitute the garment fabric. In this case, the fabric must be able to stretch one half its length, then return without being distorted.

Test the fabric by cutting a strip 3″ wide and 14″ long. If it will stretch to 21″ without too much strain, you can use it in place of ribbing. However, if the fabric does not have enough

stretch, you should insert a zipper at the center of the shirt back. Directions for "Exposed zipper through a neck trim" are in Chapter 8.

Assemble the shirt (darts, shoulders)

Close the underarm darts if your pattern has them. Next, stitch the shoulder seams; make narrow knit seams, using one of the methods given in Chapter 3. Press the completed seams to one side.

Prepare the ribbing

Cut a strip of ribbing, wide enough to give you the desired neck finish. Cut a double thickness across the tube of ribbing; then cut along one fold to open the tube. This gives you one long strip.

Crew neck—Cut strip 3″ wide.

Mock turtleneck—Cut strip 4″ to 4½″ wide.

Turtleneck—Cut strip 9″ to 10″ wide.

You need the same length for all three neck finishes. Choose one of the following methods to determine length needed.

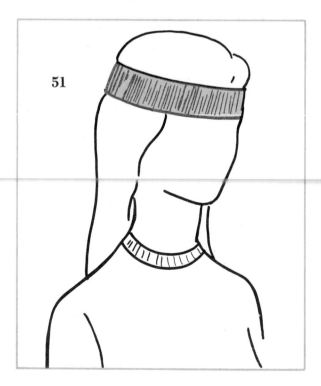

51

Method 1: Fold ribbing in half lengthwise and stretch it firmly around your head. (**FIG. 51**) Mark this amount, then add an extra ½" for seam allowances.

Method 2: With a tape, measure both your head circumference and neck circumference. Fold the ribbing strip in half lengthwise, and mark off your neck measurement with a pin. (**FIG. 52**)

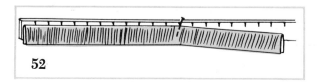

52

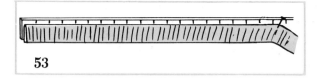

53

Stretch this marked amount to see if it will extend to the head measurement, plus ½". (**FIG. 53**)

If ribbing stretches that far without causing runs, use the neck measurement for length. If there is too much strain, you must add to the length. If ribbing stretches much beyond the head measurement, you can use 1" to 1½" less for length. Hold the adjusted length in position around your neck to make sure it isn't too tight.

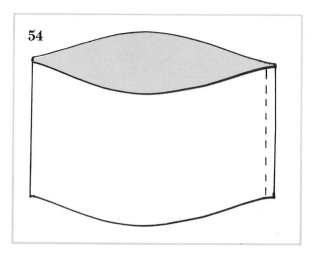

54

NOTE: Various ribbings have different amounts of stretch. The length that you need for one ribbing is not necessarily the length you will need for another. Always measure to be sure you have enough length to go over the head.

To join the ribbing, place the right sides of the strip together; straight stitch across the narrow ends with a ¼" seam allowance. (**FIG. 54**)

Press the seam open with your fingers. Fold the strip in half lengthwise, with cut edges together and with the right side out.

Apply the ribbing

Divide the ribbing into four equal sections by placing a pin at the seam and another pin directly opposite. Fold the ribbing in half so that these two pins touch; place another pin at each new fold. (**FIG. 55**) It is important to be accurate in measuring.

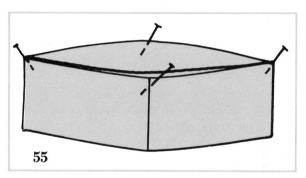

55

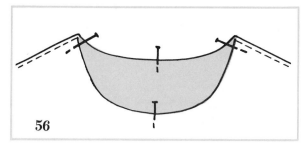

56

Divide the neck edge of the shirt into four equal sections. Place pins at the center front and center back. Fold the shirt so that these two pins are together and the cut edges of the neckline are lined up. Place pins at the two new folds (shoulder seams will not fall on the pin marks). (**FIG. 56**)

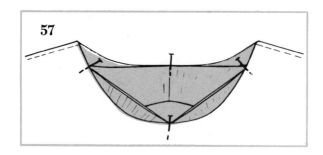

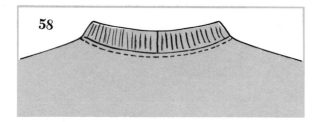

pattern to sleeve. These marks help you distribute the sleeve ease.

Pin the sleeve to the arm opening with right sides together, matching all marks (shoulder point, notches, etc.). (FIG. 59)

Place the fabric under your machine presser foot, with the arm opening on the top and sleeve on the bottom. Make a narrow knit seam. Stretch the arm opening to fit the sleeve in the cap area. Trim away any excess seam allowance.

With the shirt wrong side out, slip the ribbing inside. Pin the right side of the ribbing to the right side of the neck edge, matching division marks. The seam in the ribbing should line up with the center back of the shirt. (FIG. 57)

Stitch a ¼″ seam along the neck edge, with the shirt on the bottom and the ribbing on top. Start your stitching at center back; stretch the ribbing to fit each section and sew around the neck opening. Make a second stitching to complete a narrow knit seam.

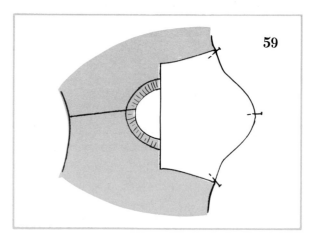

Press the neck area from the wrong side so the seam allowance goes down into the shirt. Let your steam iron shrink out any puckering.

On a crew neck, you can topstitch around the back to keep the seam allowance in place. Use a regular straight stitch for this—with no stretching. Stitch from shoulder to shoulder, about ⅛″ below the neck trim. (FIG. 58) Do not topstitch a turtleneck or mock turtleneck finish.

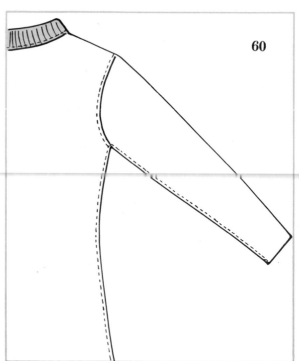

Attach sleeves

You can add the sleeves in casual knit tops or shirts before you close the underarm seams. This is a quick and easy method.

Make sure you have transferred the shoulder seam position and other sleeve markings from

NOTE: For better knit garments, use the conventional method for setting in sleeves. Finish the underarm seams of both garment and sleeve first, then set the sleeve into the armhole.

Stitch the side seams

Pin the side seams and sleeve seams together. Match stripes if you are working with a striped fabric.

Start stitching at the bottom of the shirt. Stitch around underarm curve and out to the edge of the sleeve. (FIG. 60) Trim the excess seam allowance if necessary, and press seam to one side.

Choose a hem finish

You can hem sleeves and the bottom edge of a knit top or shirt by machine or by hand (See Chapter 3). Or you can finish them with ribbing, which is used on many ready-made garments. (FIG. 61)

To finish sleeves with ribbing, trim away the hem allowance. Measure around your arm at the point where the sleeve ends. Cut a strip of ribbing 3″ to 4″ wide and ½″ less than your arm measurement.

Sew the ribbing together as you would in making a neck trim; fold it in half lengthwise. Turn the sleeve inside out. Divide the sleeve opening and the sleeve trim in half; pin trim in place with the right sides together. Stretch the ribbing to fit and stitch with a narrow knit seam.

To finish the bottom edge with ribbing, the shirt should be a straight-cut design; it should not be tapered to fit the waist. Cut away the hem allowance, and measure around the bottom edge of the shirt. Cut a strip of ribbing 4″ to 5″ wide and 4″ less than the bottom edge measurement.

Sew the ribbing together as you would in making a neck trim; fold it in half lengthwise. Divide the bottom edge of the shirt and the ribbing into four equal sections. Pin ribbing to shirt with right sides together, matching division marks. Sew with a narrow knit seam.

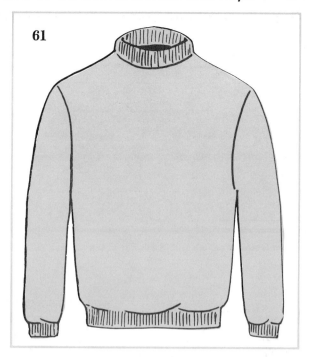

61

THE SHELL

You can wear a sleeveless shell under suits and with separate skirts and pants.

Pick a pattern—cut the fabric

Use a basic shell pattern. Choose one with underarm darts if you are working with a doubleknit and want a trim, tailored fit. The shell will have an exposed zipper, 7″ to 9″ long, at the center back. If your pattern has a center back seam, you can eliminate it by folding it out of the way and placing the pattern on a fabric fold.

Assemble the garment

First, insert the zipper at center back. Follow directions for "Exposed zipper in a slash" in Chapter 8.

Stitch the darts, if any. Sew the shoulder seams together and press. Finish the neck and armholes before you close the side seams; you'll find trim ideas and directions in Chapter 8. For instance, you might use ribbing, piping or an over-edge trim of contrasting or self-fabric.

Complete the bottom edge of the shell with a regular knit hem or with another finish. If you use an over-edge trim on the neck and armhole, consider a mock over-edge finish (see Chapter 8) for the hem; these look well together.

THE TANK TOP

This low-cut top is great for warm weather, and you can complete one in about a half hour.

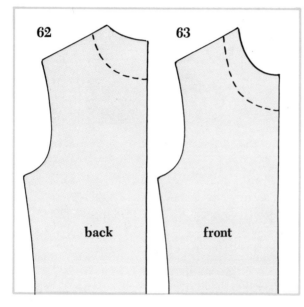

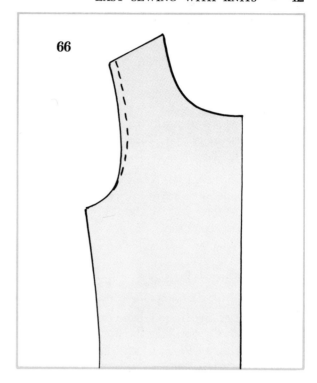

Adjust the pattern

Start with your shell pattern (with or without a dart) and make a few changes.

First, lower the front and back necklines the desired amount. (**FIGS. 62 and 63**)

Then, straighten the shoulder seam by dropping it ¼″ at the neck edge. (**FIGS. 64 and 65**) This gives you a better fit around the neck.

The arm opening also can be made larger by shortening the shoulder seam at the arm opening. (**FIG. 66**)

Assemble the top

Sew the shoulder and side seams. The easiest way to finish the neck and arm edges is to turn them under ½″ and topstitch them. Many times two rows of topstitching look better than one. You can make two rows of straight stitches or zigzag—or use a double needle for a quick finish.

You also can use other trims, such as piping and over-edge trim, on the neck and armholes. See Chapter 8 for ideas and directions.

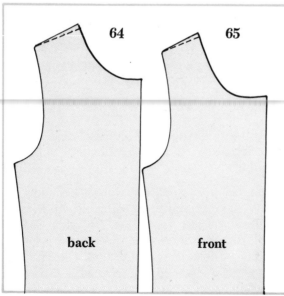

Simple knit pants
Shirt with mini-placket

5

How to Fit and Sew Women's Pants

Knit pants are fun to make and a joy to wear. Once you have a pattern adjusted to give you a custom fit, you will be able to whip up a pair of knit pants in one hour! What could be quicker—and who doesn't need more pants? For an easy project, try the simple knit pants with a fold-over, elastic waistband and no zipper. Of course, you can make pants with a separate waistband, if you wish.

GENERAL TIPS

Use these guides for selecting fabric and pattern and for adjusting seam allowances.

Choose the fabric

When you select material for pants, look for a knit that will hold its shape. This is important for the knee and seat areas. You'll find doubleknits are most satisfactory.

Polyester doubleknits are practical because you can wash and dry them by machine. They come in a variety of textures and patterns; so, you can have both dressy and casual pants. Wool doubleknits work up easily and are dressy, but they must be dry-cleaned. Double-knit acrylics are used for pants, but you should wash and dry them carefully to prevent fuzz balls and excessive shrinkage.

Doubleknit nylon was one of the first fabrics used for knit pants, and it is very comfortable and inexpensive. It does not keep a crease, however, and it will bag in the knee and seat areas. Nylon is useful for Bermudas and children's pants. It also is comfortable for activities that do not require a "just-pressed" look. Usually, you can make pants of doubleknit nylon one size smaller than pants of other doubleknits because the fabric has so much stretch.

Doubleknit cotton and cotton blends are fine for shorts and Bermudas; but, they will give you baggy knees in long pants.

NOTE: Preshrink all knit fabric to be used for pants. See "Fibers for knits" in Chapter 1 for guides.

Seam allowances

Use ⅝″ seam allowances for knit pants if the fabric will hold a press. This gives you a smooth line over the hips. Use narrow knit seams only when the fabric tends to roll and will not press flat.

Check your pattern to see what seam width is allowed. Most patterns have a ⅝″ seam allowance. Some special patterns for knits allow only a ¼″ seam; adjust your pattern, if necessary, by adding to the seam edges.

Pattern size

Buy a pants pattern according to your hip measurement. The waistline can be adjusted easily, if necessary.

SIMPLE KNIT PANTS

This easy pattern has a fold-over waistband with elastic. There are no darts or zipper. As you look through pattern books, check the small line drawings for a waist finish similar to the one sketched here. (FIG. 67)

In some pants patterns with a fold-over waistband, both front and back leg sections are cut in one piece; there is no side seam. For your first pair of pants, it is best to use a pattern with two pattern pieces for the leg. This

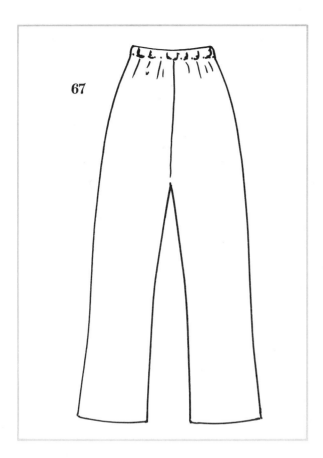

tract this total from the pattern measurement.) Remove the excess equally from the side seams and the center back seam; this involves six seam edges. Divide the excess amount of ease by six, and take off that amount from each seam edge. Do not change the center front seam. (**FIGS. 68 and 69**)

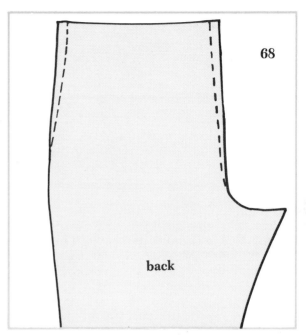

back

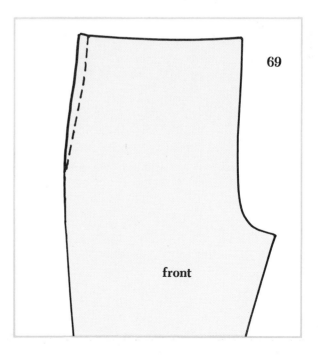

front

allows you to alter your pattern at the side seams.

Check the pattern—make adjustments

The various pattern companies allow different amounts of ease in pants patterns. Compare your body measurements with your pattern and adjust the pattern where necessary. Remember not to include the seam allowances when you measure a pattern for fit.

WAIST CIRCUMFERENCE: The pattern for a fold-over waistband style should be at least 4″ larger than your actual waist measurement. If your hips are more than 11″ larger than your waist, allow 5″ to 6″ of ease in the waist.

Many patterns from large companies allow too much ease in the waist circumference; you should correct these patterns before you cut the fabric. To alter, determine the amount of excess ease. (Add the 4″ to 6″ of ease you need to your waist measurement, then sub-

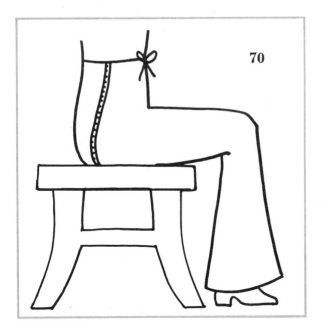

70

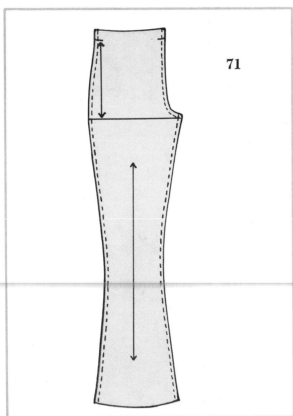

71

CROTCH DEPTH: To check this measurement, tie a string around your waist and sit on a flat surface. Place the end of a tape measure at your side on the string; take the tape down over the hip curve, under the body to the flat surface. (**FIG. 70**) Add 1″ to this measurement for the crotch depth.

Check the crotch depth on the *front* pattern piece. Measure from the waistline to the deepest part of the crotch. Draw a horizontal line across the pattern piece if your pattern does not have this line; follow the illustration as a guide. (**FIG. 71**)

Add depth by slashing the pattern at the alteration line; spread the two pieces apart as needed. (**FIG. 72**)

Subtract depth by folding the pattern along the alteration line. (**FIG. 73**)

Alter both front and back pattern pieces equally.

HIPS: Measure the largest part of your hips, and determine how far this measurement falls below your waistline. Locate your hip on the pattern by measuring down from the waistline mark. Check the pattern width at

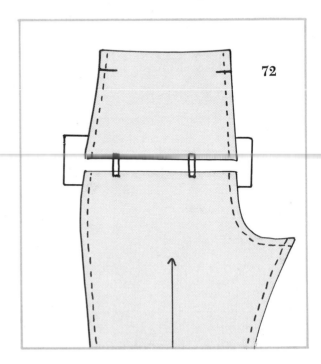

72

WAISTBAND ALLOWANCE: For a fold-over waistband, you need at least 1½″ above the waistline marking on the pattern.

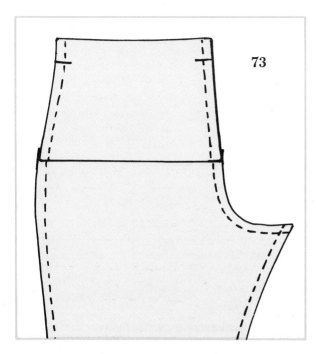

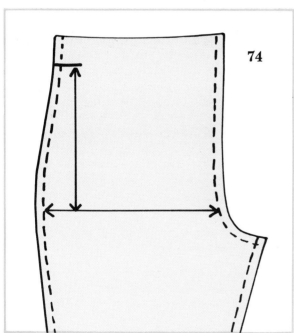

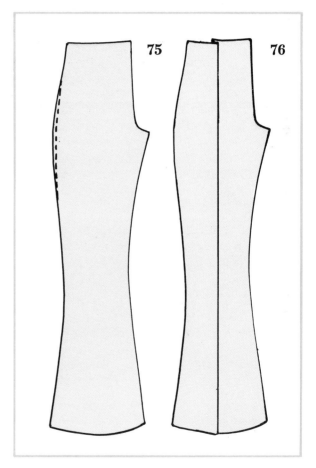

ure the same as your hips. The first time you make the pattern, however, it is best to allow the extra 1″. You can remove any excess ease when you do the string fit after pants are assembled. (The string fit is described later in this chapter.)

Alter the pattern pieces along the side seams if there is a small change to be made. (FIG. 75) For a large adjustment, make a vertical fold (or slash) down the pattern piece. (FIG. 76) Alter both front and back pattern pieces equally.

this point. (FIG. 74) Measure both back and front pattern pieces, and double the total to get the full hip width.

The pattern should be 1″ larger than your hips. If you like a slim fit, you may not want this ease. In that case, the pattern will meas-

RISE: If your figure is round in the front or round in the back, you may need extra fabric to compensate for it. You can add up to 1″ at the top of the center front seam and/or center back seam. Taper the line back to the side seam. (FIGS. 77 and 78) You will check this addition in the final fitting.

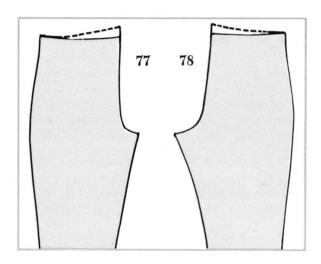

When in doubt, add the extra fabric. If you don't need it, you can trim it away after the fitting.

CROTCH CURVE: The need for this alteration often shows up in the first fitting. If the back of your pants pull down when you sit, you probably need to lengthen the back curve slightly. If you are very flat in front and back, you may need to trim some of the curve from both front and back sections.

Lengthen or shorten the crotch curve, if needed, by adding or subtracting at the inside leg seam. (FIGS. 79 and 80)

LEG CIRCUMFERENCE: You should have at least 1″ of ease in all leg areas. If you have a full

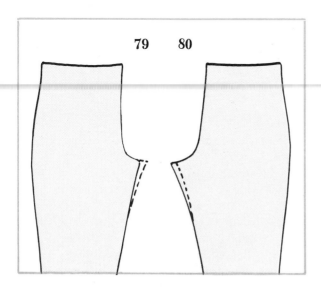

upper thigh, add extra length to the crotch curve and continue this addition down to the knee area. (FIG. 81)

LEG LENGTH: Decide how long you want your pants. Usually, wide-leg pants are worn longer than straight-leg pants.

Measure your body from the waistline down to where you want your pants to end; add 1½″ to 2″ for hem. Check your pattern and adjust. (FIG. 82) Cut across pattern and spread to add length; fold pattern to shorten.

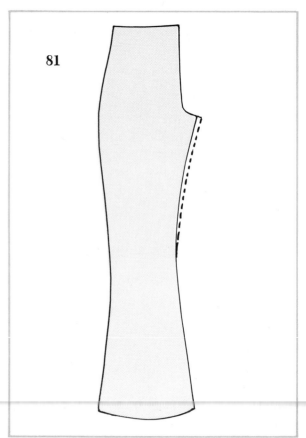

Decide on leg style

If you have a straight-leg pattern, you can adjust the width of the leg to give you different styles. Straight legs and stove pipes are 18″ to 21″ around the bottom. Flared or belled legs are 23″ to 26″. If you can't decide how wide you want the pants, measure a pair of ready-mades that you like.

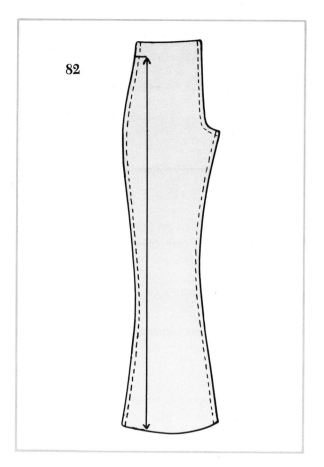

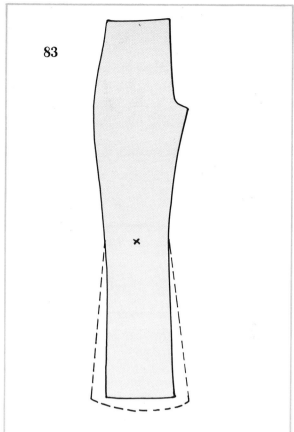

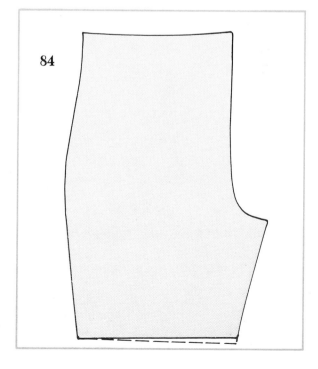

To alter the pattern for flares or bell bottoms, you must establish the knee location. Any flare will begin at the knee and go out equally on each side. Measure down from the waist to where your knee bends. Mark this location on the front and back pattern pieces.

Decide how much extra width you want to add to the pants leg, then add one-fourth of that amount to each leg seam. Draw the bottom as a curve, rather than a straight line when you make wide legs. (FIG. 83)

You can make hostess pants with wide pajama legs by starting the fullness at the hip and inside crotch seams. Add equally to all four pattern edges.

When you change a pattern for Bermuda shorts, make the bottom leg line ½″ longer at the inside leg seam. (FIG. 84) This will eliminate a hiked-up look when you wear the shorts.

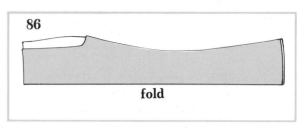

86

fold

Cut the fabric

Solid color fabrics for pants can be cut double. Fold your fabric in half, using a lengthwise rib to help you follow grain. Pin pattern pieces to the fabric using a "with nap" layout. (**FIG. 85**) Make sure the grain line of the pattern is parallel to a lengthwise rib.

If your fabric has a stripe or a design that should be matched, cut the pattern from a single layer of fabric. Make sure you cut a right and left front, and a right and left back. Do this by cutting one pants front with the printed side of the pattern up. Then turn the pattern over and cut the other front with the printed side down. Use the same procedure when you cut the pants back.

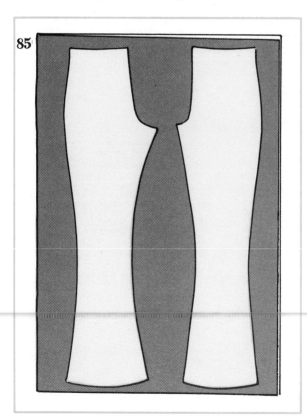

85

Assemble the pants

NOTE: When you use a pattern for the first time, do not press creases or seams until after you assemble the pants and do a string fit. Once you have adjusted a pattern to give you a perfect fit, you can stitch and press as you go.

FRONT CREASES: Set the creases in the front leg pieces before you sew any seams. Fold each front piece in half, matching leg edges. (**FIG. 86**) The crease goes straight up the front to the waist. You can make a sharp crease by using a moist press cloth and a warm iron. Never place the iron directly on the right side of the fabric.

You can use a double machine needle at this point to stitch along the crease line, if you

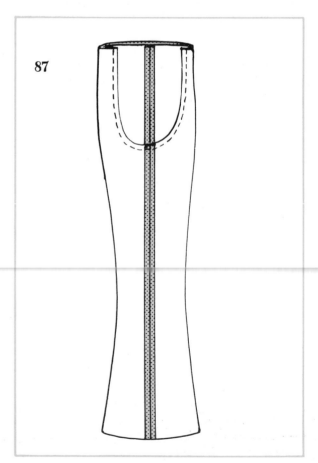

87

wish. Spread the pants leg out flat, with the right side up. Stitch down the center crease line with matching thread.

If you want a sharper edge, you can stitch along the edge of the crease while the pants leg is folded. Do this after the pants have been completed, so the stitching will catch the turned hem and keep the line sharp.

Of course, you may prefer no crease at all. In that case, go on to the next step.

SIDE SEAMS: Pin and sew the side seams. Press each seam in the closed position first in order to embed the stitches. Then press the seams open.

INSEAM: Pin and sew the inner leg seams and press. A sleeve board is useful when you press this seam.

BACK CREASES: Turn each completed pants leg right side out. Fold each pants leg along the front crease, and smooth it flat on the ironing board. The side seam and the inseam should be directly on top of each other. Press the back crease only up to the crotch area.

CROTCH SEAM: Have one pants leg wrong side out and one pants leg right side out. Slip one leg inside the other so the right sides are together. Place pins at the inseam, in the crotch curve, and at the top of the pants.

Stitch together with one long seam. (FIG. 87) If you are using a straight stitch (instead of an automatic stretch stitch), you must stretch the fabric quite firmly as you sew around the crotch curve. This will produce the stretch seam needed in this area.

Trim the seam to ¼" in the curved area, then zigzag or straight stitch the edges together. (FIG. 88) Press the remaining seam allowance open.

The string fit

Try on your pants, and tie a string snugly around your waist to hold them up. Stand in front of a mirror; pull the pants up all

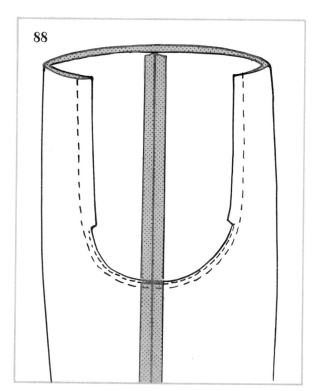

88

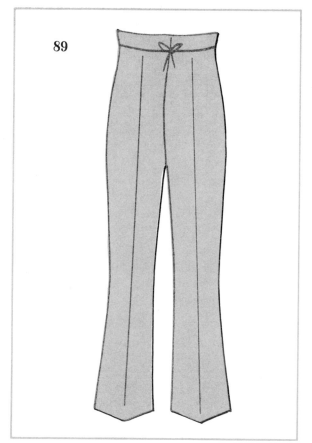

89

around the waist until you have a smooth fit. (FIG. 89) Mark the waistline by putting a row of pins directly below the string.

If you have taken your measurements and adjusted your pattern correctly, you should have at least 1½″ above the pins for a fold-over waistband. Trim away any excess fabric, and correct your pattern to correspond with the new cutting line.

NOTE: The 1½″ allowance will position the fold-over elastic waistband above your waistline (as with a separate waistband). However, you may find it more comfortable to have the elastic waist-band *end* at your waistline. If so, allow only ¾″ of fabric above the waistline pins.

Correct any fitting problems

Even though you measure and adjust your pattern, there often are fitting problems that

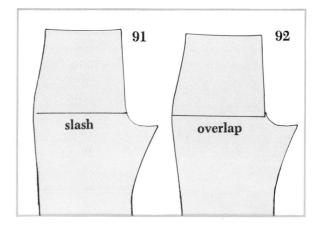

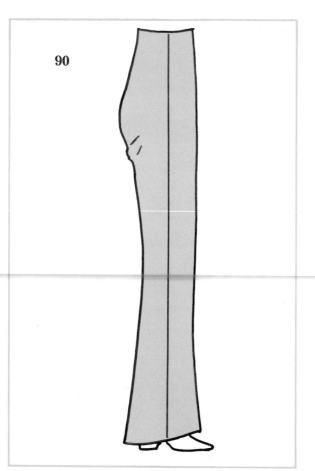

show up only when you try on the pants. Many corrections can be made simply by taking up or letting out part of a seam. In other cases, you will have to take out seams and recut a section of the pants. However, if you correct your pattern at the same time, you should be able to avoid this problem the next time you make a pair of pants.

BAGGY SEAT: (FIG. 90) You can correct this by taking a dart across the lower hip area of the back pattern piece.

Slash the back pattern piece from center back to, but not through, the side edge. Make this

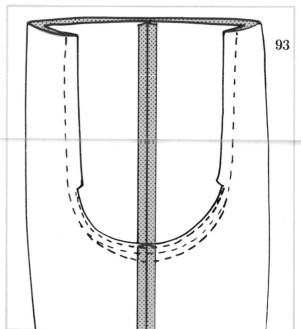

slash in the crotch curve area where the notches are located. (FIG. 91) Overlap the slash ½″ or slightly more, if needed. (FIG. 92) Tape in place, then redraw and trim the overlapped edge at the center back so it is even. Next, recut the back of the pants to fit the altered pattern.

You can stitch the crotch curve a bit lower, if needed, to compensate for the length taken out by the dart. (FIG. 93)

On your paper pattern, add a bit more height at the top of the center back seam; then, you won't have to sew the crotch lower when you make your next pair of pants.

VERTICAL WRINKLES IN THE FRONT CROTCH AREA: (FIG. 94) These may result from the pants being too short at the center front seam, or from having more fabric than necessary in the front crotch area.

If the center crotch seam is too short, the pants will pull in and be uncomfortable in the crotch. You can correct this by adding extra fabric at the top of the center front seam. Raise the waistline mark at center front, giving extra length to this seamline. Adjust your paper pattern to reflect this change. (FIG. 95)

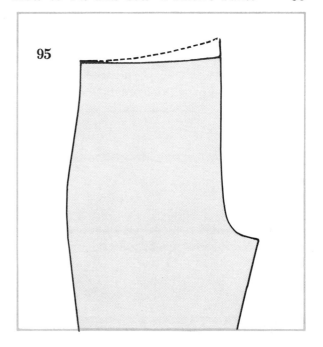

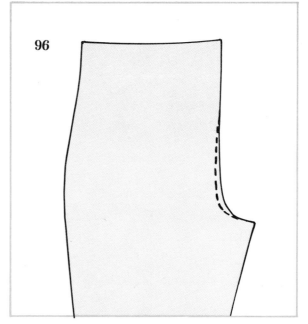

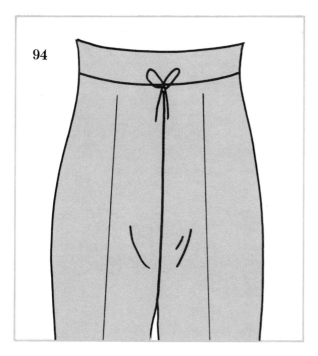

If the pants are not pulling, but you still have vertical wrinkles, try on the pants inside out. Pin the crotch seam wider until you get rid of the extra fabric that is causing the problem. Sew the new seam, being careful not to make the crotch curve lower. Adjust the paper pattern to correspond to this new curve. (FIG. 96)

Finish the fold-over waistband

Use ¾" elastic that can be dry-cleaned and is resistant to chlorine bleach. Cut a strip 1" to 2" smaller than your actual waist measurement. Join the elastic with a ½" overlap and stitch securely. (The elastic should fit snugly around your waist, yet stretch enough to slide over your hips.) Divide the elastic circle into four equal sections and mark.

Pin the elastic to the inside of the waistline, matching each mark with a seam. Position the elastic so that the edge is ⅛" below the fabric edge. Stitch along the *lower* edge of the elastic, using a wide zigzag stitch; stretch the elastic to fit the fabric as you sew. If you use a simple straight stitch, you must stretch both the elastic and the fabric as you sew. (FIG. 97)

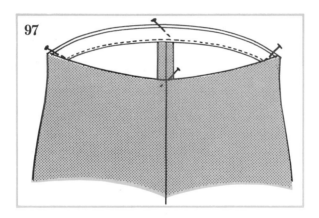

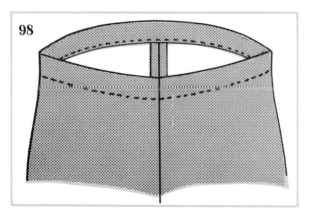

Turn the elastic and fabric to the inside of the pants; make only one turn. The elastic will be completely covered by the fabric. Attach the edges of elastic and waistband fabric to the pants. This stitching will be along the actual waistline. Stretch the elastic as you stitch, and sew with a wide zigzag. If you use a simple straight stitch, stretch both elastic and fabric as you sew. (FIG. 98)

Hem the pants

The knit hem (Chapter 3) is recommended for knit pants. It is invisible and quick to do. Topstitching can be used around the bottom of the pants legs, too. Use a matching or a contrasting thread, and do two or three rows of stitching, about ½" apart. To make a coordinated outfit, use the same type of topstitching on a matching top.

PANTS WITH SEPARATE WAISTBAND

If you prefer pants with darts and a separate waistband, you can use a regular pattern. You may be able to omit a zipper in this style, also. To check, see **NOTE** under "Skirt with separate waistband," Chapter 6. Follow directions for "Apply the closed waistband" in the same chapter.

PAJAMAS FOR CHILDREN

You can make pajama pants with a ribbed leg band by altering a child's pants pattern. Taper the leg so it measures about 4" larger than the ankle measurement. Cut a strip of ribbing about 6" wide, and sew it to the pants leg, using the neckband technique (see Chapter 4). The ribbing strips should be long enough to allow the foot to slip through. The pattern can be made even simpler by overlapping the side seams of the paper pattern. This eliminates two seams and makes the pants quicker to sew.

Skirt with separate waistband
Top with crossed-over V

6
How to Fit
and Sew Skirts

There is no limit to the skirt style you can make from knit fabrics. Straight, A-line, flared, pleated and even circle skirts work out beautifully. In most cases you can eliminate the zipper. The easiest style to make is the simple knit skirt with a fold-over waistband; but you can make skirts with separate waistbands, too.

GENERAL TIPS

Some guides concerning fabric, seam allowances and pattern size are given first. These apply to all types of skirts.

Choose the fabric

Doubleknits are the best choice for skirts because they hold their shape and will not sit out. You sometimes see straight skirts made from sweater-type knits; these are attractive, also.

Seam allowances

Use ⅝″ seam allowances whenever possible. Press seams open to give you a smooth line over the hips. You will need to add to the seam allowance if your pattern provides only ¼″ seams.

Pattern size

Buy the pattern according to your hip measurement, then adjust the waist as necessary.

SIMPLE KNIT SKIRT

This style is ideal for knits, and it goes together very quickly. It has a fold-over waistband with elastic; there are no darts and no zipper.

Pick a pattern

Most large companies have skirt patterns with fold-over waistbands; these often are paired with a tunic or overblouse. Usually the skirts are straight or A-line, but a few are flared. When you look through the pattern books, check the small line drawings for the waist finish sketched here. (FIG. 99)

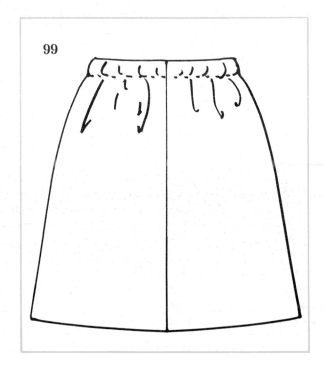

99

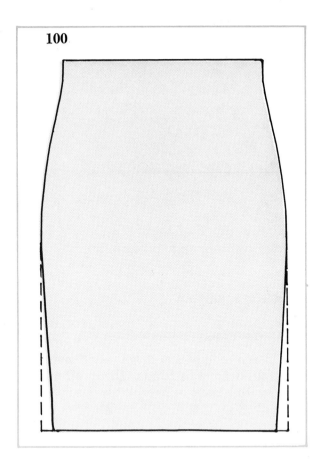

100

figure. You will need at least 4″ to 6″ of ease. Many large company patterns allow more. Wait until you fit the skirt before you take out any extra fullness. You may want the dirndl appearance that some patterns have.

WAISTBAND WIDTH: You will need 1½″ above the waistline mark for a fold-over waistband finish.

Cut and assemble the skirt

For layout guides, see Chapter 2. Stitch the skirt seams and press them open.

101

The smaller pattern companies also have this style. On some patterns the side seams are slightly tapered at the hem. This is meant for use with stretchy sweater knits that tend to flare out as they are worn. If you use such a pattern for a doubleknit fabric, straighten the side seams to eliminate the taper. (FIG. 100)

Check the pattern

HIPS: Measure your hips around the largest part, then measure your pattern at the same hip location. (Be sure to measure inside the seam allowances.) The pattern should be 1½″ larger than your hips. The ease is recommended for doubleknit fabrics to prevent the skirt from "cupping" across the back. If you are using a very stretchy fabric, you may need less.

WAIST CIRCUMFERENCE: This varies according to your pattern style, the fabric and your

The string fit

Pull the skirt over your hips for a fitting. Tie a string around your waist (along the waistline mark of the skirt), and stand in front of a mirror. The skirt should hang from your waistline in such a way that the side seams are at right angles to the floor. (FIG. 101)

If the side seams swing to the front or back, you have a fitting problem at the waist or hipline. Adjust the skirt at the waist until the side seams hang straight. Place a row of pins just below the string to mark the adjusted waistline.

On some patterns designed for knits, you will have only one pattern piece for both front and back skirt sections. These require shaping at the waistline for a good fit. Mark any alterations on your pattern.

You should have 1½" above the waist pin line for a fold-over waistband. Trim any excess, and adjust your paper pattern.

If you decide there is too much fullness at the waist, divide the excess among all seam allowances and taper all seams equally.

Finish the fold-over waistband

Use ¾" elastic that can be dry-cleaned and is resistant to chlorine. Cut a strip 1" to 2" smaller than your waist measurement.

Follow directions in "Finish the fold-over waistband" section of "Simple knit pants," Chapter 5.

Hem the skirt

See Chapter 3 for guides.

SKIRT WITH SEPARATE WAISTBAND

This is a closed waistband with elastic; there is no zipper. The technique can be used with knit pants, also.

NOTE: Not everyone can wear this type of skirt (or pants). If your hips are more than 11" or 12" larger than your waist, or if you are using fabric with very little stretch, you may need a zipper opening and a lapped waistband. If so, follow your pattern directions for this finish. If you are not sure about a zipper, you can wait until you fit the garment.

Pick a pattern

Choose your favorite skirt style—from a straight cut with waistline darts to a wide flare. Use any well-fitting conventional pattern or a pattern designed especially for knits.

Check the pattern

HIPS: Measure your hips around the largest area. For a doubleknit fabric, the pattern should be 1½" larger than your hips. A stretchy fabric may require less ease.

WAIST CIRCUMFERENCE: The pattern should have 1" to 2" of ease. Use the full 2" if your hips are wide in relation to your waist, or if you are working with a firm fabric.

Cut and assemble the skirt

You can omit a center back seam in a straight skirt if you place the seamline of the back pattern piece on a fold of the fabric.

Sew any darts first; press them toward the center of the skirt. Stitch seams of the skirt and carefully press them open.

The string fit

Pull the skirt over your hips for a fitting, as described in "The string fit" under "Simple knit skirt."

At this point you will know if a zipper is necessary. If there is too much strain on the fabric, you should insert a zipper in the left side seam and use a lapped waistband; follow your pattern directions. If you can pull on the skirt without strain, you can proceed without a zipper.

There should be ⅝″ of fabric above the pin line for seam allowance. Trim away any excess, and adjust your paper pattern accordingly.

Apply the closed waistband

Cut a waistband 4″ wide across the stretch of the fabric, and 2″ larger than your waist measurement. Place the right sides together and stitch with a ½″ seam. (**FIG. 102**) Press the seam open.

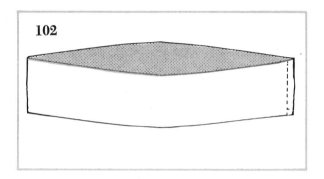

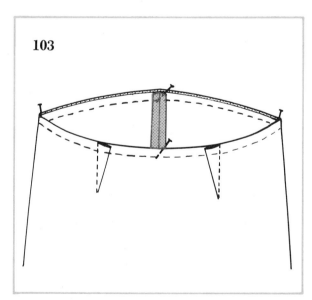

Divide both waistband and skirt into four equal sections. Turn skirt wrong side out. Pin the right side of the waistband to the right side of the skirt, matching the divisions. The waistband seam should be at the center back of the skirt. Stitch with a ⅝″ seam allowance; have machine set at 9 stitches per inch. (**FIG. 103**) Stretch both pieces of fabric as you sew. Remember that this line of stitching must stretch enough to go over your hips.

Next, add the elastic. Use 1″ elastic that can be dry-cleaned and is resistant to chlorine. Cut a strip ½″ larger than your actual waist measurement. Join the elastic in a circle with a ½″ overlap and stitch securely.

Divide both elastic and waistband into four equal sections. Pin elastic to the waist seam allowance, matching division marks. Keep the lower edge of the elastic slightly above the first stitching.

Stretch the elastic to fit and stitch it to the seam allowance only; use a wide zigzag stitch. If you use a simple straight stitch, you must stretch both the elastic and the waistband as you sew. (**FIG. 104**)

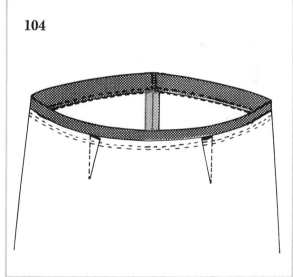

Pull the waistband up and over the elastic; fold it to the back. Hold waistband in place with pins on the right side, just below the seamline.

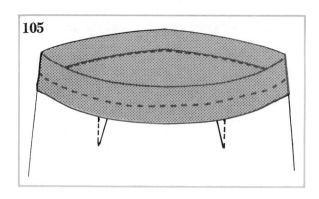

105

Stitch in the seam groove from the right side. (**FIG. 105**) Stretch the fabric if you are using a simple straight stitch. A zipper foot is a help for this stitching.

Trim away any excess seam allowance from the back of the waistband.

Hem the skirt

See Chapter 3 for guides.

A. V-neck shirt with insert
B. Mitered V-neck top
C. Placket with collar

7

Try Some Neckline Variations

You can customize a new pattern or give your basic patterns a new look by changing the neckline style. It's an easy way to add variety to one pattern. This chapter shows you how to convert a round neckline to a V-neck, to a V-neck with an insert, to a placket opening (with or without a collar) or to a mini-placket (combination of the V-neck and placket). Use these neckline variations on dresses for yourself and on shirts and tops for everyone in the family.

V-NECKS

One advantage of a V-neck is that you can use a strip of self-fabric for the trim, rather than trying to find ribbing that matches. The neck opening is large enough to pull over your head; so the self-fabric does not have to be very stretchy. You can use ribbing, of course, but self-fabric usually is more attractive.

By learning how to cut a V to any length, you eliminate the need for many different patterns. You save money and keep down the clutter in your sewing area.

Pick a pattern—cut the V

Your pattern can have set-in or raglan sleeves. If you buy a pattern with a V-neck, follow it to cut your fabric. If you use a basic top or dress pattern, follow the lower, crew neck markings (Chapter 4) when you cut the fabric.

To make a V-neck on a set-in sleeve garment, fold the front section (fabric) in half along the center front. Cut the V to the desired length, starting at the center front fold and ending at the neck edge. (FIG. 106)

If you use a raglan sleeve pattern, first cut out the fabric and sew the sleeves to the front and back sections; then, fold the garment down the center front. Cutting line for the V starts at the center front fold and ends at the neck edge in the middle of the sleeve sections. (FIG. 107)

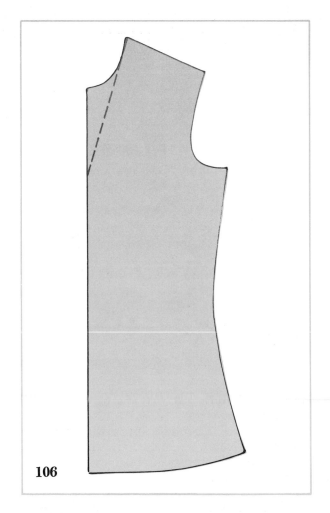

106

NOTE: The depth of the V is up to you, but the opening must be large enough to pull over your head. You can cut it a bit deeper than you want the finished opening to be, because the trim will fill in 1½" to 2" at the V-point.

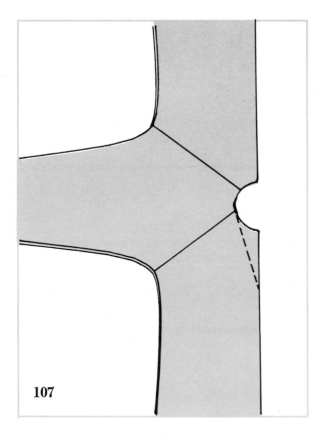

107

Prepare the trim

Trim can be self-fabric, contrasting fabric or ribbing. Cut a 3″ strip across the greatest stretch of the fabric. You will need enough trim to go around the V-neck, plus about 4″. Fold the trim in half lengthwise, wrong sides together, and pin. Do not press the trim at this point.

To keep the neck edge firm and to hold it against your neck, you will stretch the trim slightly as you stitch it to the garment. It is important that the trim strip measure less than the neck opening, especially when you use very stretchy fabric or ribbing. It also is important to measure and use the same amount of trim on both sides of the V; otherwise, the point of the V will pull to one side.

To measure the neck edge, insert a pin from the wrong side of the garment, ½″ below the point of the V. Measure along the ¼″ seamline from this "point" pin to the shoulder seam (A). Then measure from this shoulder

seam to the opposite shoulder seam (B). (**FIG. 108**) Make sure the fabric is flat and not stretched when you take these measurements.

On one end of the trim strip, mark off 1″ with a pin.

Determine length of trim you need for the first side of the V; follow the guide below.

Self-fabric
- For an adult, use ⅜″ less trim than the measured distance.
- For a child, use ¼″ less.

Ribbing trim
- For an adult, use ¾″ less trim than the measured distance.
- For a child, use ½″ less.

NOTE: The above measurements are for firm self-fabric trim. If the self-fabric is very stretchy, follow the measurements for ribbing.

On the trim strip, measure the first side of the V and mark with a pin.

Determine length of trim you need across the back of the neck. Measurements are the same for both adults and children. (Guide follows).

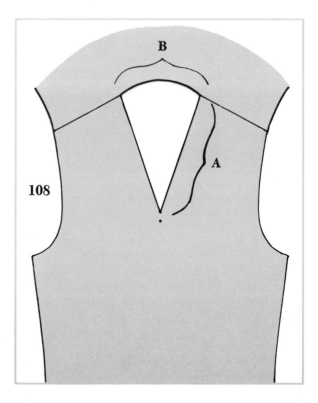

108

Self-fabric • Use ½" to 1" less trim than the measured distance; subtract the lesser amount if fabric is firm.

Ribbing trim • Use 2" of ribbing for every 3" of neck curve.

NOTE: If you are using self-fabric that is very stretchy, follow the measurements for ribbing.

On the trim strip, measure length needed for the back neck section and mark it with a pin.

Next, measure trim length for the other side of the V and mark it with a pin. Give yourself another inch at the end of the strip. Trim strip should look like **FIG. 109.**

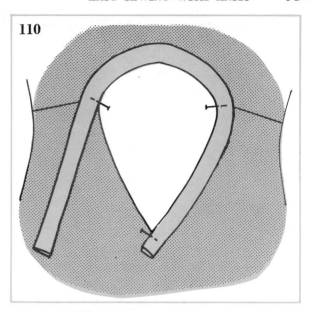
110

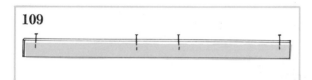
109

Choose a finish

THE MITERED V: Trim is joined with a seam at the V-point.

Place the right side of the trim against the right side of the garment, with cut edges even. Have the first 1" mark on the trim over the "point" pin on the garment; insert the "point" pin through the trim. Use a ¼" seam allowance.

Pin the next mark on the trim to the shoulder seam. Take the trim around the back of the neck, and pin the next measured mark to the opposite shoulder seam. (**FIG. 110**) Now you are ready to stitch.

Begin stitching at the point of the V; use a straight stitch on your machine and a ¼" seam allowance. Stitch with trim side up. Stretch the trim to fit as you stitch up the side of the V. Continue stitching across the back to the opposite shoulder, stretching the trim to fit. Stop stitching and leave the machine needle in the garment.

To complete the V, lift the free end of the trim (where you began the stitching), and

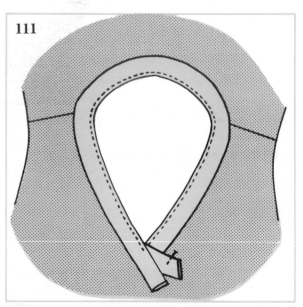
111

pin it out of the way. Insert a new "point" pin from the back of the garment exactly at the point where you began stitching.

Pin the last section of trim in place. Put the "point" pin through the trim at the last mark, using a ¼" seam allowance. Then, continue stitching from the shoulder to the point of the V. (**FIG. 111**)

NOTE: Stitching lines should meet at the point of the V for a neat finish. (**FIG. 112**) Be fussy here, and correct the stitching if necessary.

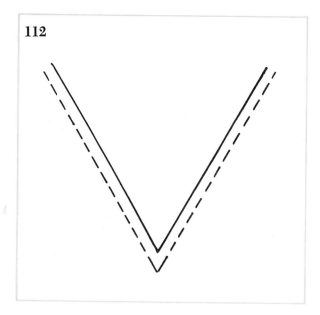

112

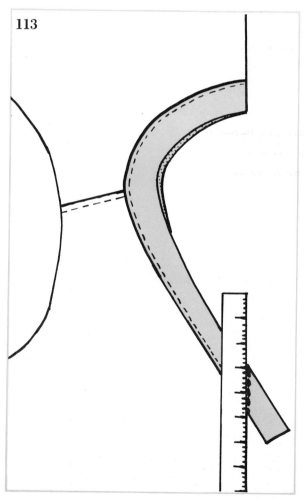

113

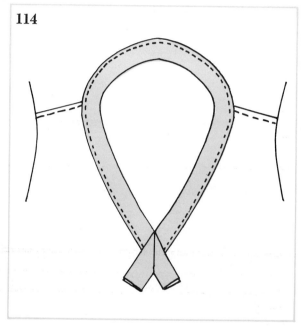

114

Clip into the point of the V, and turn the trim so the seam is on the inside. Fold the garment down the center front, right sides together. Place a ruler along the fold, extending it over the trim. (FIG. 113) Draw a line on the trim, following the edge of the ruler; stitch along this line for a perfect miter.

Press the mitered seam open, and press the seam allowances down into the garment. (FIG. 114) Do a second stitching along the seam allowances with straight or zigzag stitches; catch the trim ends to the seam allowances at the V. Cut away excess trim ends, and your mitered V-neck is completed. (FIG. 115)

THE CROSSED-OVER V: Trim crosses at the V-point. It crosses right over left for a woman, left over right for a man. Directions and illustrations are for a woman's garment.

Pin the right side of the trim against the right side of the V, with cut edges even. The 1″ mark on the trim should be placed over the "point" pin, using a ¼″ seam allowance on the trim. Pin the trim at the shoulder seam and across the back to the other shoulder seam.

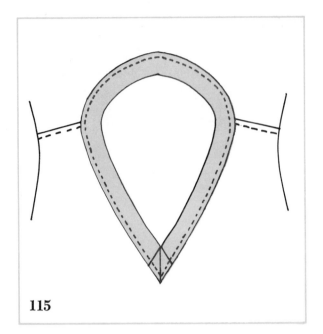

115

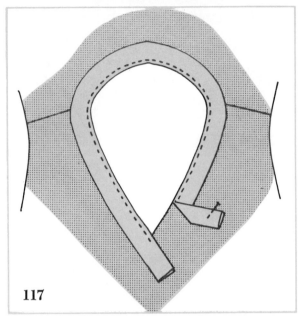

117

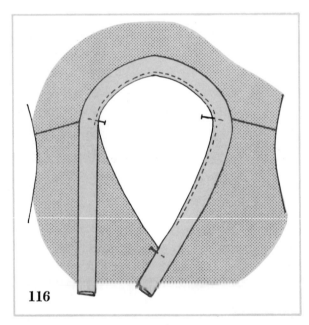

116

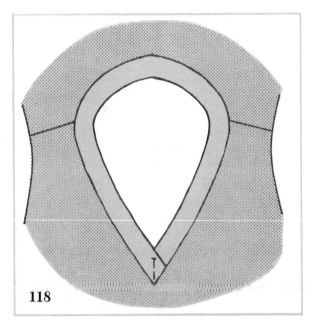

118

Stitch with trim side up. Begin stitching 2″ above the point of the V. (For a man's shirt, begin stitching at the V and continue around the neck; trim will be in correct position.) Stitch up to the shoulder seam and around the back of the neck, stretching the trim to fit. (**FIG. 116**) Stop stitching at the opposite shoulder seam; leave machine needle in the garment.

Lift the free end of the trim strip (at the beginning of the stitching), and pin it out of the way. Insert a new "point" pin from the wrong side of the garment, ½″ below the point of the V. Place the last mark on the trim over the "point" pin, still using a ¼″ seam allowance; pin securely. Finish stitching from the shoulder seam to the point of the V. (**FIG. 117**)

Clip the garment down to the point of the V, and turn seam to the inside. Lay the garment on a flat surface, right side up. Unpin the free end of the trim and position it behind the last section of trim, already stitched in place. Adjust the trim ends until they lie flat at the V; pin in place. (FIG. 118)

Fold the garment back and close the open seam (the 2″ you left open at the begin-

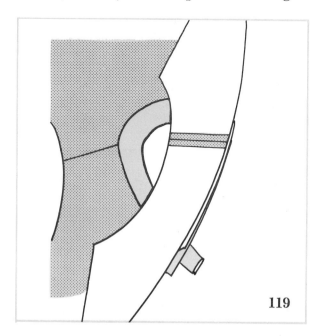

119

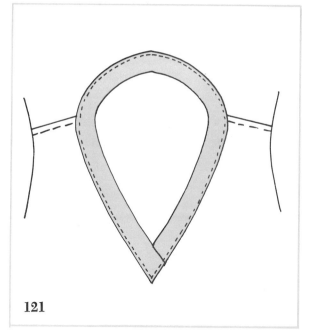

121

ning). Stitch from the 2″ above the V down to the V. Follow the ¼″ seam allowance; this will catch both sections of the trim to the garment. (FIG. 119)

Press the neck trim from the wrong side so seam allowances go down into the garment. (FIG. 120) Do a second stitching along the seam edges with either a straight stitch or a zigzag. Trim the excess ends for a neat finish. (FIG. 121)

V-NECK WITH INSERT

This style combines a low V cut on the garment with a high round neckline on the insert.

Pick a pattern—cut the V

The top or dress pattern must have set-in sleeves. You can use a crew neck or turtleneck finish. Decide on the neck style, and cut the fabric accordingly.

To cut the V, fold the garment front down the center and draw a line from the middle of the shoulder to the lowest point of the V. (FIG. 122) Cut the V quite deep (2″ above the waistline is a good length).

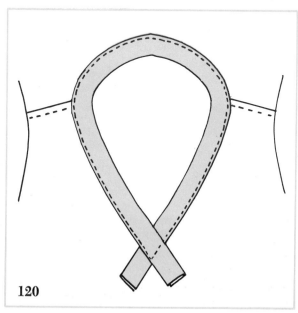

120

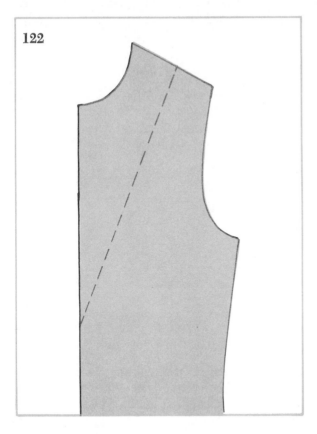

122

Cut the insert

Use the V cut-out section as a pattern, and cut the insert from a contrasting fabric. Add

123

½″ for seam allowances along both sides of the V; follow exactly along the neck and shoulder edges. (FIG. 123)

Apply the trim

Trim for the sides of the deep V can be either self-fabric or ribbing; you will need two strips of trim 3″ wide. Insert a pin from the wrong side of the garment, ½″ below the point of the V. Measure along the ¼″ seam-line from the "point" pin to the shoulder seam.

Determine amount of trim you need for each side of the V from the guide below. (This is for a V that ends about 2″ above the waist-line.) Add 1″ extra to each strip for overlap.

Self-fabric
- For an adult, use ⅝″ less trim than the measured distance.
- For a child, use ½″ less.

Ribbing trim
- For an adult, use 1″ less trim than the measured distance.
- For a child, use ¾″ less.

Work with the garment front only, and sew the prepared trim to each side of the V. At the V-point, use either the mitered or crossed-over technique, described earlier in this chapter. Use ¼″ seam allowances; do not make a second row of stitching along the edge at this time. Press the trim so that seam allowances go out into garment.

Add the insert

Pin the right side of the insert to the wrong side of the garment front; line up the cut edge of the insert with the edges of the trim. Pin through the trim at 2″ intervals. (FIG. 124)

Fold back the garment front; stitch directly over the trim seamline, catching all layers of garment, trim and insert. (FIG. 125) Sew from the shoulder down to the point of the V, pivot the fabric around the needle and stitch up to the other shoulder edge.

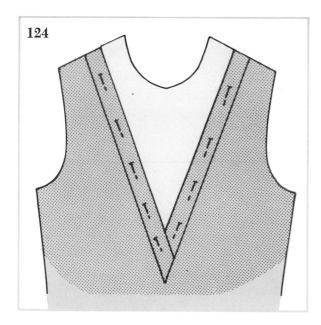

124

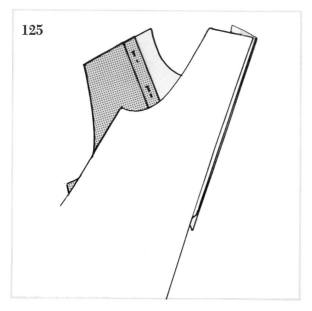

125

Do a second row of stitching along the seam edges, using either a straight stitch or a zigzag. You have completed the garment front; you are ready to join the shoulder seams and complete the neck trim.

PLACKETS

Placket openings of various lengths work well on knit garments. Use a short placket with a collar for a man's golf shirt, a woman's top or a child's shirt; use a longer version for a dress opening. Without a collar, you can finish the placket and neck opening with an over-edge trim.

Pick a pattern

You can adapt a basic knit top or dress pattern for cutting plackets and placket facings; there is no need to invest in new patterns. Use the high neckline on your basic pattern for all placket variations. Finish the neck edge with a collar or with an over-edge trim.

Placket with a collar

The length of this placket is up to you. For a man's golf shirt, the placket is about 9″ long. For a dress opening, 21″ is a good length. Use a ¼″ seam allowance at the neck edge.

CUT THE COLLAR: Make the collar from one large rectangle of fabric. Measure around the seamline of the neck edge. (Do not include seam allowances.) Cut a rectangle of fabric

126

as long as this measurement and 7″ wide. This is your complete collar pattern; it will be folded down the center to form the upper collar and undercollar. (FIG. 126)

You can make the collar pointed by adding extensions to the basic pattern. Measure 1″ to 3″ out beyond the edge of the collar at the fold line; redraw the edges at an angle. (FIG. 127) The distance between A and B must not change; that is the line to be stitched to the garment. The farther out you extend the collar points, the more pointed you make the collar.

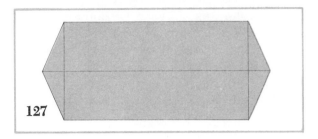

127

MAKE THE COLLAR: Fold the collar lengthwise with right sides together. Stitch the ends of the collar with ¼" seam allowances. (**FIG.** **128**)

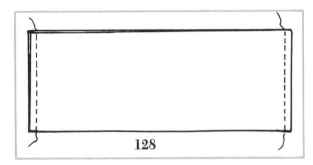

128

Turn the collar to the right side. Press the collar, rolling the seam allowances under so they will not be visible from the right side. (**FIG. 129**) The undercollar will develop a bulge in the middle because of this rolling; carefully steam out the fullness and press so the cut edges of the collar are even. If you choose to topstitch the collar, do it now.

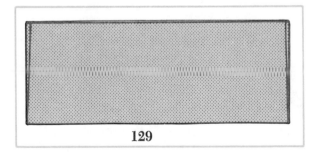

129

Make a ⅛" to ¼" cut in the *undercollar* at the center back. Use ⅛" for a lightweight knit and ¼" for a heavy knit. Trim the undercollar in a gradual curve, wide at the center cut, tapering to nothing at the side seams. (**FIG. 130**)

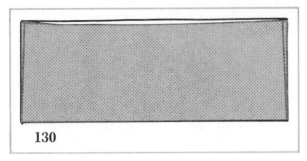

130

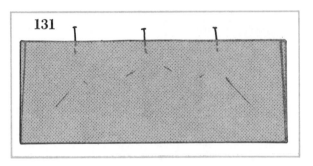

131

Divide the unfinished edge of the collar into four equal sections; pin the upper collar and undercollar together at these marks. (**FIG.** **131**) If you complete all the steps correctly, you will have a new bulge—this time in the upper collar. This gives your collar a permanent shape and a smooth roll.

132

<u>DRAW A PLACKET BOX</u>: Mark the center front on your paper pattern. Then draw a box around this center front line, 1½″ wide (¾″ on each side of center front) and as long as you want your placket opening. (**FIG. 132**)

<u>CUT THE FACINGS</u>: Use a piece of pattern paper or tracing paper 12″ wide and 8″ longer than the placket box. Along the length of the paper, make a 2″ fold, and place the folded edge on the outside line of the box. (**FIG. 133**)

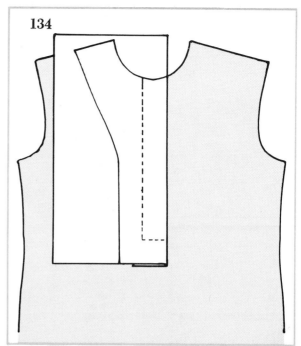

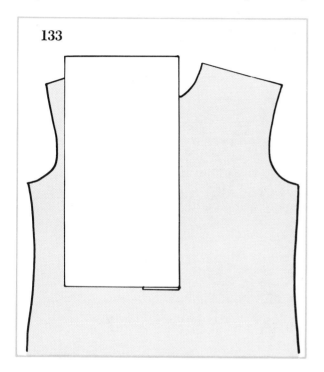

Position the paper so it covers the neck curve of your basic pattern, plus 4″ of the shoulder line. The bottom of the paper should be at least 2″ below the box.

Trace along the neck curve and then 3″ along the shoulder line. From here, draw a curve down the pattern front to the bottom of the paper so it ends 4″ from the fold. (**FIG. 134**) Cut along the lines you have drawn; unfold the paper. The placket facing should look like **FIG. 135**. Use this pattern to cut a right and a left facing from your fabric. Use it also to cut two pieces of interfacing; for these, use only part of the placket pattern—from fold to the straight edge.

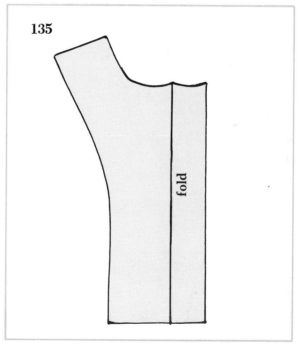

<u>ADD A PLACKET STAY</u>: On the paper pattern, divide the box lengthwise into three ½″ sections. Draw a wedge at the bottom that is 1″ deep and slants to each corner. (**FIG. 136**) Cut a stay (from firm, woven fabric; see

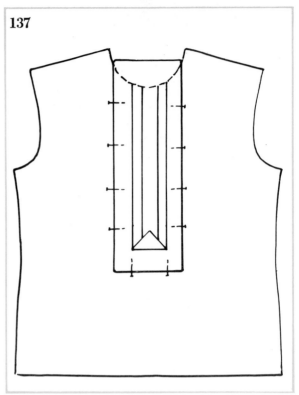

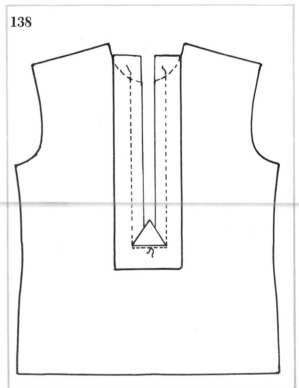

Chapter 3) that is 4″ wide and 2″ longer than the box. Trace the box design onto the stay fabric.

Mark the center front line on the garment by pressing a crease that is 1″ shorter than the box. Lay the stay fabric on the wrong side of the garment front section. Center the tracing over the garment crease, and pin securely in place. (FIG. 137) Make sure the bottom of the design box is on or parallel to a stripe, or that it follows the cross grain of the fabric.

Use a matching thread and 12 stitches to the inch to sew along the outside lines of the box. Start at the center point of the bottom of the box, and stitch up to the neck edge. Again, start at the center point of the bottom of the box and stitch up the other side. (FIG. 138)

Cut along the inside lines of the design and remove this center section of fabric; but, do not cut all the way into the corner of the box at this time.

PREPARE THE FACINGS: Fold each placket facing along the fold line, wrong sides together, and press. Open each facing and secure the interfacing to the small section; bond it in place or stitch it to the facing along the edge. (FIG. 139) This interfacing provides support for buttons and buttonholes.

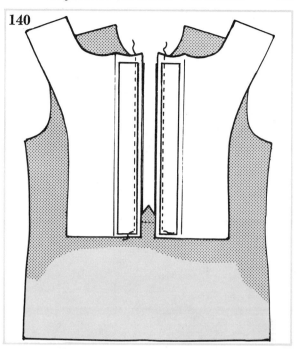

140

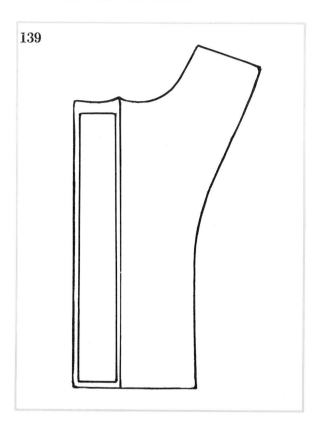

139

STITCH THE PLACKET: Place the right sides of the facings against the right side of the garment; line up the cut edges. Pin in place, and turn the garment to the wrong side.

Stitch on top of your first stitching lines. Go from neck edge to the corner of the box on each side. Backstitch in the corners to make ends secure. Now, cut all the way into the corners on the garment, but do not cut the seam allowances on the placket facings. (FIG. 140)

Press the facings so that seam allowances go out against the garment. Lay the garment, wrong side up, on a flat surface. Fold the facings on the pressed-in fold lines, and arrange

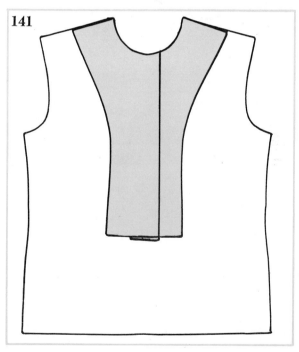

141

them so they fill the opening. (FIG. 141) (Outside of finished garment should have the lap right over left for a woman; it should be left over right for a man.) Notice that the neck facings follow the neck curve.

Turn the garment to the right side; tuck the wedge down inside the garment. By hand, catch the lower folded edge of the top facing to the edge of the placket opening. (FIG. 142) This will hold placket in place during the final stitching.

Lift the garment front until you see the wedge lying on top of the placket facings. Stitch across the base of the wedge, catching it to both facings. (FIG. 143)

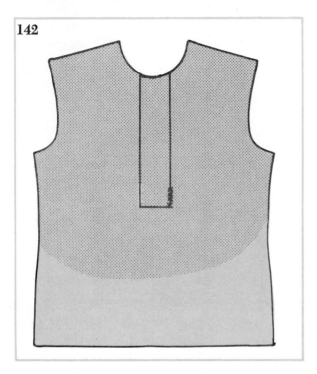

142

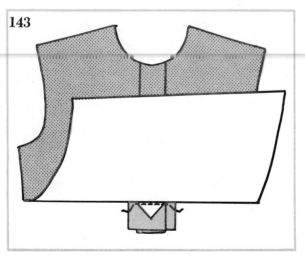

143

Press lightly from the wrong side and remove the hand stitches. Trim the stay fabric close to the stitching lines.

STITCH SHOULDER SEAM: Join the shoulder seams of the garment and press them.

ATTACH THE COLLAR: Divide the neck opening of the garment into four equal sections. With pins, mark center back and center front; then place pins halfway between. Keep in mind that the center front of the garment is in the middle of the placket, not at the edge. Pin the collar to the garment with the underside of the collar against the right side of the garment; match the division marks. Collar should meet at center front. Keep the placket facing free, and sew the collar to the neck edge with a ¼" seam allowance.

Turn the facing back from the front fold line, so the right side of the facing is against the collar; pin it in place. Make sure the amount of placket extending past the collar is the same on both sides. Sew the facing in place by stitching over your original seamline.

Grade the seam allowances, and turn the facings right side out. Press the back neck seam allowances down inside the shirt. Topstitch around the back of the neck just below the seam to hold the seam allowances in place.

MAKE THE BUTTONHOLES: If you wish to have buttonholes, add them now. Make buttonholes vertical; center them in the placket. (See "Machine buttonholes," Chapter 8.)

Placket with over-edge trim

This variation of the placket does not have a collar; so, the full facings are not necessary.

CUT THE FACINGS: Cut two pieces of garment fabric, 4" wide and 2" longer than the finished placket. These strips are the placket facings. (Garment neck and placket edges will be finished with a separate ½" trim.) Also, cut two strips of interfacing, 2" wide and 2" longer than finished placket.

MAKE THE PLACKET: Follow directions for "Draw a placket box" and "Add a placket stay." (See "Placket with a collar" earlier in this chapter.)

Fold the two facing strips of fabric in half lengthwise with the wrong sides together and press well. Slip interfacing between each facing strip and bond it in place or stitch it to the facing along the edge. Place the facing strips on the right side of the garment; line up cut edges of strips with cut edges of box. Pin in place. (FIG. 144)

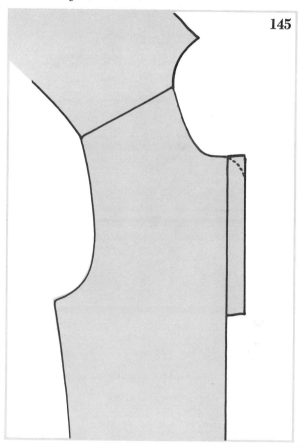

145

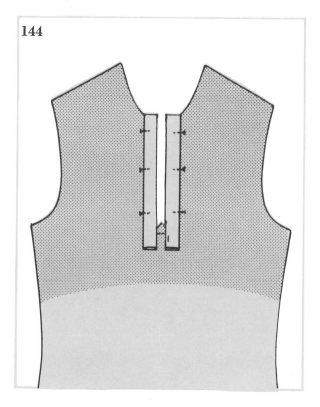

144

Turn the garment to the wrong side. Stitch down your original seamlines from neck edge to the corners of the box; backstitch to make ends secure. Now, cut into the corners of the wedge, but do not cut the placket facing seam allowances.

Stitch the shoulder seams together and press. Fold the garment along the center front and center back. Pull the two facing strips out so that one is on top of the other. Round off the top corners of the placket facings. (FIG. 145)

APPLY THE TRIM: Cut a strip of trim across the stretch of the fabric, 2½" wide. The trim can be cut from self-fabric, contrasting fabric or ribbing.

Place the right side of the trim against the right side of the placket and neck; cut edges of the trim should line up with edges of the placket and neck. Stitch along the trim ½" from the edge. Ease the trim around the curve at the placket top, and stretch it slightly around the neck curve.

Check the stitching to see if it is even; correct it if necessary. Turn the trim over the stitching and press; then fold it to the inside of the garment. Catch it in place by stitching in the seam groove on the right side. Cut away excess trim from the inside of the garment.

FINISH THE PLACKET: Arrange the placket pieces with the proper lap, and pull the small wedge to the inside. Catch the edge of the

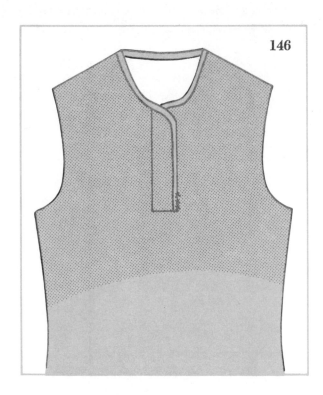

THE MINI-PLACKET

One of the quickest neck finishes for a woman's knit top is the mini-placket. It's a combination of the V-neck and the placket; the neck opening is cut V-shape, and there is a lapped placket below the V-point.

Pick a pattern—cut the V

Use a set-in or raglan sleeve pattern with a high neckline and cut your fabric. Fold the front garment piece in half, and cut the V. (FIG. 148)

NOTE: Do not cut lower than you want the finished neck opening to be. You will be using very narrow trim; it will not fill much of the V-point.

Press a crease down the center front of the garment, 1" shorter than the finished placket. Stitch the shoulder seams together and press them open or to one side.

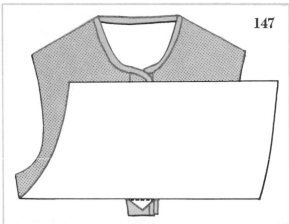

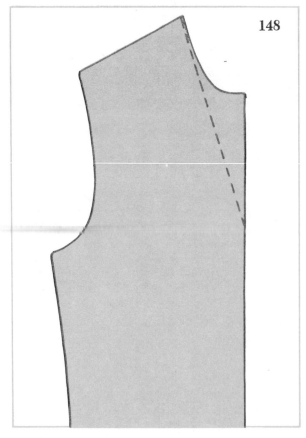

placket facing to the side of the opening with a few hand stitches. (FIG. 146)

Lift the garment front until you expose the wedge. Stitch across the base of the wedge through the two facing pieces. (FIG. 147) Trim away excess stay fabric.

MAKE THE BUTTONHOLES: Finish the placket with buttons and buttonholes; make the buttonholes vertical. (See "Machine buttonholes," Chapter 8.)

Measure the trim

Cut a strip of trim across the stretch of the fabric, 1½″ wide. Fold it in half lengthwise, wrong sides together, and press lightly. You will need enough trim to go around the neck opening and down both sides of the crease, plus about 3″ extra.

Make the placket

Mark the bottom of the placket with a pin. Place the prepared trim on the right side of the garment front with the cut edges against the center crease. Let 1″ to 2″ of trim extend below pin that marks the bottom of the placket. (FIG. 149)

Stitch the trim to the garment with a ¼″ seam allowance. Start the stitching line at the pin. Keep cut edges of trim along the center crease, and stitch up the trim. Ease the trim around the point of the V, and continue stitching around the neck. Stretch the trim slightly as you sew it to the back of the neck so that it will curve. Continue stitching down the other side of the neck until you reach the

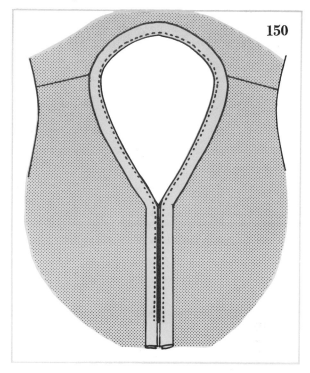

150

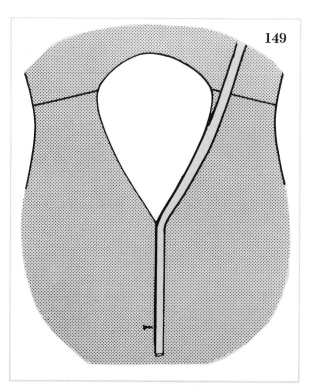

149

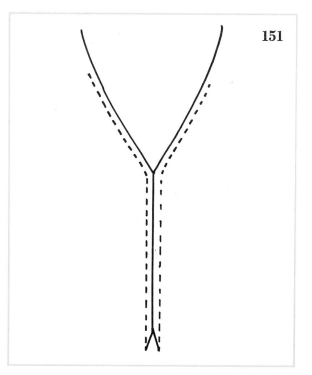

151

pin at the bottom of the placket. Remember to ease the trim as you stitch around the point of the V. (FIG. 150)

The beginning and end of the stitching line should be directly opposite each other. Correct them if they are not. Secure these points with backstitching. Slash down the center front crease to within ¾" of the end of the stitching. Then cut to the end of the stitching lines to form a wedge. (FIG. 151)

Working from the right side, arrange the trim in its finished position. (Lap right over left for a woman.) Tuck the free ends to the inside at the bottom of the placket, and pin the overlapped trim together. Baste the trim in position at the bottom of the placket to hold it for the final stitching. (FIG. 152)

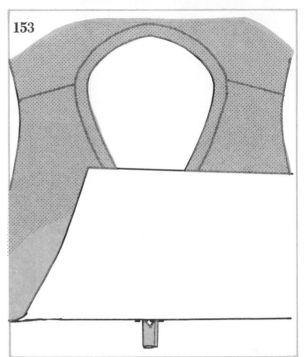

153

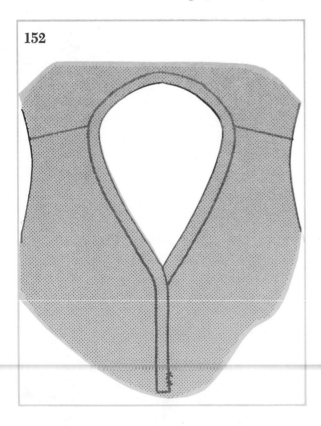

152

Lift up the front of the garment until you see the wedge lying on top of the trim strips. Carefully stitch across the base of the wedge catching it to the trim strips. (FIG. 153)

Do a second row of stitching around the seam edges and press the seam allowance down into the garment. Cut away any excess trim at the bottom of the placket.

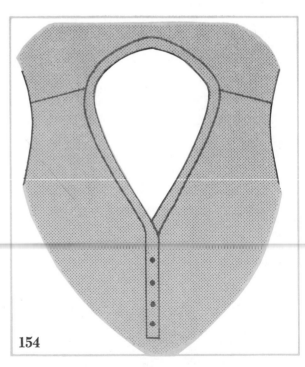

154

Close the placket with small buttons. You can sew them through both layers of the placket if you do not need buttonholes. (FIG 154)

8

How to Apply Zippers, Trims and Buttonholes

One basic pattern can be the basis of an interesting wardrobe. Variations in trims at neck, sleeves and hems, as well as different uses of zippers and buttonholes, will give each garment an individual look. This chapter covers three ways to use exposed zippers, eight ideas for trimming garments and two methods of making buttonholes.

ZIPPERS

Knit skirts and dresses usually have a one-piece front and back. If you need a zipper, you probably insert it in a center back (or center front) slash; this gives you an exposed zipper. Directions follow for applying an exposed zipper in a slash—first in a garment *without* a deep neck trim, and then in a garment *with* a deep neck trim. A third exposed zipper application is in a shoulder seam. Try to match the zipper color to the fabric, and preshrink the zipper before you stitch it in place.

Exposed zipper in a slash

In this application, you sew the zipper in a slash at center back before you stitch any seams.

ADD A STAY: Lightly press a crease down the center back of the garment (1″ shorter than the zipper length); this is a guideline for centering the zipper. Place the zipper on the crease, with the top of the zipper teeth at the neck seamline. Insert a pin in the garment to mark the bottom of the zipper teeth. Remove zipper and put aside until later. (FIG. 155)

Use stay fabric that is preshrunk (see Chapter 3). Cut a piece of stay fabric 3″ wide and 2″ longer than the zipper. Draw a line the length of the zipper down the center of the stay fabric. (FIG. 156)

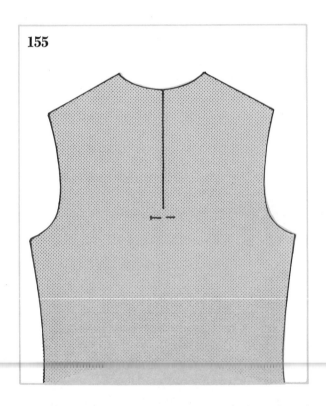

155

Pin the stay fabric against the right side of the garment, with the drawn line directly over the center back crease. (FIG. 157) Position the bottom of the line at the pin that marks the bottom of the zipper. Stitch along the drawn line from the bottom to the top, using 12 stitches to the inch.

Now stitch a rectangle around the center line. Go down one side, ⅛″ from the center line;

stitch the length of the drawn line. Turn and stitch across the bottom to ⅛″ beyond the center line. Turn again and stitch up the other side, keeping ⅛″ from the center line. (**FIG. 158**)

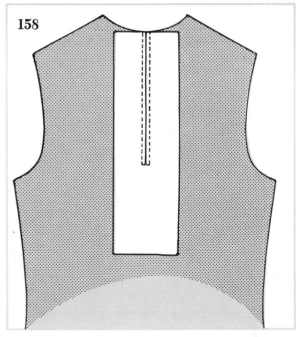

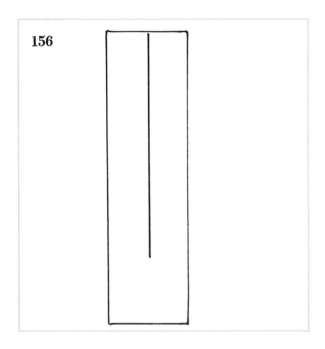

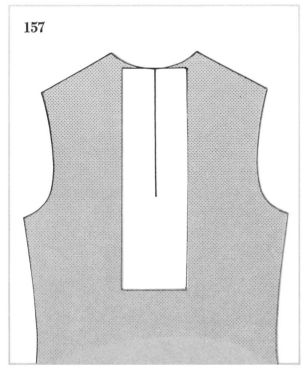

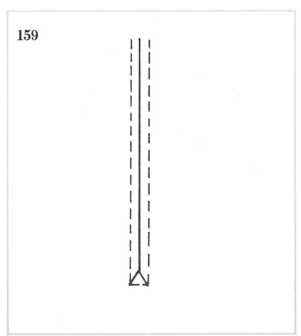

Slash down the center line to within ½″ of the bottom; cut into the corners, making a wedge. (**FIG. 159**)

Turn the stay fabric to the wrong side and press so that none of it shows on the right side. You have a neatly faced slot. (**FIG. 160**)

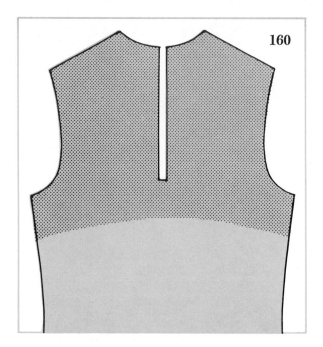

160

STITCH THE ZIPPER: Pin the zipper in the slot; make sure the metal stop at the bottom of zipper is exposed. Lift the lower edge of the garment until you see the ends of the zipper tape and the wedge. Stitch across the base of the wedge, securing it to the zipper tape. (**FIG. 161**)

Unpin one side of the zipper, but leave zipper in place. Fold back that side of the garment until you see the stay fabric (with zipper un-

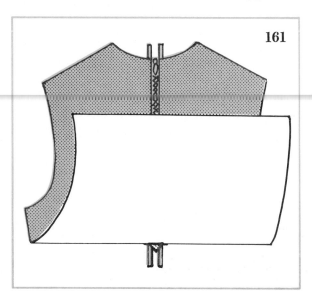

161

derneath) and the original stitching line. Use a zipper foot, and stitch the garment to the zipper tape by sewing up this same stitching line (**FIG. 162**); stitch from bottom to the top. Keep the cut edge of the garment parallel to the zipper tape (you should be able to see this through the stay fabric). Correct your stitching from the zipper tape side if the stitching isn't straight.

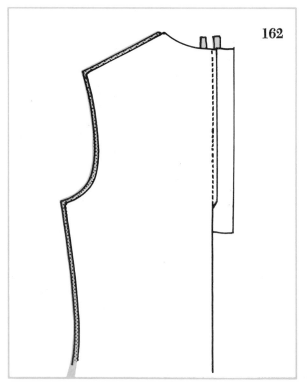

162

Unpin the other side of the zipper, and fold back the other side of the garment. Stitch the zipper from the bottom up.

NOTE: It is important that you stitch both lines in the same direction.

Trim stay fabric close to seamlines.

FINISH THE NECK EDGE: Sew the shoulder seams together and press them. Use a narrow trim or a facing to complete the neck edge.

Exposed zipper through a neck trim

You may want a zipper in a knit top or dress with a high neck trim; this gives you a larger neck opening to pull over your head. Or a zipper may be necessary when you use self-fabric for the neck trim; most knit fabric does not have enough stretch to pull over your head.

Follow these directions for applying a zipper through a crew neck or turtleneck. Attach the trim first, then insert the zipper.

PREPARE THE TRIM: Use special ribbing or self-fabric. Cut the trim strip 3″ wide for a crew neck, 4″ to 4½″ wide for a mock turtleneck and 9″ to 10″ wide for a full turtleneck.

The length of the trim will vary with the amount of fabric stretch. Generally, the length should be 1″ less than the neck seam of the pattern to keep the trim snugly against your neck. This measurement may be too short for firm trim or too long for stretchy trim. Try the measured strip around your neck to see how it feels and looks. Adjust the length if needed. Do not add a seam allowance when you cut this trim; the exposed zipper will separate the two edges.

Fold the trim in half lengthwise, wrong sides together, and press a crease at the center fold. The crease will be a guideline for zipper placement and for finishing the trim.

Open the trim and butt the cut edges together (let edges touch, but not overlap). Join cut edges by hand or with a machine zigzag stitch. (FIG. 163)

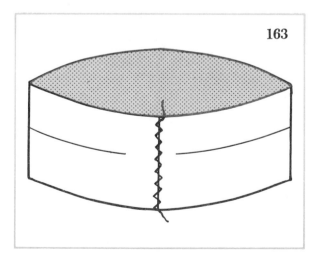

163

Divide one edge of the trim into four equal sections and mark with pins; have one mark at the joined edges.

ATTACH THE TRIM: Sew the shoulder seams of the garment together; press them open or to one side, depending on the fabric and seam you use. Divide the neck edge of the garment into four equal sections and mark with pins.

Turn the garment wrong side out. Slip the prepared trim inside the neck edge of the garment with the right sides together. Place the joined edges of trim at the center back, and pin the division marks of trim and neck edges together. Stitch with a narrow knit seam (refer to Chapter 3). Press the seam up into the trim (the trim is not folded double at this point).

APPLY STAY AND ZIPPER: Follow directions for "Add a stay" and "Stitch the zipper" under "Exposed zipper in a slash" earlier in this chapter.

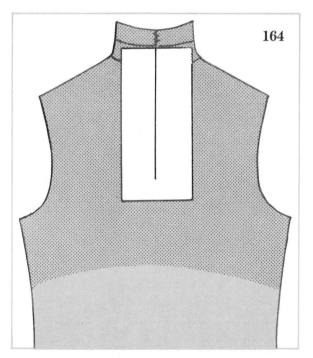

164

NOTE: In this application, position top of zipper and top of stay fabric at the center fold on the neck trim. (FIG. 164) When you are ready to

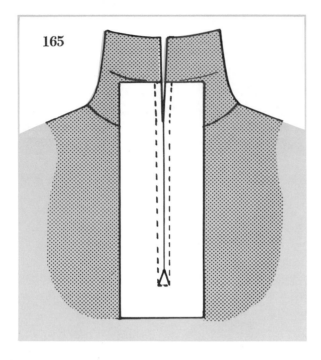

165

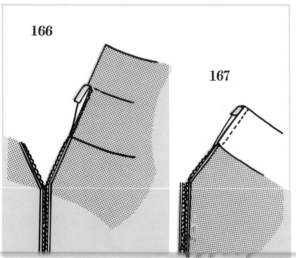

166

167

the neck seam. (Zipper teeth are inside the folded trim.) Stitch along the original zipper seamline, through the zipper tape and both layers of trim fabric. (FIG. 167)

Cut away the excess zipper tape, and turn the neck trim right side out. Zipper teeth are exposed for a neat finish.

Pin the loose edges of the neck trim in place; make sure that ¼″ of the trim extends below the neck seamline on the inside of the garment. Finish the neck trim by stitching in the seam groove from the right side (see Chapter 3).

Exposed zipper through a neck trim—shortcut version

In the preceding method, you do the final stitching on the neck trim after you insert the zipper. In this method, you have the trim completely in place before you insert the zipper. This shortcut method is fine for a basic knit top with ribbing trim.

Cut trim and butt narrow ends; stitch. Fold trim lengthwise. Divide both neck edge and trim into four equal sections; match the divisions, with trim seam at center back. Stitch together with a narrow knit seam.

Add zipper; refer to "Add a stay" and "Stitch the zipper" under "Exposed zipper in a slash"

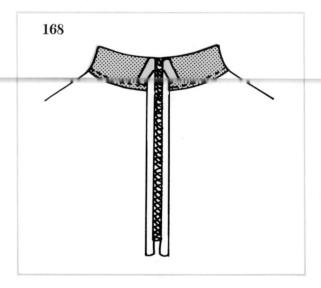

168

slash the center back opening, slash through the stitches that hold the neck trim together. (FIG. 165)

FINISH THE TRIM: Open the zipper. Unfold the neck trim so it is flat and right side up; this turns zipper teeth away from center back. Turn down excess tape. (FIG. 166)

Fold the neck trim over the zipper teeth so that the right sides of the trim are together, and the bottom edge of the trim is ¼″ below

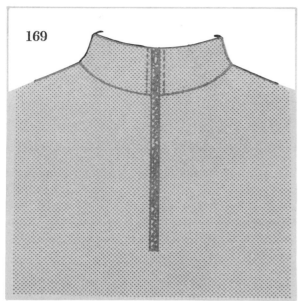

169

in this chapter. Place zipper in the slot, with the top of the zipper teeth at the top fold in the neck trim. After zipper is stitched in place, fold the zipper tape ends to the inside of the garment (**FIG. 168**); topstitch through the trim to hold tape ends in place. (**FIG. 169**)

Zipper in a shoulder seam

Use a shoulder seam zipper with a turtleneck or mock turtleneck finish and a set-in sleeve. The zipper is exposed in the left shoulder seam; so, a good color match is important. Match neck trim to garment since zipper is exposed in the neck finish, too.

The zipper should be long enough to extend from the top of the finished neck trim, along the shoulder seam and just past the edge of the shoulder. You will stitch across the zipper teeth; buy a nylon zipper so that you will not damage your machine needle.

CUT THE FABRIC AND TRIMMING: Cut out the garment, using the high neckline on your pattern. Close the right shoulder seam, then measure the distance around the neck edge.

Cut a strip of matching trim that is 4" to 4½" wide for a mock turtleneck or 9" to 10" wide for a full turtleneck. You will stretch the trim as you stitch it to the neck edge.

The strip should be about 1" shorter than the neck opening. Try the measured strip of trim around your neck to check the size; you may need to cut firm knits a bit longer and stretchy knits a bit shorter.

ATTACH THE TRIM: Fold the trim in half lengthwise, wrong sides together; press the fold. Open the trim to the full width and divide one edge into four equal sections. Divide the garment neck edge into four equal sections. Pin the division marks together, starting at the open shoulder seam. Stitch the trim to the neck edge, right sides together. Press seam allowances up into the trim.

INSERT THE ZIPPER: At left shoulder seam, place the zipper against one seam edge of the garment, right sides together. Position top of the zipper teeth at the fold line of the trim, and have zipper teeth running along the seamline. Use a zipper foot; stitch on the zipper tape side, close to the teeth. (**FIG. 170**)

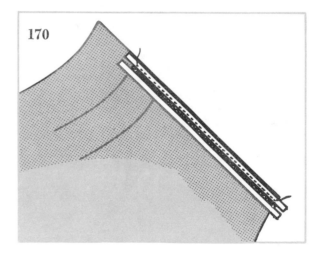

170

Pin the free edge of the zipper to the free edge of the garment shoulder, right sides together. Position top of zipper teeth at fold line of the trim. Stitch as you did the first side. (**FIG. 171**) Make sure the neck seams are directly opposite each other on the zipper tape and that the neck seam allowance is into the trim area when you stitch across it.

Unzip the zipper, and fold the tape ends down and away from the zipper teeth. Fold

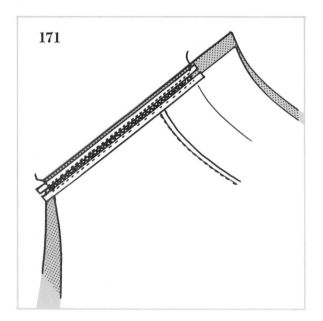

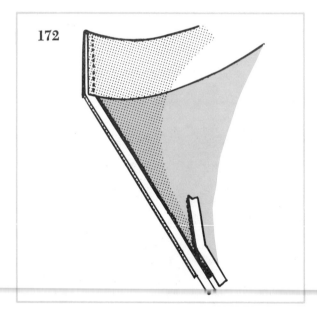

in place. Close the zipper and set the sleeve into the arm opening. Double stitch across the zipper area, and cut away any excess zipper.

TRIMS

You can finish garment necks, sleeves and hems with plain hemming or facing—or with special trimming effects. Here are directions for using a fake-cuff hem, an over-edge trim, a mock over-edge trim, piping, a ribbing edge trim, and topstitching. The chapter also tells you how to make corded belts, loop buttonholes, gathered short sleeves, and how to use ribbing for collars and cuffs.

Fake-cuff hem

This hem variation is for sleeves and for the bottom edges of tops, sport shirts and pants (straight-cut garments, rather than flared styles). The hem is easy to make and looks as though you added a separate cuff. Allow an extra ½" in the hem width for this finish.

Turn the hem under; make a double fold. (FIGS. 173 and 174) Each turn should be 1¼" wide for a sleeve and 1½" wide for the bottom edge of a shirt or pants.

Stitch ¼" from the edge of the fold (FIG. 175); then unfold the hem and press. (FIG. 176) The stitching catches the raw edge in the fold and you have a clean finish on both sides of the garment.

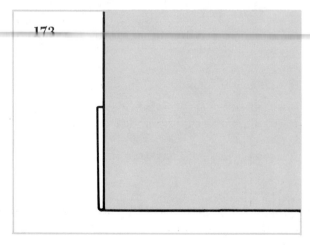

the trim over the zipper so that the right sides of the trim are together and free edge of trim is ¼" below the neck seam. (Zipper teeth are inside the folded trim.) Stitch as close to the zipper teeth as you can. (FIG. 172) Cut away excess fabric in the corner, and turn the neck trim right side out.

FINISH THE TRIM: Pin the free edge of the neck trim over the neck seam; stitch in the seam groove from the right side to hold trim

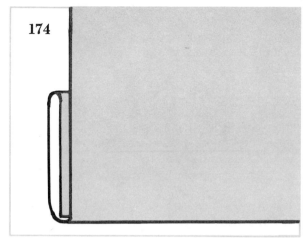

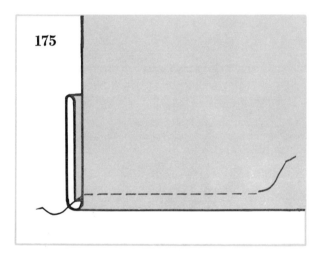

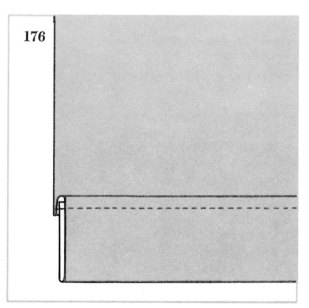

Over-edge trim

Use this attractive trim around neck and arm openings, along jacket edges and around hems. The over-edge trim is a separate strip of fabric that actually binds a cut or folded edge (FIG. 177); you cut away all seam allowances before you apply the trim.

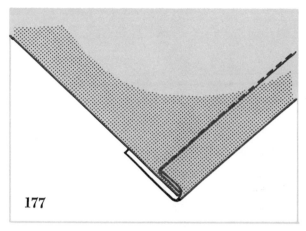

THE TRIM: Use a strip of matching or contrasting fabric, and cut across the fabric so that the strip has maximum stretch. Decide how wide you want the finished trim. For a neck or armhole, ½″ is a good width; you may want a wider width for a jacket edge. Cut trim strips four times as wide as the finished trim will be, but never less than 2½″. (A narrower width is difficult to handle.) Have the strips as long as the garment edges you will bind; join strips with a bias splice if necessary.

GENERAL DIRECTIONS: Cut away the seam allowances on the garment edge where you will add trim. Place one edge of the trim along the edge of the garment, right sides together. Stitch on the trim side. Your stitching depth determines trim width. For instance, if you stitch ½″ from the cut edge, finished trim will be ½″ wide. Correct stitching if it is uneven.

Turn trim over the stitching line and press. Wrap trim around garment edge and fold to the inside. Catch trim in place by stitching in the seam groove from the right side. Use a short stitch (18 per inch). If the trim is a contrasting color, put thread that matches the garment on the machine top and thread that matches the trim on the bobbin. After you complete the stitching, cut away excess trim.

You should stretch the trim slightly as you stitch around an inside curve (such as the

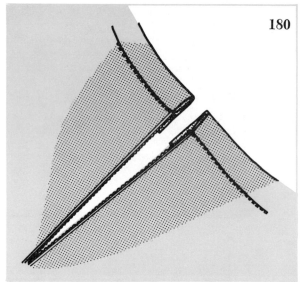

180

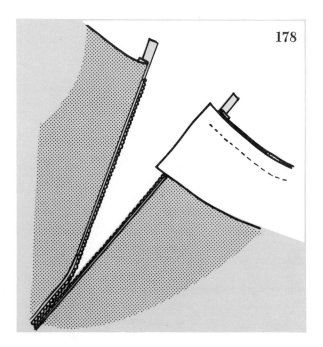

178

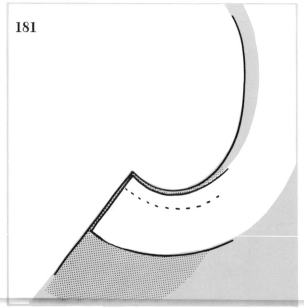

181

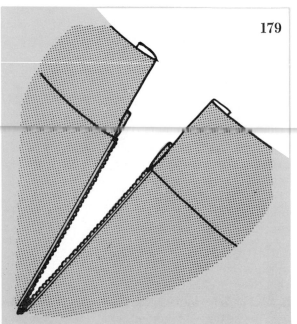

179

neck); do not stretch trim along a straight edge. Ease the trim slightly as you stitch around an outside curve (such as a lapel).

ORDER OF WORK: For a *neckline*, first insert the zipper and close the shoulder seams. Open the zipper. Position trim, leaving ½″ extending beyond the zipper at both ends. (FIG. 178) You will fold these ends in when you turn and finish the trim. (FIGS. 179 and 180)

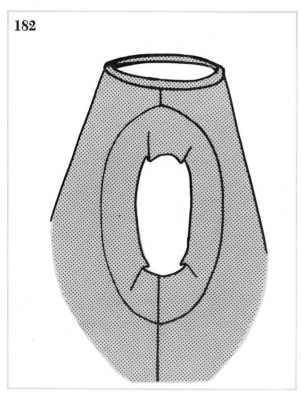

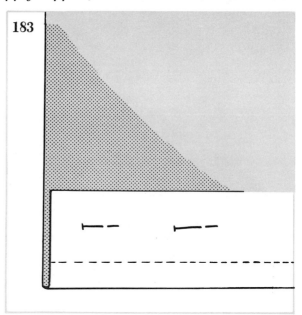

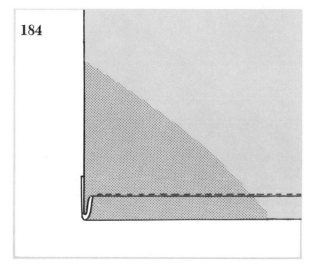

For a *sleeve or hem,* stitch one edge of the trim (**FIG. 181**), then close the sleeve or side seam. (**FIG. 182**) Turn trim to the inside and stitch in the seam groove.

Mock over-edge trim

This looks like over-edge trim, but it is made without adding a separate strip of fabric. You can use it on a straight edge that does not have much curve. It works well for hems on tops, shirts or dresses that do not flare. Allow a 2″ hem on the garment when you cut the fabric.

Fold up a 2″ hem, right sides of the fabric together. Stitch along the fold, ½″ from the edge. (**FIG. 183**)

Unpin the hem and press the free end down to cover the folded edge. Wrap the free end around the folded edge to the inside of the garment. Catch the hem in place by stitching in the seam groove from the right side. (**FIG. 184**) Cut away excess fabric on the inside.

Piping

A narrow piping trim is fine for neck and arm openings. It can be of the same or contrasting fabric.

THE TRIM: Cut the trim strip across the stretch of the fabric, 1¼″ wide. Cut the length the same measurement as the edge to be finished, plus seam allowances; you will not stretch trim as you apply it.

GENERAL DIRECTIONS: Use ¼″ seam allowances on garment edges to be finished. On the

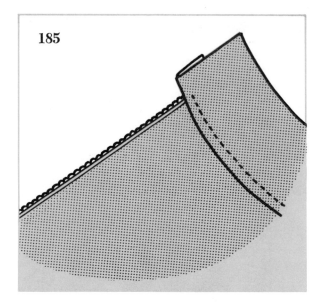

185

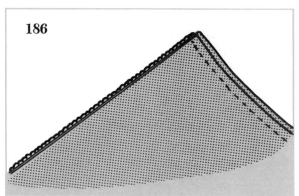

186

At the *armhole*, position trim and do the first stitching, then close the side seam. Turn piping to finished position and do the final sewing.

Ribbing edge trim

You can use ribbing to trim sleeveless arm openings as well as the sleeve and shirt edges and necklines that are discussed in Chapter 4.

THE ARMHOLE: First, cut seam allowance to ¼". Since you will add 1" of ribbing, cut away an additional 1" from the armhole. (FIGS. 187 and 188) Cut fabric; stitch shoulder and side seams.

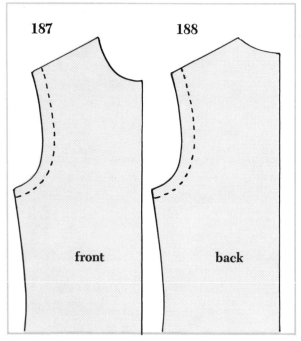

187   188

front   back

trim, make a fold lengthwise, ⅜" deep, wrong sides together. Place the edge of the smaller section against the garment edge, right sides together. Stitch a seam, ⅛" from the edge of the trim fold, catching trim to garment. (FIG. 185)

Press the trim to the inside. Catch down the free edge of the trim with a row of topstitching (FIG. 186), or with hand stitching on the inside.

ORDER OF WORK: At the *neckline*, first insert zipper in garment; close the shoulder seams. Then position trim; leave ½" extending beyond the zipper at each end. (You will turn these ends in before you do the final sewing.) Do the first stitching, turn trim to the inside and do the final sewing.

THE TRIM: Cut a strip of ribbing 2½" wide and 2" to 3" smaller than the arm opening. Join narrow ends of the ribbing with a ¼" seam; press the seam open with your fingers. Fold ribbing, wrong sides together, and divide it into four equal sections.

Turn garment wrong side out. Divide the arm opening into four equal sections, and slip the prepared ribbing inside. Pin the division marks together. (FIG. 189) Stitch with a narrow knit seam, stretching ribbing to fit.

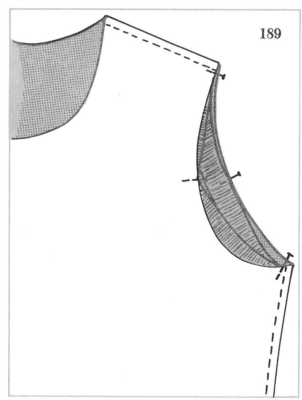

189

Press trim from wrong side so that seam allowances go into the garment.

Topstitching

Use this easy finish on sleeves or the bottom edges of garments. Thread your machine top with buttonhole twist (a heavy silk thread). Adjust tension and stitch on the right side. Stitch several rows, about ½" apart.

If you do not have buttonhole twist, use two strands of regular thread. Most newer machines hold two spools; or, wind two bobbins with the thread and stack them on one spindle.

Corded belt and button loops

Turn a strip of garment fabric into a corded belt or into button loops to use on a plain dress or pantsuit. A corded belt also makes an interesting tie closure for a vest.

CUT THE FABRIC: Use a strip 1" to 1½" wide; cut it along the lengthwise grain of the knit.

CORDED BELT: You will need cotton cording, twice the length of the fabric strip. Fold the fabric strip in half lengthwise, right sides together. Slip the cord down along the fold. (FIG. 190) Position cord so that half the length extends out beyond the end of the strip.

Stitch across the end of the strip, catching the cord in the stitching. (FIG. 191) Backstitch here to make it secure.

Stitch down the length of the strip, using a zipper foot. (FIG. 192) Keep the cord along the fold, and stretch the fabric as you sew. Trim the seam allowance close to the stitching line.

Turn the strip of fabric by pulling on the end of the cord. As you turn the strip, you automatically thread the other half of the cord through it (FIG. 193); this saves you time. Turn in the raw ends of the belt and catch them by hand. You can tie a small knot in each end of the belt.

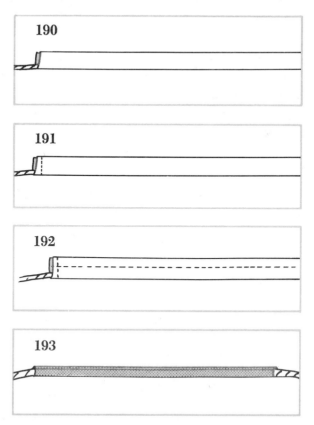

190

191

192

193

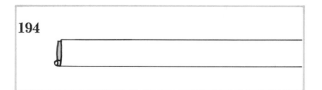

194

195

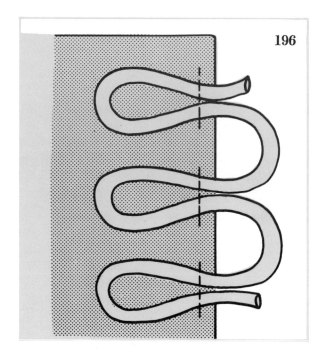

196

BUTTON LOOPS: When you make button loops, you will not need to cord them. Fold the fabric strip in half lengthwise, right sides together. Use strong string that is 1″ longer than the fabric strip. Slip the string into the fabric along the fold, with 1″ extending beyond the end. (FIG. 194)

Stitch across the end of the strip and down the length. (FIG. 195) Use a zipper foot; keep string close to the fold and stretch fabric as you stitch.

Trim the seam allowance, and pull the strip through to the right side. There will be no string inside. Use this long strip to form but-

ton loops. Baste them into position before you sew the garment facing in place. (FIG. 196)

Gathered short sleeves

To make this full sleeve for a girl's top or dress, cut the bottom edge of the sleeve slightly wider than usual, then stitch ribbing to the edge. (FIG. 197)

Cut the sleeve edge about 3″ larger than the arm circumference. Use FIG. 198 to help you alter the sleeve pattern. Add equally to both sides.

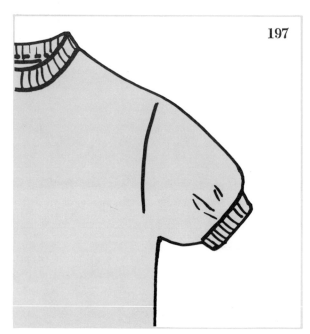

197

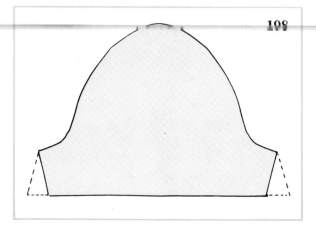

198

Cut a strip of ribbing 3″ wide and ½″ less than the arm circumference. Stitch the narrow ends of the trim together with a ¼″ seam; press the seam open with your fingers. Fold the ribbing in half lengthwise, and divide it into four equal sections.

Divide the sleeve into four equal sections. Pin the ribbing to the sleeve edge, right sides together, with divisions matching. Stretch the ribbing to fit the sleeve in each section; stitch with a narrow knit seam.

Ribbing for collar and cuffs

Use matching or contrasting ribbing to make collars and cuffs for knit tops and dresses. This type collar will stretch over your head, just like a crew or turtleneck; you can slip your hand through the cuff so that no closure is needed.

Use the high neckline on your basic pattern when you cut the garment. Adjust the sleeve length to accommodate the extra length the cuff will add.

THE COLLAR: Cut a strip of ribbing 10″ wide, and stretch it firmly around your head to determine how much length you need. Remember, this collar has to pull over your head.

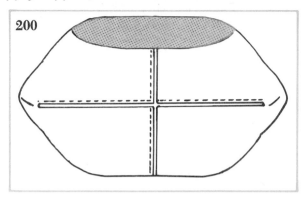

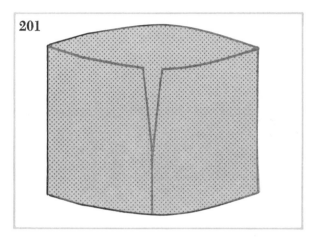

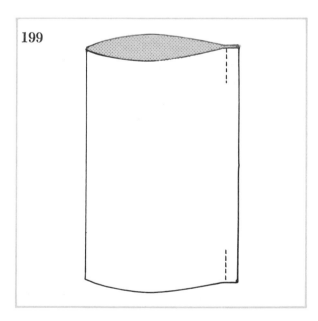

Fold fabric along the 10″ width, right sides together. Stitch down from the top edge 1″, and up from the bottom edge 1″. (FIG. 199) Backstitch at the beginning and end of these stitching lines so they will be secure.

Refold the collar lengthwise so that it looks like FIG. 200. Close the remaining opening by stitching from each end to the center. Do not cross the center seam.

Turn the collar to the right side. It should look like FIG. 201.

Divide both the collar and the neck edge of the garment into four equal sections. Pin them, right sides together, with the collar seam at the center front. Stitch with a narrow knit seam. (FIG. 202)

CUFFS: Make a cuff as you do a collar—only the measurements are different. The strip of cuff fabric should be about 10″ wide and ½″ less than your wrist measurement.

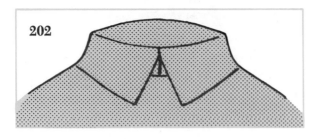

202

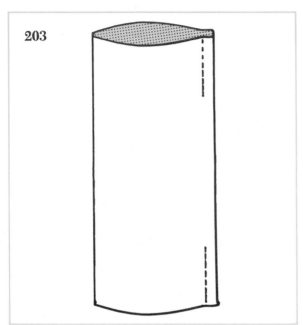

203

Bound buttonholes

Fabric-edged buttonholes are easy to make in knit fabric. If you've had trouble with bound buttonholes, you should be pleasantly surprised with this method.

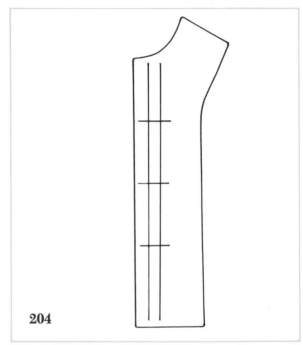

204

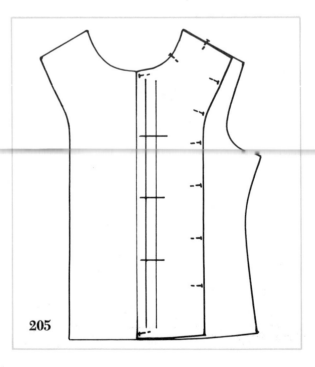

205

For each cuff, fold along the 10″ width, right sides together. Stitch down from the top edge 2½″, and up from the bottom edge 2½″. (FIG. 203) Backstitch at the beginning and end of the stitching lines.

Refold cuff and stitch (as for collar). Turn to the right side. Divide both the sleeve edge and the cuff in half and mark with pins. Slip the cuff inside the sleeve so that right sides are together. Position the cuff so the wings of the cuff will be on the outside of your arm. Stitch cuff to sleeve with a narrow knit seam.

BUTTONHOLES

You'll find both bound and machine-made buttonholes on knit garments. The nature of knit fabrics suggests that you modify the buttonhole techniques you use on woven fabrics.

MARK THE GUIDELINES: You begin the bound buttonholes before you do any other sewing on the garment. Make buttonholes from the right side; use an interfacing for support.

Trace the buttonhole markings from the pattern onto the interfacing. Extend all horizontal and vertical lines, so the interfacing looks like FIG. 204. Position the interfacing on the wrong side of the garment. Match center front lines and pin securely. (FIG. 205)

Stitch along the traced lines, using a contrasting thread and a basting stitch on your machine. Stitch all horizontal lines in the same direction, and stitch all vertical lines in the same direction. This keeps the lines true.

MAKE BUTTONHOLE STRIPS: Change to a thread that matches your garment, and set the machine for 12 stitches to the inch.

Cut a strip of fabric 1″ wide and long enough to give you 6″ for each buttonhole. Fold the strip in half lengthwise, wrong sides together. Stitch along the length of the strip, about ⅛″ from the fold. (FIG. 206) Trim the folded strip, so it is twice the width of the stitched section (or ¼″ wide). (FIG. 207)

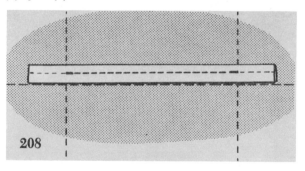

208

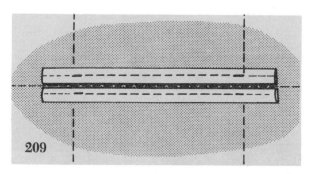

209

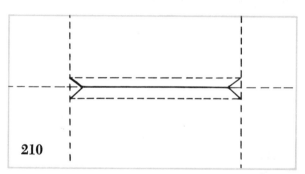

210

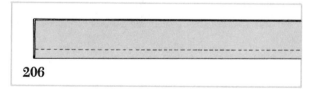

206

207

You need two fabric strips for each buttonhole. Cut each strip the width of a buttonhole, plus 2″.

STITCH THE BUTTONHOLES: Work with garment right side out. Place the *cut edges* of a buttonhole strip along the buttonhole line. Stitch down the center of the strip (directly over previous stitching) between the vertical lines. (FIG. 208) Start and stop exactly on the verti-

cals, and backstitch or knot the thread; this stitching determines the finished width of the buttonhole; so, do it carefully. Correct the stitching from the wrong side, if necessary.

Take a second buttonhole strip; butt the cut edges against cut edges of the strip already in place. Stitch the strip as you did the first one. (FIG. 209)

Turn the garment to the wrong side. Open the buttonhole by cutting between the two rows of stitching. Cut to within ½″ of the end, then make a good-size wedge by cutting into each corner. (FIG. 210) Hold the buttonhole strips out of the way; cut only the garment and interfacing.

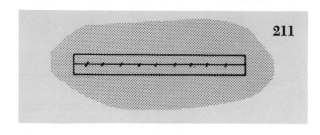

211

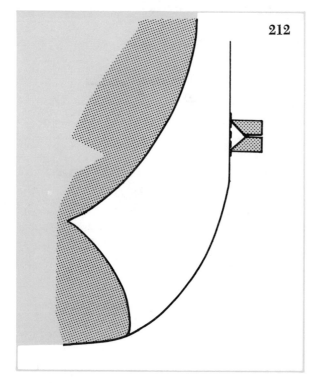

212

Press buttonholes from the wrong side; never press from the right side. Leave the buttonholes at this point; assemble the garment and complete the collar and neck edge.

To finish a bound buttonhole, arrange the garment facing in place, and pin between the buttonholes. From the right side, stitch completely around each buttonhole. Use a short stitch (20 stitches to the inch) and a matching thread. Guide the needle along the seam groove that joins the buttonhole strip to the garment. Start stitching on a side of the buttonhole, not in a corner; overlap the stitching where it meets.

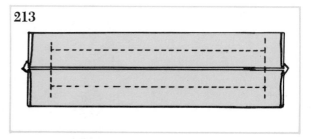

213

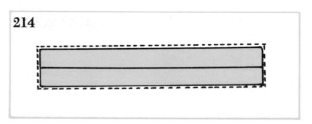

214

Push the strips through to the wrong side, and pull them taut. Baste the lips of the buttonhole closed. (FIG. 211)

Turn the garment to the right side. Fold back one edge until you see the wedge lying on top of the buttonhole strips. (FIG. 212) Stitch across the base of the wedge, catching it to the strips. This stitching forms the corners of the buttonhole; so, make it secure.

Fold back the other side of the jacket, and stitch across the base of the other wedge in the same manner.

Trim the ends of the strips to ¼". Hold your scissors at a sharp angle and make a slanted cut. This grades the layers of fabric to eliminate bulk. (FIG. 213)

On the facing side of the jacket, you have stitched a small box. Carefully open the box and trim it away, close to the stitching line. (FIG. 214) This gives a flat, neat finish, and the edges will not ravel.

Machine buttonholes

If you want machine buttonholes, make them after the garment is completed. Use interfacing to add support, and work buttonholes through garment and facing at the same time. Use a long stitch length on your machine so that stitches are not too close together. Very close stitches will cause ripples on the buttonhole edges. Make a sample buttonhole to help you adjust stitch to fabric.

Jacket with buttonholes
in over-edge trim

9

Helps for Sewing
Women's Jackets

Jackets and suits made from doubleknit fabrics are comfortable to wear
and easy to sew. This chapter offers general tips on fabrics and patterns
for women's jackets. It also has step-by-step directions for finishing a
cardigan jacket with over-edge trim and for making vertical buttonholes
along that trim.

GENERAL TIPS

You can shortcut a few steps when you make women's jackets of knit fabric. For instance, you can omit underlinings and linings. That saves you work and preserves the stretch and soft look of the knit at the same time. However, you'll probably want interfacings to keep the collar and front edges firm. Here are helps for choosing fabrics and interfacings; for adjusting your pattern; and for determining buttonhole position, size of buttons and buttonholes.

Pick a pattern

Choose a suit or jacket style in a conventional pattern or a special pattern for knits. Follow your pattern instructions for general construction methods, and for any tailoring techniques you may need for such things as rolled lapels and a tailored collar.

Choose the fabric and interfacing

Doubleknit that is firm and medium-to-heavy weight is best for a suit or jacket. Polyesters and wools are recommended; some acrylics can be used if they have enough body. Preshrink the fabric, using the method suggested for the fiber. After you've made the garment, you can preserve its new appearance by having it dry-cleaned, even if the fabric is washable.

Add firmness to a jacket front with a woven interfacing fabric that is cut on the straight grain; this supports buttons and buttonholes. For a collar, use a woven interfacing fabric that is cut on the bias. Small areas, such as pocket flaps, need a lightweight interfacing; a press-on type is fine for these, but don't use it for jacket fronts.

Adjust the pattern

If your pattern has a bust dart, check the location and correct it, if necessary. (See "Bust dart location" under "Fit and ease guide" in Chapter 2.) Make any other adjustments for fit. Amount of ease you need will depend on how you plan to wear the jacket—over tops and sweaters, or as a top itself with no extra layers underneath.

When the jacket opening has a straight edge, you can cut the jacket front and the facing as one piece. This eliminates front seams and reduces bulk. Some patterns are designed this way, or you can join the two pattern sections yourself. Pin the facing section to the jacket front, overlapping seamlines of jacket and facing.

Buttonhole placement

You can determine buttonhole placement for yourself; follow the guides in this chapter. For making buttonholes, either bound or by machine, see Chapter 8.

On a single-breasted jacket, one buttonhole is at the bustline—unless the garment style or the size or number of buttons makes this impossible. If there is no buttonhole at the bustline, you may need a concealed snap to prevent gapping.

You can shift the buttonhole lines on a conventional pattern, and this often is necessary when you alter a bust dart. Buttonhole locations are not marked on many special patterns for knits; so, you must add them.

Follow these basic guides for correct buttonhole placement:

• If your jacket is single-breasted with an open lapel, place the first buttonhole at the bustline.

• If your jacket is double-breasted, place the first buttonhole 1″ to 2″ below the bust.

• If your jacket buttons all the way to the neck, place the first buttonhole near the neckline. Take one half the width of your button, plus ¼″, and measure this distance down from the finished neck edge.

• If your jacket is fitted, place a buttonhole at the waistline.

To insure a correct fit in a single-breasted jacket or coat, start buttonholes ⅛″ beyond the center front line (toward the front opening); sew buttons to the center front line on the left side of the jacket. If you make a double-breasted jacket, locate the buttons and buttonholes an equal distance from center front line.

Button size

Find the center front line on your pattern. The distance from center front to the finished jacket opening governs the size of button. The button should be no wider than the distance between these two lines. If you choose a larger button, you must increase the width between the lines; width should be one half the width of the button, plus ½″. This prevents the homemade look that you get when buttons are too close to the edge of the jacket —or when they hang off. Decide on button size before you cut your fabric; you can add width from center front to jacket edge, if necessary.

Buttonhole width

Determine the buttonhole opening by measuring the button diameter and adding ⅛″. This works for a fairly flat button.

If you have a round button, or one with a high dome, use the following method to get the buttonhole width. Take a narrow strip of paper (about ¼″ wide), and wrap it around the thickest part of the button. The buttonhole width is one half this measurement.

CARDIGAN JACKET WITH OVER-EDGE TRIM

You can change a regular jacket pattern into a cardigan style by eliminating the collar. Button the jacket front, or give it a Chanel look with no buttons.

The over-edge trim can vary from ¼″ to 1¼″ in width. It can be even wider if the trim fabric is very stretchy. The finished width of the trim is determined by the distance from garment edge to your stitching line. For example, if you stitch ½″ from the edge, the finished trim will be ½″ wide.

Adjust the pattern

If you are adapting a jacket pattern, place the facing pattern piece in position on top of the jacket front piece. Draw a new style line; the easiest line to work with is a V. (FIG. 215) Cut both facing and jacket pieces along this new line.

An over-edge trim actually binds the cut or folded edges of a garment; no seam allowance is turned under. So, you should cut away seam allowances in all areas where you plan to use the trim. This will be down the jacket front and around the neck edge. If you also wish to trim the sleeves and jacket bottom, remove the hem allowances (or fold them out of the way).

On a jacket that buttons, an over-edge trim should not go past the center front line. For instance, if you want a finished trim 1″ wide, you must have at least 1″ from center front to the jacket edge.

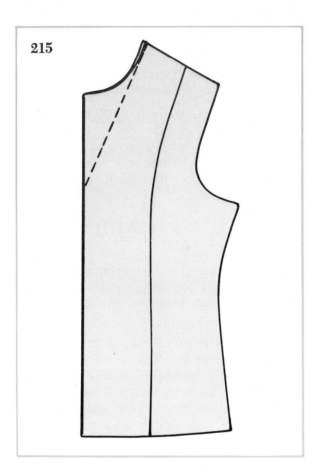

215

The Chanel-type jacket, with no buttons, looks best if the jacket does not meet at center front. To adjust your pattern, trim away 1″ beyond the center front line. Alter both facing and jacket front sections.

Assemble the jacket

Sew the shoulder seams of the jacket and facings, and press them open. For an attractive finish, overcast by machine the free edge of the facing.

Pin the facing to the jacket, *wrong* sides together. The jacket is easier to handle if you stitch these two sections together before you apply the trim. Straight stitch or zigzag close to the neck and front edges.

Apply the trim—miter the corners

For cutting and applying trim, see "Overedge trim" in Chapter 8.

Occasionally, you have a square corner to turn; so, you miter the trim to give a flat finish. You attach trim by first stitching toward the corner from one side, then stitching toward the same corner from the adjoining side. Finally, you stitch the miter.

Place the trim on the right side of the garment, and stitch the desired width. Do not stitch all the way to a corner; leave the seam width from stitching to corner. (FIG. 216) For example, if you are stitching ½″ from the garment edge, end your stitching ½″ back from the corner.

By hand, run the trim along the jacket edge to the corner, and along the adjoining edge for 3″. As you do this, a triangle of fabric will form at the corner. Pin the trim in place, keeping the triangle formed. (FIGS. 217a and 217b)

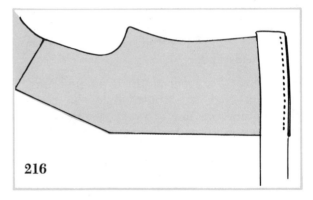

216

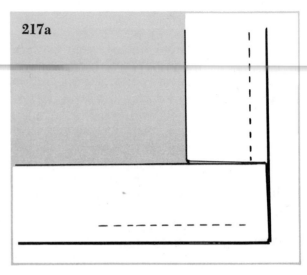

217a

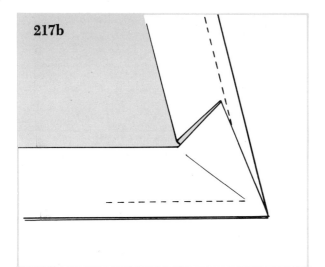

217b

stitching to garment edge. (FIG. 219) Stitching line will be halfway between garment edge and the line.

Now, draw a short line on the trim, connecting the end of the stitching with the new line at the edge of the trim fold. (FIG. 220) Stitch along this short line.

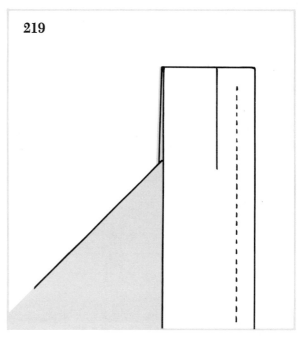

219

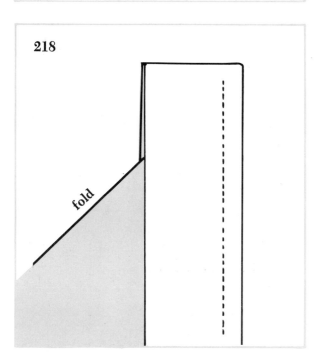

218

fold

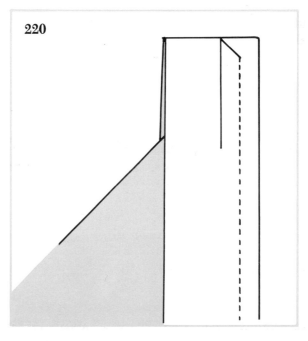

220

From the 3″ mark on the next edge, stitch toward the same corner. For this, work on the facing side, with the trim against the machine. The two stitching lines should meet in the corner.

Fold the garment so the two stitched edges are together (right-angle fold). The trim should be flat and look like FIG. 218.

Draw a line on the trim, parallel to the stitching line and double the distance from the

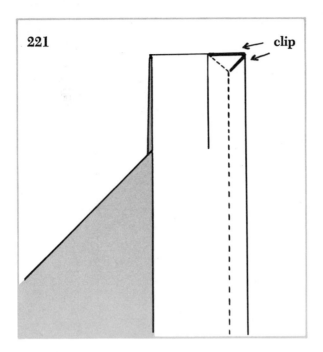

the trim on a line parallel to the fold of the jacket. (**FIG. 222**) Trim seam allowance to ¼"; press seam open with fingers.

Continue stitching the trim to the garment, mitering where needed. Press the trim out over the stitching line, then fold it inside the jacket. Arrange the back of each corner into a miter (if you have not stitched it), and catch it down as you stitch in the seam groove.

Buttonholes in the over-edge trim

This buttonhole technique works for any width trim. A small ball button is best with a narrow trim; a button ¾" or 1" wide can be used with trims 1" or wider when finished.

The buttonholes will be vertical. Test the button size you need by cutting a slit in a

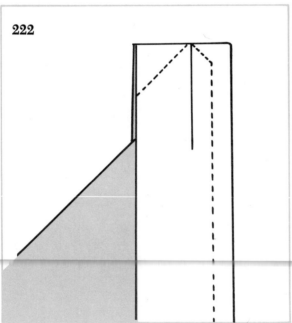

Slash the trim on the lines indicated. (**FIG. 221**) Trim excess fabric; leave a ¼" seam allowance along the stitching. Press seam open with fingers. This lets the trim lie flat when turned.

You also can miter the back of the trim that will be turned inside the jacket. Stitch along

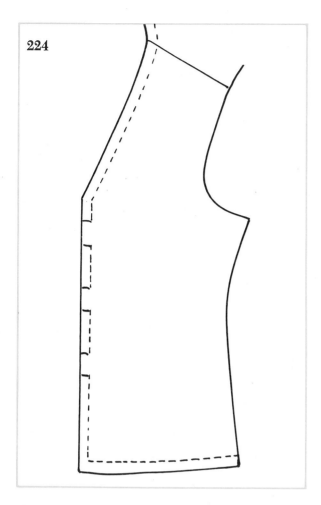

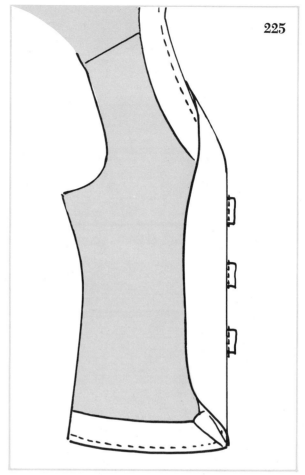

scrap of fabric and slipping it over the button. Mark the buttonhole length and placement on the right front of the jacket. When you stitch the jacket and facing together along the edge, do not close the buttonhole areas. If you want buttonholes to be at center front, you must stitch trim on the center front line.

Sew the over-edge trim to the jacket, following previous instructions. Stitch to a buttonhole marking, and stop; leave buttonhole areas open. (FIG. 223) Backstitch at the top and bottom of each buttonhole.

Clip the jacket and facing fabric to the stitching line at the top and bottom of each buttonhole; do not cut the trim fabric. (FIG. 224)

Turn these little flaps into the jacket so they are sandwiched between the jacket and fac-ing. Carefully fold the facing back against the jacket front so you expose the flaps. (FIG. 225) Sew the flaps together; trim them to ¼".

Press the trim over the stitching line. Wrap trim around the jacket edge and fold it to the inside. Catch trim in place by stitching in the groove from the right side. Do not stitch across buttonhole openings. Backstitch at the top and bottom of each buttonhole.

Cut away the excess trim on the inside of the jacket, *except* at buttonhole openings. This will form a flap at each buttonhole. (FIG. 226)

Cut these flaps to the width of the trim; then, tuck them between the two layers of trim. Catch the folded edges together with small hand stitches.

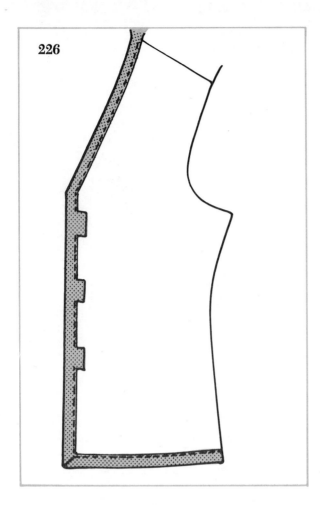

226

Finish the jacket

If you use over-edge trim on jacket front, back and sleeves, apply trim to each section before you close the side seams and sleeve seams. Press trim out over garment edge. Pin side seams and sleeve seams with trim in opened position; stitch. Fold the trim to the inside; catch it in place by stitching in the seam groove on the right side of the jacket.

If you use over-edge trim only on the jacket front, the trim will end at the side seams. Completely finish the trim, then pin jacket front to jacket back at the side seams. Match hem markings. Jacket back is not hemmed; it will be longer than the jacket front.

Fold up the back hem allowance so that it wraps over the jacket front at the side seams. Stitch the side seams, catching all layers; this makes a neat finish on the inside of the jacket. (See FIG. 237, Chapter 10.)

A. Pullover and cardigan sweaters made from sweater bodies
B. The alpaca sweater made from alpaca knit fabric

10

How to Sew Your Own Sweaters

You can duplicate sweaters you buy in the store—if you can find the sweater fabrics. Knit yardage for alpaca sweaters and sweater bodies for cardigans and pullovers are available in many fabric stores that specialize in knits. You cut these knit fabrics and stitch them together by machine.

This chapter tells you how to make an alpaca cardigan, a classic cardigan and a pullover. Use the same directions for remaking old sweaters into small sizes; this is a money-saver if you can take your husband's worn sweaters and recycle them for the children. Directions here are for classic styles, but you can use the same techniques to make other sweater styles, as well.

SWEATERS FROM ALPACA

You'll find the alpaca sweater a rewarding garment to make. It looks professional and costs only a fraction of a ready-made. It can be cut for either a man or a woman. Alpaca makes a great golf sweater because it is lightweight and can be worn the year around.

Alpaca is an animal fiber and should be treated like wool. Sometimes it is blended with wool; check the bolt ends to know what you are buying. Dry cleaning, rather than hand washing, is recommended for alpaca and alpaca blends. It is not necessary to pre-shrink the fabric, but you should spread it out on a flat surface overnight before you cut out the garment, so that the yarns can relax.

Alpaca knit comes in a tube form with an imperfect fold along one edge. (This is formed by a row of loose stitches; fabric looks as if it had a flaw along the fold.) Open the tube by cutting along this fold, you will have a flat piece of fabric to work with.

Place the pattern—and cut

Use a special pattern that is designed for the alpaca-style sweater. If you can't find a pattern, you may be able to trace one from a sweater you already have.

Place the pattern pieces so the grain line of the knit is running up and down the sleeve and body pieces. Pattern pieces will be crosswise, rather than lengthwise, on the fabric.

The sleeve pattern for many alpaca sweaters is long and full, and the sleeve drapes over the cuff. You can make the sleeve more conventional by cutting it the exact sleeve length and leaving the bottom edge about 3″ larger than the wrist measurement. (FIG. 227) Use the same amount of ribbing for either sleeve style.

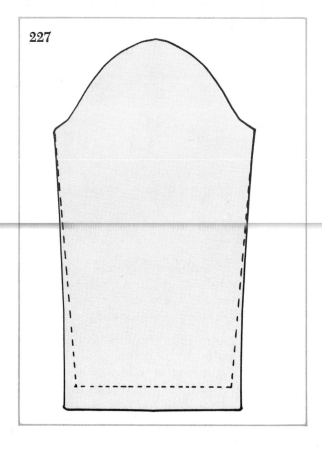

227

You will notice that the back pattern piece is 4″ shorter than the front piece. The front will be hemmed up 2″, while 2″ of ribbing will be added to the back. The sweater back and front then will be the same length.

Make the welt pocket

If you want pockets in the sweater, put them in before you sew the shoulder seams.

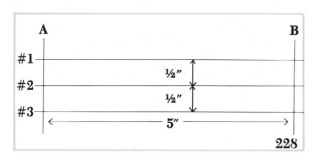

The alpaca pocket is located on the sweater front, 3″ from the side and 5″ up from the finished hem. It is 5″ wide. Mark the correct locations on the wrong side of the fabric.

Cut two pieces of stay fabric 4″ by 7″. Cut two pieces of alpaca, 7″ by 8″, for the pockets; the grain lines should run up and down, parallel to the 8″ side of the pocket.

Enlarge the pocket design (**FIG. 228**) for a pattern, and trace it onto the stay fabric pieces; use exact measurements.

Pin the stay fabric in place on the wrong side of the sweater front. Line #1 should be directly on top of the pocket opening mark. (**FIG. 229**) Stitch along the pocket design, using a long stitch length and a contrasting thread. Stitch all parallel lines in the same direction so that the fabric will not shift.

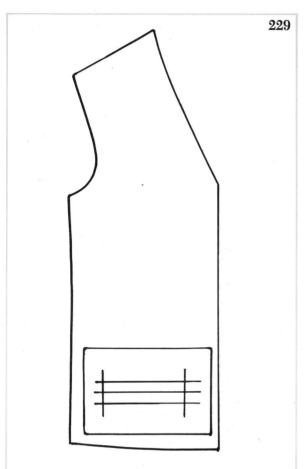

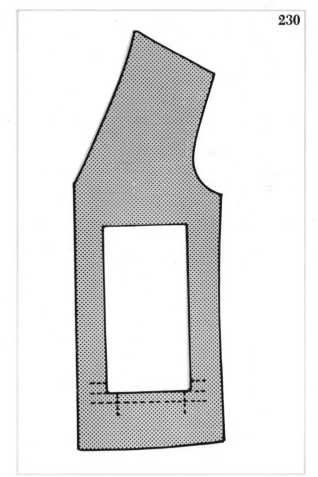

Change to a matching thread and set the machine for 12 stitches to the inch.

Work on the right side of the sweater, and place the bottom edge of the pocket piece along line #2. Center it over vertical lines A and B, with right sides of fabric together. (FIG. 230) Pin in place.

Turn the sweater to the wrong side. Stitch along line #1 between vertical lines A and B. Backstitch at both ends of the line.

Turn the sweater to the right side. Fold down 1″ at the free end of the pocket (this will form the welt). Then, place the folded edge on line #3. (FIG. 231) Pin in place.

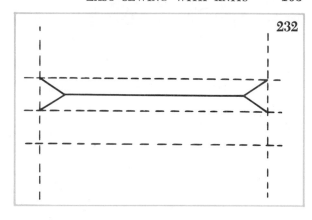

Pull the pocket fabric through to the wrong side and arrange it into position. Baste the pocket closed (FIG. 233); have the edge of the welt pulled up to the top of the opening. Press from the wrong side.

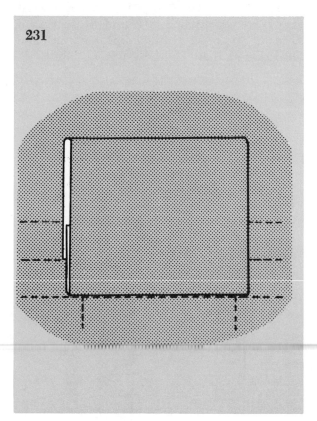

231

Turn the sweater to the wrong side and stitch along line #2 between vertical lines A and B. Backstitch at each end. Slash the pocket open between lines #1 and #2, cutting a large wedge at each end. (FIG. 232) Cut only the stay fabric and the sweater fabric; do not cut the pocket fabric.

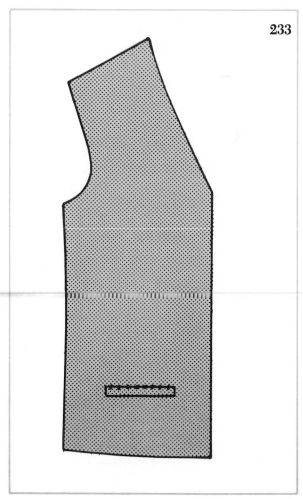

233

With the right side of the sweater up, fold back one side until you see the wedge on top of the pocket pieces. (**FIG. 234**) Straight stitch along the base of the wedge, making it secure. Continue the stitching down the

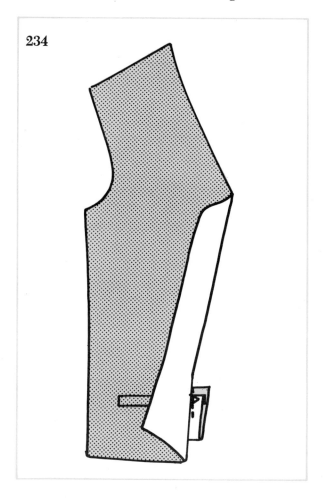

234

full length of the pocket to close it. Finish the seam edge with a second row of straight or zigzag stitches.

Complete the opposite side of the pocket in the same manner. Press from the wrong side. Remove basting stitches, and trim away any excess pocket or stay fabric.

NOTE: This pocket method also can be used for other knit garments. It makes a nice pocket in a man's sport shirt, for instance. You can make the pocket wider by changing the measurements of the pocket design and adjusting the size of the pocket and stay pieces.

Join the shoulder seams

Sew the shoulder seams with ⅝″ seam allowances. Stretch the seams very little, even if you use a straight stitch on the machine. The alpaca fabric is thick and spongy, and it stretches some just by going under the presser foot. If you use a straight stitch, you can strengthen the shoulder seam by making another row of stitches in the same seamline, or by sewing a piece of seam tape into the seam. Cut the tape the same length as the shoulder line on the pattern; stitch on the tape side, rather than the sweater side. Do not stretch the fabric when you apply the seam tape.

To finish the seam, trim the back seam allowance in half; push the front seam allowance past it toward the back of the sweater. Make a welt seam by topstitching on the right side, ¼″ behind the shoulder seam. (**FIG. 235**) Or, you can do this stitching by hand on the wrong side, if you prefer.

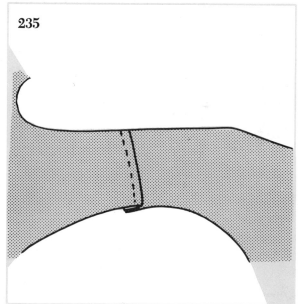

235

Set in the sleeves

Fold the sleeve in half, and mark the center top. Pin that mark to the shoulder seam and sew the sleeve in place. Distribute sleeve ease evenly around the arm opening. Stretch the seams very little as you stitch.

Apply back ribbing

Measure the width across the bottom of the sweater back. Use two-thirds of this measurement to cut a piece of alpaca ribbing.

NOTE: If special alpaca ribbing is not available, you can use the same measurements for a piece of self-fabric. Cut the strip of alpaca fabric 4½″ wide; grain of the alpaca should go across the strip, rather than lengthwise.

Fold the alpaca ribbing or self-fabric trim in half lengthwise, right side out. Divide both the trim and sweater back into four equal sections. Pin trim to the right side of the sweater with cut edges together. (**FIG. 236**) Match the division marks, and stitch.

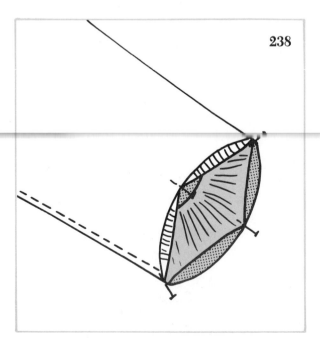

237

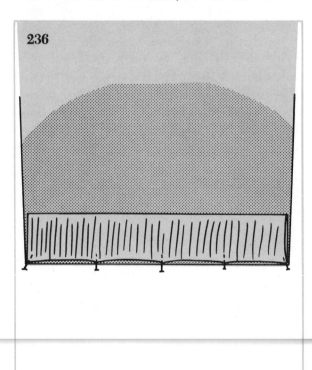

236

238

Close the underarm seam

Pin sweater front to sweater back, right sides together; the front will be 2″ longer than the sweater back. Fold the front hem up so that it wraps around the back ribbing; stitch the underarm seam. (**FIG. 237**)

Unfold the bottom corner. Hem the sweater front by hand with a catch stitch.

Sleeve cuffs

Make each cuff by cutting a piece of ribbing or self-fabric 6″ long and stitching the cut edges with a ¼″ seam allowance. (Use 6″ of ribbing for the cuff on sweaters of all sizes, for both men and women.)

Press the seam allowance open with your fingers. Fold the ribbing lengthwise, wrong sides together, so that you have a double tube of ribbing. The cuff is much smaller than the sleeve opening, but they will go together easily if you divide the bottom of the sleeve and the cuff into four equal sections before you pin them together. (FIG. 238) Stretch the cuff to fit the sleeve, and straight stitch around the edge. Do a second row of straight or zigzag stitching.

Front trim and buttonholes

Special knit trim for alpaca is 1″ wide and is finished along both edges. If you have this

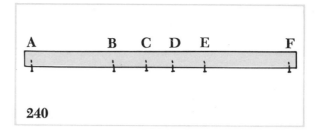

240

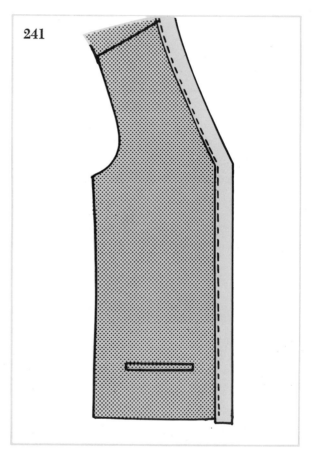

241

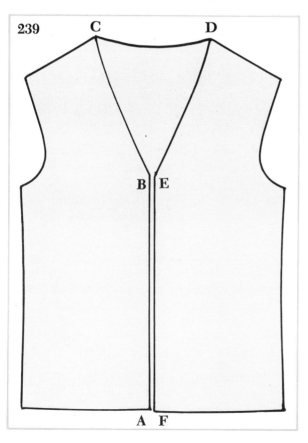

239

commercial trim, use it for the front of the sweater. Otherwise, you can use self-fabric for the front finish.

SPECIAL TRIM FOR THE FRONT: First, press the trim with steam to reduce shrinkage, then measure the length you need. Take measurements from the paper pattern, rather than from the sweater; the sweater edges may have stretched a bit. Measure the distance between A and B, B and C, C and D, D and E, and E and F; do not include seam allowances in these measurements. (FIG. 239)

Transfer these measurements to your trim. (FIG. 240)

Place the wrong side of the trim on the right side of the sweater, with a ⅜″ overlap. Pin the pre-measured marks in their proper places, then pin the rest of the trim securely. There will be 2″ of trim extending below the front edges of the sweater, which already has been hemmed. Stitch ⅛″ in from the edge of the trim, stretching slightly as you sew. (FIG. 241) This makes a ¼″ seam allowance along the sweater edge.

Press the trim to the wrong side of the sweater, leaving the edge of the trim visible from the right side. (FIG. 242) Turn up the ends, and catch them in place by hand.

The trim should be caught down around the back of the neck and 2″ below the shoulder

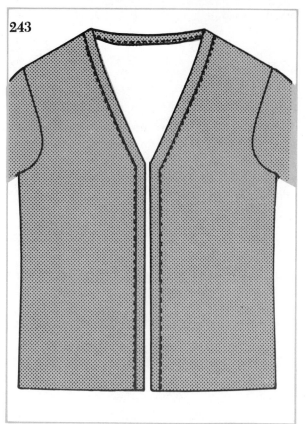

243

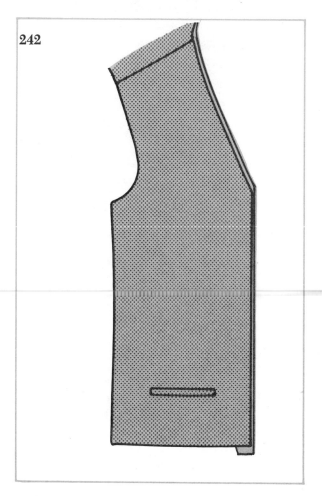

242

seam. Do this by hand or use the blind hemming stitch on your machine. The buttons and buttonholes will hold the trim in place down the sweater front.

Mark the buttonholes on the trim side of the sweater; make them vertical. Place a piece of stay fabric between the two layers of sweater fabric, and work buttonholes from the trim side by machine. See "Machine buttonholes" in Chapter 8.

SELF-FABRIC FOR THE FRONT: Cut the trim on the cross grain of the fabric, and make it 3½″ wide. Because this trim is so stretchy, you must cut it shorter than the front opening of the sweater. You will stretch the trim to fit as you stitch it to the sweater edge; this makes a firm neck edge.

Take the measurements for the sweater front exactly as you would for commercial trim; then reduce the amounts for each section by one-fourth.

Place the right side of the open trim strip on the right side of the sweater, with edges together. Pin the pre-measured marks in place; turn up trim ends. Stretch the trim to fit as you sew with a ½″ seam allowance. Fold the trim over the seam allowance and to the back of the sweater; keep seam allowances inside the trim. Stitch in the seam groove from the right side. (**FIG. 243**)

You can fold the raw edge of the trim and catch it in this seam groove stitching. Or, you can complete the seam groove stitching; then, fold under the raw edge of the trim and catch it down by hand.

Work the buttonholes from the right side; slip pieces of interfacing between the alpaca layers to support the buttonholes and buttons. See "Machine buttonholes" in Chapter 8.

SWEATERS FROM SWEATER BODIES

You can make many sweater styles from a sweater body. This tube of sweater knit has one edge finished with ribbing. You use the edge along the bottom of the sweater and sleeves to get a professional look and to eliminate a hem.

General guide

Sweater bodies are made from various kinds of yarns, and they come in solid colors, stripes and intricate jacquard patterns. Some have an extra piece of ribbing attached to the bottom rib; this gives you additional trim for the neck or front. Sometimes you can buy an extra piece of ribbing that was knit especially for the neck finish; it will be 16″ to 18″ long.

You can cut and sew sweater bodies like other knit fabrics without fear of having them ravel. They present no special problem if you handle them correctly. You'll find that sweater bodies vary in size; be sure you buy as many as you need to complete your garment. Often, one is enough, but sometimes you need two, or even three, to make a complete sweater.

BUY OR TRACE A PATTERN: There are special patterns for sweaters. However, if you can't find one, it is possible to trace a pattern from a sweater you already have. For a pullover, you also can use your basic knit top pattern; cut the high neckline.

Adjust the body and sleeve pattern pieces so they will be the exact finished length. You will be using the ribbed edge of the sweater body as the bottom of the sleeves and the sweater; this makes it difficult to adjust length once the fabric is cut.

Many cardigan sweaters have no side seams. This shortens sewing time, and any front-opening sweater pattern can be adapted to this style. To eliminate the side seams, overlap these seams on the pattern and pin or tape the pattern sections together. You will

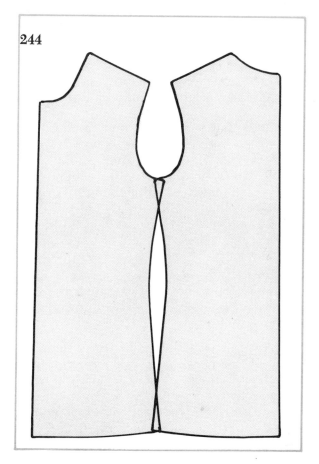

244

place the center back of the pattern on a fold of the sweater fabric. The front of the pattern should be ¾″ wider than the back of the pattern to allow for the button overlap. Your pattern will look like FIG. 244.

PREPARE THE FABRIC—AND CUT: Cut along the imperfect fold (the row of loose stitches along one edge), and open up the tube. Steam the sweater body to press out any bulges and to straighten the ribbed edge.

Sweater bodies usually can be cut double, unless you are working with a stripe or a pattern that must be matched. If the sweater has a front opening, the straight edge should be cut directly up a rib of the knit; this is best done by cutting one layer of fabric at a time.

SEWING SWEATER KNITS: Stitching on sweater knits will take some experimenting. You want a stretchy seam, but one that is flat. A rippled seam results from too much stretching and stitches that are too close together. You may have to lighten the pressure on the presser foot when you stitch bulky knits. Too much pressure stretches the fabric as it feeds through the machine, and this causes ripples.

The seam that works with one sweater knit will not necessarily produce a good seam on another type of sweater knit. Make some sample seams on scraps until you find the right combination of stitch length, stretch and pressure.

Assemble the cardigan

Sew the shoulder seams first. If there is a lot of stretch in the knit, you can sew a piece of seam tape into the shoulder seam to stabilize it.

NECK TRIM: The method of applying the neck finish will vary with the type of trim you use. Look at some ready-made cardigan sweaters to see how the neck trims are finished. Determine the amount of trim you need by stretching the folded ribbing around your neck until it is comfortable and looks

good. Allow for the ¾″ overlap on each front section of the sweater, and cut the trim. Divide the trim and the neck edge of the sweater into four equal sections. Pin together, matching division marks, and stretch the neck trim to fit evenly as you stitch.

FRONT TRIM: Apply the front trim next. It can be either 1″ grosgrain ribbon or a special knit braid, also 1″ wide. You will have to use what is available. If you have grosgrain ribbon, shrink it before you sew it to the sweater front; otherwise, the front will ripple after the sweater has been washed or cleaned.

Fold the sweater down the center back, and measure the length of the fold. Use this meas-

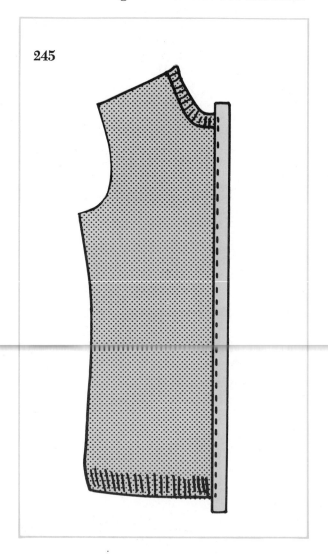

245

urement to cut two pieces of trim. (Include the neck ribbing in this measurement.)

Pin the wrong side of the trim against the right side of the sweater with a ¼″ overlap. Leave 1″ of trim extending beyond the top and bottom edge. Ease the cut edge of the sweater to fit the front trim; many times the sweater stretches a bit as you handle it. Stitch along the edge of the trim with a straight stitch. (FIG. 245) Turn the trim to the inside of the sweater and press.

FINISH THE SWEATER: Fold under the ends of the trim and catch them in place by hand. Mark the buttonholes on the trim side; make them vertical. If you use a knit braid for the trim, insert a piece of interfacing between the two layers of knit. This will support the knit fabric and keep it from stretching out of shape as you make the buttonholes. Grosgrain ribbon does not require interfacing. See "Machine buttonholes" in Chapter 8.

Sew the underarm seam of the sleeve and set it into the arm opening. Sew the buttons in place, and you have a new cardigan sweater.

Variation: You can make a V-neck cardigan for a man by using the knit braid for the front trim. Follow directions for applying the alpaca front trim.

Pullovers—crew and turtleneck

Use the high neckline if you cut the sweater from a basic top pattern. Cut out the sweater. Stitch the shoulder seams; sew in a piece of seam tape if the knit has a lot of stretch.

For a crew neck or a turtleneck, you need a piece of ribbing that matches the sweater body and is about 4″ wide; one edge must be finished. This makes a very professional-looking neckline.

Cut the ribbing strip 3¾″ wide. Measure the length you need by stretching the trim around your head, and add ½″ for seam allowances. Stitch the narrow ends of the ribbing together with a ¼″ seam. Press the seam open

with your fingers; do not fold the ribbing lengthwise.

FOR A CREW NECK: Divide both ribbing and sweater neck into four equal sections. Place the right side of the ribbing against the wrong side of the neck edge, unfinished edges together. Match the divisions; pin.

Stretch both neck and ribbing as you stitch a ½″ seam; use a straight stitch set at 9 stitches to the inch. Then, make another seam ½″ below the first one. (FIG. 246)

Pull the ribbing over to the right side of the sweater, and pin the finished edge of the ribbing along the bottom seamline. (FIG. 247) Catch the edge down by hand, using a backstitch. For this, unravel a piece of yarn from the scraps of the sweater body and use it for thread; steam press the yarn first to get rid of wrinkles.

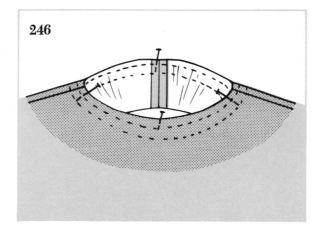

246

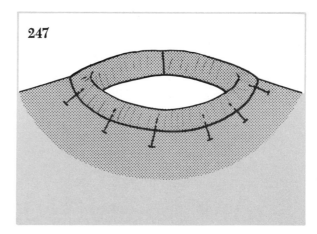

247

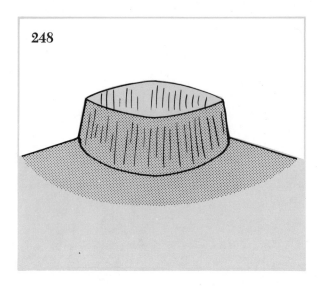

248

FOR A TURTLENECK: Follow directions for a crew neck, but stitch just one seam at the neck edge. Use a ¼″ seam allowance. Fold the ribbing over to the right side, and catch down by hand. (**FIG. 248**)

Or, you can apply the ribbing for a turtleneck in reverse. Place the right side of the ribbing against the right side of the sweater, unfinished edges together. Pin and sew. Then, fold the ribbing to the wrong side. The handstitching is then on the inside of the neck edge.

FINISH THE SWEATER: Sew sleeve to sweater. Close the side seam and sleeve seam in one continuous stitching.

11

How to Fit
and Sew Swimsuits

You can make swimsuits from knits for the whole family and save at least
half the cost of ready-mades. If you have trouble finding a suit that fits
well, you'll get the extra bonus of a good fit from your custom-made one.
Here are guides for making women's one-piece, two-piece and tank-top
suits and for making men's swim trunks.

GENERAL TIPS

Give special attention to the pattern size, the fabric and other materials you choose for a swimsuit.

Pick a pattern

Buy a special pattern designed for fabrics that stretch to fit. This type of pattern is cut smaller than your actual measurements. A conventional pattern for fabrics with no stretch is cut larger than body measurements and includes ease for movement. A suit made from a conventional pattern using a stretchy knit fabric would be much too large; you'd probably lose it as soon as you hit the water.

When you choose a pattern from one of the small companies that design patterns exclusively for knits, you usually buy according to a woman's hip measurement and a girl's ready-made clothing size. For men and boys, buy according to the waist measurement. Most of these patterns are made for a fabric with 20 percent stretch; so, a 15″ strip of fabric should stretch to 18″. If your fabric doesn't stretch that much, use a larger pattern. If the fabric stretches much more than 20 percent, use a smaller pattern.

Check your pattern for seam allowance width; this varies with different companies.

Choose the fabric

Swimsuit fabrics may be one-way stretch (crosswise stretch only) or two-way stretch (crosswise and lengthwise stretch). The two-way stretch is all-purpose. It can be used for any type of swimsuit, and it is a *must* for a one-piece design.

The one-way stretch is limited to trunks for men and boys, and to two-piece suits for women and girls. The stretch goes around the body; it does not make a comfortable one-piece suit.

Most swimsuit fabrics are nylon, but you'll find some of acrylic, polyester and combinations with spandex.

Preshrink all swimsuit fabrics. When you make a child's suit, put the fabric through the washer and dryer. (You'll probably wash and dry this suit later.) If you don't ordinarily dry an adult's suit in the automatic dryer, use only the wash cycle to preshrink the fabric.

For swimsuit linings, there are special knit fabrics. Usually, you line the crotch section of a suit. You may want to line the complete suit, especially if it is white or of a light-weight fabric. Use the suit pattern to cut lining pieces to the same shape and size as the suit pieces they line.

Other materials

Most swimsuit patterns for women use bra cups and elastic. Choose the types that will give you best results.

BRA CUPS: You'll find a variety of styles in bra cups. There are sew-in and pin-in types, cups with push-up pads, and special cups for the woman who has had breast surgery.

Try to find cups made from molded polyester. These are soft and spongy and are covered with fabric. They can be put through the washer and dryer, and are not affected by salt water or chlorine; look for the label that tells you this.

NOTE: Some bra cups are made of very rigid plastic. Do not put this type in a dryer; it will melt.

The easiest bra style to handle has a wide margin of lining fabric around the two cups. You can sew the unit into the suit and achieve a professional look.

The bra for a bikini suit usually is made from a fiberfill padding fabric. You can buy the padding by the yard and make the bra cups yourself. Follow instructions in your pattern.

ELASTIC: Buy special elastic to use in a swimsuit. It resists chlorine and holds its shape when wet. This elastic comes in widths of ¾″, ⅜″ and ¼″. Check your pattern for width or combination of widths you need.

Most two-piece suits use ¾″ elastic at the waist opening. Some use this same width at the leg, while others call for ⅜″ leg elastic. The ⅜″ width is more comfortable for the leg, especially if your upper thighs are heavy. You can substitute the ⅜″ elastic, even if your pattern calls for ¾″. Just trim away the extra ⅜″ from leg opening. Make this adjustment on your pattern before you cut the fabric; it is more accurate than trying to trim the fabric edges after the suit is assembled.

Sewing notes

Your machine should be free of lint and well oiled. You'll need a sharp, fine (size 11) needle, or a ball-point needle, to sew closely knit swimsuit fabric. A dull needle does not easily penetrate the fabric; it might cut a thread and cause the fabric to run. Use polyester thread for a strong seam.

The automatic stretch stitch and the over-edge stretch stitch on some machines are ideal for swimsuits. They produce strong, stretchy seams. If your machine does not have these special stitches, use a straight stitch, and stretch the fabric firmly as you sew.

Applying elastic

Here are some general rules for handling elastic, followed by specific directions for applying it to different sections of a swimsuit.

GENERAL PROCEDURE: Whenever you use elastic on a swimsuit, first assemble the suit and have the lining in place. Try on your suit and make any alterations needed for a snug fit. (Most swimsuits tend to stretch a bit when wet.) Then, follow these general steps:

1. Place the elastic against the wrong side of the suit, with both edges even.

2. Stitch close to the edges, using a zigzag or an automatic stretch stitch. (In some cases you will stretch a portion of the elastic; check directions for the specific section—neck, leg, etc.) If you use a straight-stitch machine, always stretch both fabric and elastic to put stretch into the stitching. (FIG. 249)

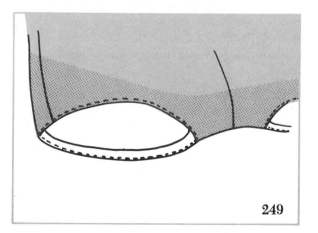

249

3. After the first stitching, make one fold. Turn the elastic and fabric to the inside. Attach the free edge to the suit, using a zigzag or an automatic stretch stitch. If you use a straight stitch, you must stretch both fabric and elastic as you sew. (FIG. 250)

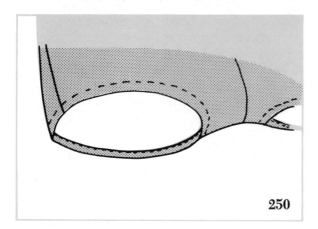

250

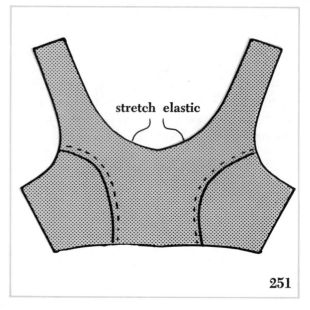

stretch elastic

251

ELASTIC AROUND THE LEG: This is the same for a one-piece and a two-piece suit.

Cut the elastic 1″ smaller than the leg opening, and leave it unclosed as you sew it to the suit. Place the elastic against the wrong side of the suit, with bottom edges even. Start at the front of the leg, stitch along the very edge; do not stretch elastic in the front leg section. When you stitch the elastic around the back of the leg, stretch it the 1″; this makes the suit cup in at the back and holds it in place. Follow directions under "General procedure."

ELASTIC AT THE NECK EDGE: This is the same for a one-piece and a two-piece suit. However, on a two-piece suit, leave ¾″ at the back opening free of elastic; hook fastener is sewn there.

The elastic is almost the same measurement as the suit edge. You will stretch the elastic very little—and only across the front; it is important to have a snug fitting suit before you add the elastic. Follow directions under "General procedure."

As you stitch, keep elastic and suit the same length until you reach the front neckline. You will stretch the elastic about ¾″ across the front curve of the suit (for 2″ to 3″); this holds the suit close to your body when you bend over. (FIG. 251)

ELASTIC AT THE ARM CURVE: This is the same for a one-piece and a two-piece swimsuit. Cut elastic as long as the suit edge.

Position, pin and stitch elastic to suit; follow directions under "General procedure." Be careful not to stretch the elastic in the armhole curves; stretching causes the suit to cut into your body.

ELASTIC AROUND THE WAIST: For the trunks of a two-piece suit, cut the elastic the same length as the waist opening. Overlap the ends ½″ and stitch.

Divide both elastic and waist edge into four equal sections. Pin the elastic to the inside of the suit, matching the divisions. Follow directions under "General procedure."

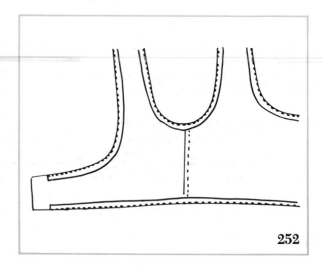

252

ELASTIC AT LOWER EDGE OF BRA TOP: Follow directions under "General procedure" for elastic; do not stretch the elastic more than the fabric as you stitch. Leave ¾" at the bra back free of elastic. (**FIG. 252**) This enables you to sew the bra hook in place without sewing through extra thicknesses.

TWO-PIECE SWIMSUIT

Patterns for two-piece suits vary in design, but the greatest difference is in the trunk style. Some have a separate crotch piece; others do not. These require different techniques when you assemble the suits.

Suit trunks without separate crotch

This style has five seams—two side seams, a center front and a center back seam and a crotch seam. The trunk is completely lined; cut swimsuit fabric and lining alike.

Stack the lining front pieces, right sides together. Stack the swimsuit fronts, right sides together. Place the swimsuit pieces on top of the lining pieces. Pin all four layers together at the center front seam and stitch a knit seam. (**FIG. 253**) If you use a straight stitch, you must stretch the fabric firmly as you sew.

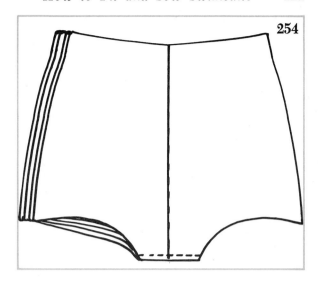

254

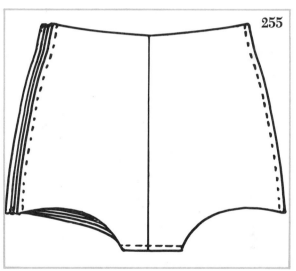

255

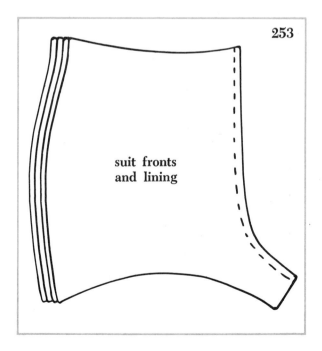

253

suit fronts and lining

Open the top layer of swimsuit fabric, and open the bottom layer of lining fabric. You have an enclosed center front seam.

Sew the center back seams of swimsuit and lining separately. Pin swimsuit back pieces, right sides together, and stitch. Pin lining back pieces, right sides together, and stitch.

The crotch seam is next. Place the swimsuit back against the swimsuit front, right sides together; pin across the crotch. Place the lining back against the lining front, right sides together. Pin all four layers together across the crotch. Stitch a knit (stretch) seam, catching all layers. (**FIG. 254**)

While the suit is in this position, close the side seams. Pin together and stitch all four layers at each side. (FIG. 255)

To turn the trunks right side out, reach down between the two layers of swimsuit fabric, and grab hold of the crotch. Pull it to the right side and you will find that all seam edges are enclosed.

Finish waist edge and legs with elastic. See "Applying elastic" in this chapter.

Trunks with a separate crotch

This design has three pieces—front, back and crotch. It is found in many women's and children's suits. You can line just the crotch, which is a simple matter, or you can line the entire garment.

TO LINE THE CROTCH PIECE ONLY: Place the right side of the crotch piece against the right side of the suit front. Place the right side of the crotch lining against the wrong side of the suit front. Line up all cut edges, and pin in place. Stitch a knit seam, taking the full width of the seam allowance. (FIG. 256) Trim the seam allowance to ⅛".

Pin the right side of the swimsuit crotch piece to the right side of the suit back. (FIG. 257)

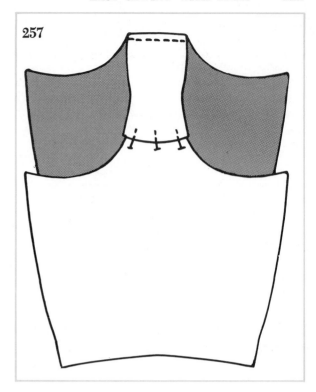

257

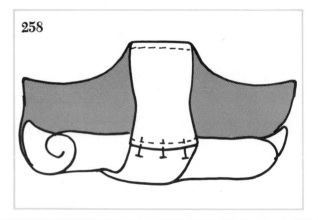

258

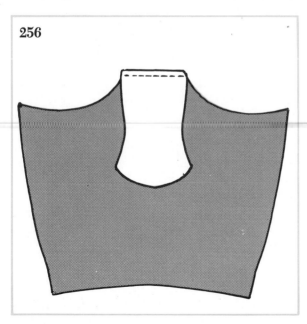

256

Place the suit on a flat surface, with the suit back on top. Roll the suit from the waist toward the crotch until you see the free edge of the crotch lining. Take this free edge and pull it around the rolled suit; pin the right side of the crotch lining to the wrong side of the swimsuit back. Stitch; trim the seam allowance. (FIG. 258)

Pull the rolled suit through the side of the crotch pieces. You have a lined crotch area with no raw seams.

To finish the trunks, pin and stitch the side seams; stitch elastic to the waist edge and legs. See "Applying elastic" in this chapter.

TO COMPLETELY LINE THE TRUNKS: Assemble the trunks, but leave the crotch seam until last. First, enclose the side seams of the suit by placing right sides of swimsuit fabric together and right sides of lining together. Stack the layers, with suit fabric on top; stitch.

When you are ready to line the crotch area, handle the suit and lining as a single layer of fabric. Follow the previous directions for lining the crotch piece only.

Finish the trunks by applying elastic to waist edge and legs.

The bra top

The bra with attached lining is the only lining you need for the top of a two-piece suit.

Assemble the top front section, according to pattern instructions. Most suits have a princess line over the bust; this goes together smoothly if you pin before you stitch. To keep the seam allowance flat and smooth over the high point of the bust, press the seam allowance toward the center of the bra; topstitch and trim any excess seam allowance.

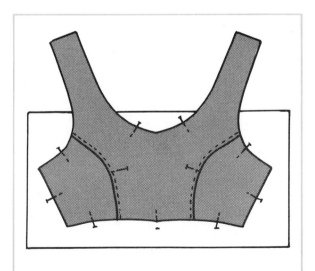

259

Sew bra cups to the suit front before you stitch the seam sides. Place the cups on a flat surface; put the suit on top, right side up. (FIG. 259) Mold the suit over the cups, and smooth out any wrinkles in the lining fabric. Pin the layers together at the suit edges.

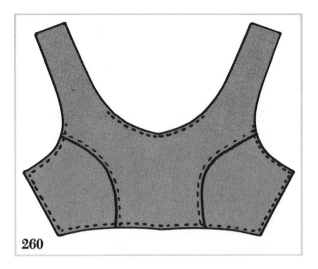

260

Stitch along these edges. Trim away excess lining fabric. (FIG. 260)

Sew the suit back to the suit front, right sides together. Pin the shoulder strap seams together and try on the bra top. The straps should be snug enough to stay in place when you swim. Adjust the width of the seam allowance, if necessary, and stitch with right sides together.

Finish the bra top with elastic; see "Applying elastic" in this chapter.

ONE-PIECE SWIMSUIT

Patterns for a one-piece suit have a brief leg or a skirt across the front, and most are designed with a flattering princess line. Use only two-way stretch fabrics for one-piece suits.

Adjust the pattern

In ready-made swim wear, you may find that a suit fits your hips, but not your bust. When you make your own suit, you can have a perfect fit—at both hips and bust.

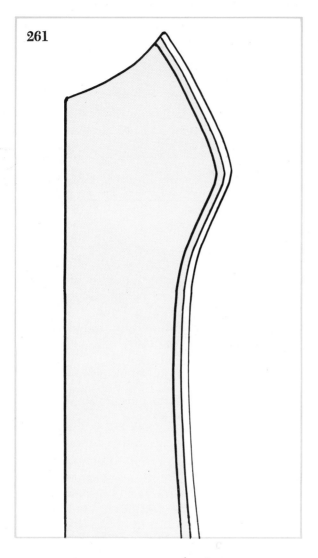

261

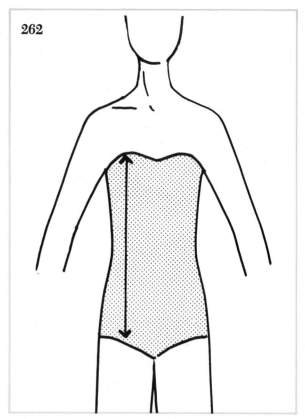

262

waist down, make the pattern alteration below the waist. If you are generally long in the body, divide the needed length equally, and add in both areas. You can shorten the pattern in these same locations, if needed.

Assemble the suit

Follow your pattern instructions for cutting the fabric and assembling the front of the swimsuit.

Select the pattern size according to your hip measurement, and alter the bust to fit. If you use a multi-size pattern, trace off your suit size, and make any needed alteration in the bust curve; you can go up or down a size by adding or subtracting at this curve. (FIG. 261)

Length is often a problem in ready-made suits, but not with the one you make. Measure your body from the top of a comfortable bra down to where brief-style panties would end. (FIG. 262) Your finished suit should be about 1″ longer than this measurement.

Check your pattern and adjust if necessary. If you are long-waisted, make the alteration above the waistline. If you are long from the

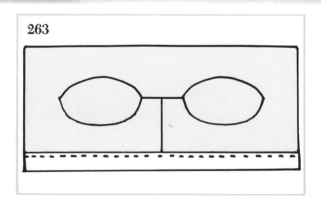

263

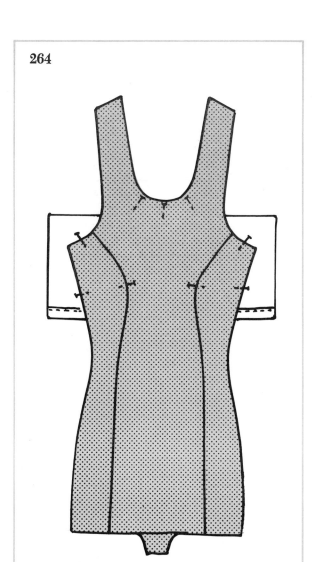

264

Sew a piece of ¾″ swimsuit elastic along the lower edge of the bra cup unit; this adds support under the bust and makes a nice finish inside the suit. Lay the relaxed elastic on top of the bra lining, and stitch. (Elastic will be against your body.) (**FIG. 263**)

Position the bra cups inside the suit, and pin them in place. (**FIG. 264**) Stitch along the edge of the suit, catching the lining fabric to the suit edge. Trim away excess lining.

Stitch all suit seams, except shoulder straps. Pin the straps together, and try on the suit. It should fit snugly and the straps should feel secure. Take a larger seam at the shoulder, or

add an extra piece of fabric, as needed. Stitch the seams.

Finish suit with elastic at leg, neck and arm edges. Follow directions under "Applying elastic" in this chapter.

TANK-TOP SWIMSUIT

Buy a special tank-top swimsuit pattern for knits. Or, convert a basic shell pattern for the top, and cut the trunks from a two-piece swimsuit pattern.

Make your own top pattern

Begin with a basic sleeveless shell pattern. Check the pattern fit, and adjust the bust dart for proper location (see "Fit and ease guide," Chapter 2). Alter the pattern by lowering the neckline at front and back and by enlarging the arm openings. (**FIG. 265**) Lengthen pattern, if needed.

265

Assemble the top

Cut the fabric. Stitch the darts and shoulder seams.

Prepare the bra cup unit by sewing a piece of ¾" swimsuit elastic to the bottom edge; let enough elastic extend from each side so that it can be hooked in back. (Elastic will be against your body when you wear the suit.) To determine length of elastic, measure around your body, with the tape under your bust. Use this measurement, less 3", and cut

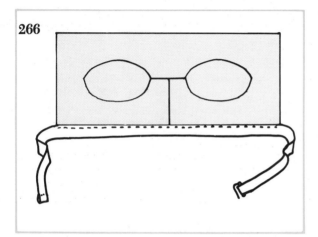

266

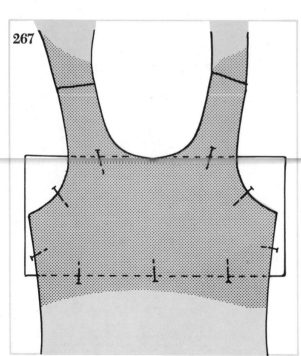

267

the elastic. Sew a bra hook on one end of the elastic; fold over and stitch the other end so that the hook will fit snugly into the fold. (FIG. 266)

Try on the bra cup unit, and hook it in back. Pull on the tank top, and adjust it over the bra unit for a smooth fit. Pin the layers together. (FIG. 267)

To attach the bra cups, stitch the lining along the neck opening of the suit. Stitch along the arm opening also if lining extends that far. Trim off excess lining along the stitched edges. Pin and stitch the side seams; do not catch the bra cups in these seams.

Finish the tank top

Elastic is not always necessary if the tank top fits well. You can finish the neck and armhole edges by turning them under ¼" and topstitching. (FIG. 268)

If you want to add elastic, use a ⅜" width; follow directions under "Applying elastic" in this chapter.

268

V-NECK SWIMSUIT

You can change a round neckline to a V-shape on a one-piece or two-piece suit. Simply adjust the pattern before you cut the fabric. Follow **FIG. 269** to alter your paper pattern. Mark the V-point about 1″ below the top edge of the pattern, then draw a slightly curved line from the V-point to the shoulder.

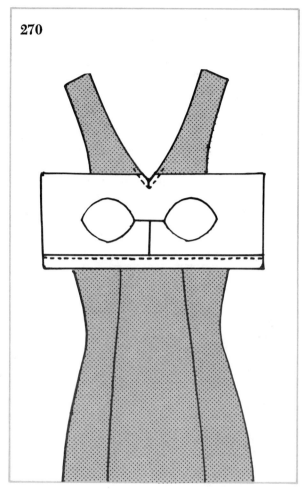

270

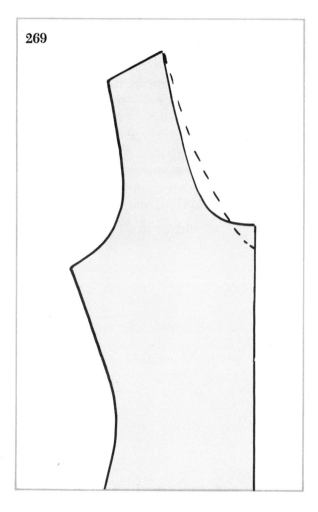

269

Attach the bra cups

Prepare the bra cup unit by laying a piece of ¾″ elastic along the lower edge; stitch. (Elastic will be against your body when you wear the suit.)

Assemble the suit, pin the bra cups in place. Trim the lining in the neck area only; it should follow the neckline of the suit.

Unpin the bra cups and place them against the outside of the suit, rounded side up. Line up the V-neck edges and stitch the bra lining to the suit, taking a ⅜″ seam allowance. (**FIG. 270**)

Clip the suit to the V point, and fold the bra cups to the wrong side of the suit. Understitch the V-neck edge, using a long stitch (see Chapter 3). Catch the bra lining to the side seam if it extends that far.

Apply the elastic

Finish the suit with elastic around the legs and arms. Follow directions under "Applying elastic."

At the neckline, do not stitch elastic into the V. Start the elastic at the shoulder where the

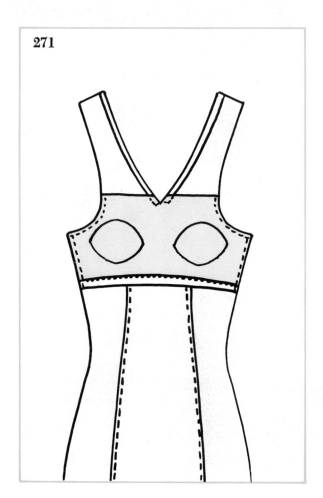

271

bra lining ends. Stitch the elastic around the back of the suit, ending at the lining on the opposite strap. Turn the elastic to the inside, and topstitch around the neck edge. (FIG. 271)

SWIM TRUNKS FOR MEN AND BOYS

You can use one-way stretch or two-way stretch fabric for men's and boys' swim trunks. Doubleknit stretch nylon probably is most readily available.

Some swim trunk patterns have a fly front. You can make this into a real fly opening. Or you can close the center front seam; leave it plain or topstitch the fly opening lines.

Check the length of pattern so that the finished trunks will be comfortable for the man who will wear them. Alter the top or bottom, wherever the length should be added or subtracted.

Men's slacks with continental pockets
Golf shirt with hidden placket

12

How to Fit and Sew Men's Slacks

Men have discovered the comfort and wearability of knit slacks—just as women have. If you learn how to make slacks for the men in your family, you stretch the clothing budget and they get custom-fitted garments.

GENERAL TIPS AND FITTING

Use these helps to select your fabric, notions and pattern. Follow the guides to check pattern pieces and to adjust them for fit.

Choose the fabric and notions

More and more menswear fabrics are becoming available in retail fabric stores; you should have no trouble finding the proper knit. Look for a masculine design and a firm knit that will hold its shape and not snag easily. Make sure any patterned or striped fabric is straight. Sometimes knits are pressed incorrectly in the finishing process, and you will have matching and grain line problems with them.

A pair of men's slacks takes 1½ to 2½ yards of fabric, depending on the size and height of the man. Check the pattern envelope for yardage information.

Besides the slacks fabric, you need about 1 yard of a firm, lightweight fabric for the pocket and waistband lining. A cotton broadcloth or a stabilized nylon tricot is satisfactory. It is not necessary to color match the lining to the slacks fabric.

Other notions you need are a 9″ or 11″ trouser zipper; ¼ yard of press-on, nonwoven interfacing; pants hooks or buttons; thread; something to stiffen the waistband. (This last item is discussed later under "The lined waistband.")

Pick a pattern

You'll find men's slacks in both conventional patterns and in special patterns for knits. You can choose straight or flared legs, continental or side-seam pockets. You may want to make slacks with several of these variations, but don't think you need a pattern for each style. You can use one pattern and change it by mastering a few basic techniques.

The correct size

Many men's slacks patterns run large when made up in knit fabric. This holds true for some of the special patterns for knits as well as most conventional patterns. Measure your pattern and adjust it before you cut the fabric.

The following guides should be helpful in choosing the correct pattern size:

• In a conventional pattern (for non-stretch fabric), use one size smaller than the man's ready-to-wear size.

• In patterns marked "for stretchable knits only," use the man's ready-to-wear size.

• In special patterns for knits that have many sizes on one pattern, there is no set rule. Some look better if you use the man's ready-to-wear size; others look better if you cut one size smaller. When in doubt, cut larger; you can always take in the seams.

Study the pattern pieces

Look at the back pattern piece and take note of a few things.

CENTER BACK SEAM: You will notice the seam allowance at center back is extra wide. (**FIG. 272**) This is the last seam to be sewn; it is wide so that you can make adjustments when you fit the waist.

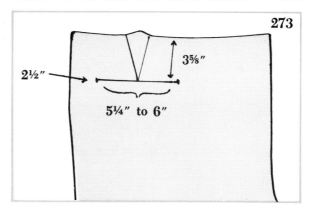

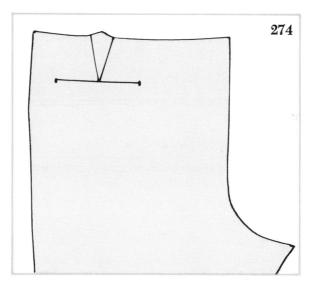

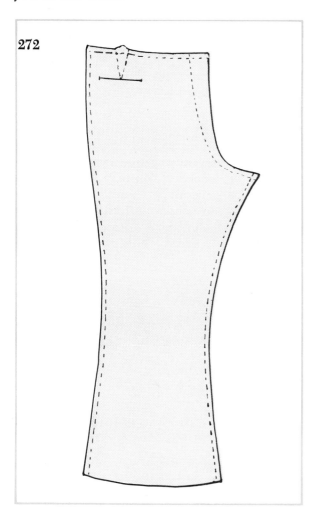

BACK POCKET LOCATION: The position and size of back pockets vary on men's ready-to-wear slacks; you can relocate pockets on the pattern to suit the wearer. If your pattern does not have back pockets indicated, you will have to mark them. Use **FIG. 273** as a guide. Draw the information on your pattern for future reference.

Usually there is a dart in the slacks back, and it is centered above the pocket. (**FIG. 274**) The tip of the dart is sewn down to the pocket line; width of the dart top should be no more than ¾″. Redraw the dart if necessary.

If the man needs more fitting than one ¾″ dart can provide, you can draw two darts above the pocket. (**FIG. 275**) Make each one ¾″ wide. Center these above the pocket.

THE FLY: Look at the front of the pattern and see what type of fly application is provided. Some special patterns for knits have a fly extension attached to the center front of the slacks. (**FIG. 276**) This is used for a very simple fly application.

If your pattern has a separate fly facing, you can tape the facing in place to the front pat-

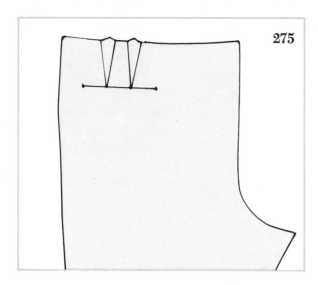

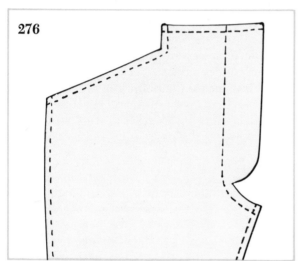

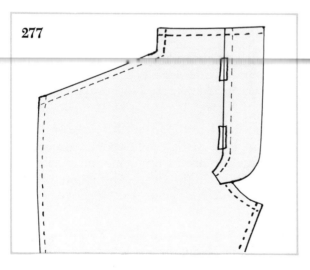

tern piece, overlapping seam allowances. (FIG. 277) This lets you use the simple fly application.

FRONT POCKET STYLE: Check the pocket style included in your pattern. You can use any of the styles discussed in this book with a little pattern adjustment. (See "Front pockets" later in this chapter.)

LEG STYLE: You can add flare to the legs of a pattern that has straight legs. Any flare starts at the knee.

Determine the knee location by measuring the man from his waist to knee, and indicate this location on the pattern. Decide how much flare he wants by measuring around the bottom of some ready-made slacks. Measure around the bottom of the pattern (don't include seam allowances); subtract this

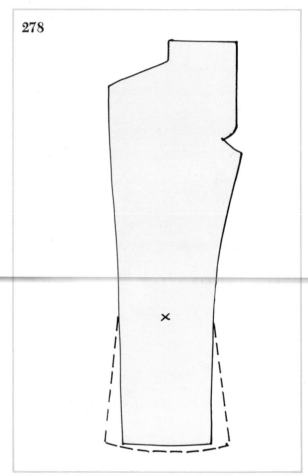

amount from the flare measurement. Divide the result by four, and add equally to all four seams. Taper the added flare gradually into the original line at the knee. (FIG. 278)

FRONT GRAIN LINE: It is helpful if the grain line is centered on the front pattern piece. It then indicates the crease line. If your pattern does not have the grain line in this position, draw it in yourself. Line up the edges of the pattern from bottom edge to the knee, and fold the pattern lengthwise. Draw the grain line on the fold line. (This is a good way to check grain line placement, too. Occasionally, it is printed incorrectly on the pattern.) A centered grain line is especially helpful when you cut a vertically-striped fabric; you can be sure a stripe runs up the crease line.

Check the pattern—make adjustments

Take measurements and alter the pattern before you cut the fabric. When you measure him, be sure the man wears a pair of slacks that fits well.

WAIST: The pattern should be 1″ larger than the man's actual waist measurement; you will ease this extra 1″ into the waistband. Measure the pattern along the waist seamline; do not include seam allowances, back darts or the fly overlap. You can make slight alterations by adding or subtracting at the side seams.

HIPS: Men tend to have a smaller waist-to-hip ratio than women; so, you probably will have little alteration in this area. A man's hip measurement generally is 6″ larger than his waist, and most patterns allow this. If the man's hips run much larger (or smaller), you can make adjustments on the side seams and in the back seat area. (See "Stride" later in this section.)

If the man has large hips, a pattern one size larger than his waist measurement indicates may give a better fit. You can take in the waist at the seamlines and with two darts instead of one on the back sections (see "Back pocket location" earlier in this chapter).

INSEAM LENGTH: Use a special tape measure that has a crotch piece attached to one end; tailor supply houses carry these tape measures.

Place the crotch piece of the tape in position, and run the tape down the inside leg seam to the bottom of the man's slacks. Add an extra 1½″ to this measurement for the hem allowance. Use this total measurement to adjust the pattern leg length.

CROTCH DEPTH: To determine crotch depth, you must first measure the side seam length. Place the end of the tape measure at the waist seam of the man's slacks; run the tape down the side seam to the bottom of the slacks. Add 1½″ for the hem. Now subtract the inseam length from the side seam length; this gives you crotch depth.

Check crotch depth on the front pattern section; pin under pocket piece in place if necessary. First, locate the point where center front and inseams meet; draw a horizontal line through this point. Measure the distance from the line up to the waist; take this measurement along the side seam. (FIG. 279) Adjust the pattern if necessary.

To add depth, slash the front pattern piece horizontally, midway between the waistline

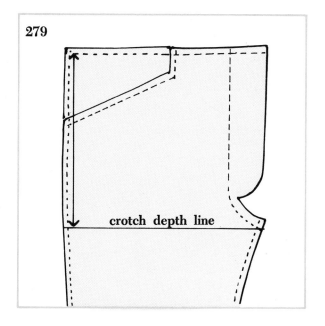

279

crotch depth line

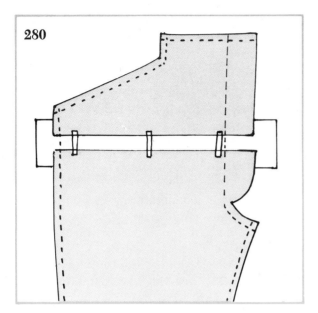

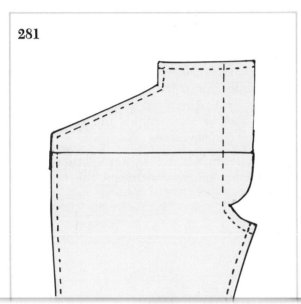

sponding change on the back piece. You also should alter the fly facing and the fly shield.

<u>STRIDE</u>: Check the back section of the pattern to see if there is enough seat room. Measure the pattern back piece from the point where the waist and side seams cross to the point where the crotch and inseam cross. (**FIG. 282**) This stride measurement for knit slacks should be half the hip measurement, less 1″.

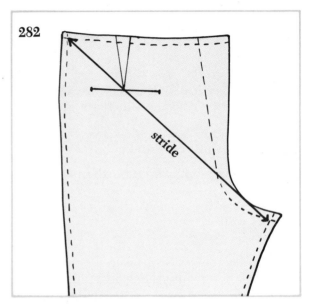

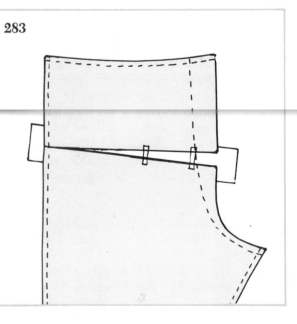

and crotch depth line. Spread the pattern apart the needed amount and tape in an extra piece of paper. (**FIG. 280**)

To subtract depth, slash the pattern and overlap the edges to take out excess depth. (**FIG. 281**) Tape the two pieces together. Or you can shorten the pattern by folding out the excess.

NOTE: If you make any alteration in crotch depth on the front pattern piece, make a corre-

If you find the pattern is too small, you can slash it midway between the waist and crotch point. Cut from the center back to, but not through, the side seam. Spread the pattern apart to increase the stride, but do not spread more than 1″. (FIG. 283) If you need to add more than 1″, go to a larger size or add width at the side seams. To reduce the stride, slash the pattern and overlap the edges the needed amount.

PATTERN FRONT: Use a critical eye to decide if the man has a fairly flat stomach, or if he is beginning to round out.

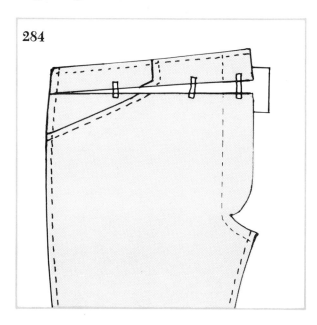

284

To accommodate any roundness, you can add to the top of the center front seam. Slash the pattern front about 1½″ below the waistline seam. Cut from the center front to, but not through, the side seam; do not cut the pattern apart. You can raise the top of the pattern 1″ or less. (FIG. 284) Tape in some extra paper to fill the gap. Straighten the pocket line if you make this alteration.

FRONT CROTCH: In order to accommodate the male figure, you should allow extra fabric on one side of the front crotch. The side will depend upon the wearer's preference; on ready-made slacks, the allowance generally is found on the left side.

Take care of this allowance when you sew the curved section of the center front seam. Make a ⅜″ seam allowance on the side where the extra fullness is needed and a regular ⅝″ seam on the other side.

MAKING THE SLACKS

Let these detailed directions help you cut and sew the slacks. Choose the style you like for back pockets, front pockets and waistband.

Prepare the fabric—and cut

Preshrink the fabric by washing or dry-cleaning according to the fiber (see Chapter 1).

Place pattern on the fabric so that the tops of all pieces face the same end. Cut fabric; use tailor's tacks to transfer markings.

NOTE: If you have made extensive alterations in the pattern, baste the leg and crotch seams together for a fitting. Adjust slacks before you set creases or stitch seams; pressed-in lines are difficult—sometimes impossible—to remove from synthetics.

Set the front crease

Press the front crease before you sew any seams. Fold the front leg pieces in half lengthwise, wrong sides together, matching cut edges at the bottom and knee. Press the fold with a steam iron and a press cloth; do not place your iron directly on the right side of the fabric. A moist press cloth helps make a sharp, lasting crease.

Back pockets—and back darts

Choose the pocket style you like. Directions follow for a single welt pocket, double welt pocket—with or without a button tab, and a waist seam pocket. If you want to add pocket flaps, refer to "Pocket flaps" in Chapter 13. To make buttonholes, refer to "Machine buttonholes" in Chapter 8.

SINGLE WELT POCKET: For each pocket, cut a piece of stay fabric that measures 2″ longer than the pocket opening and 3″ wide. Enlarge

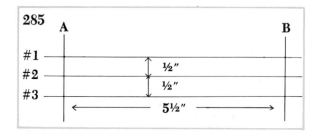

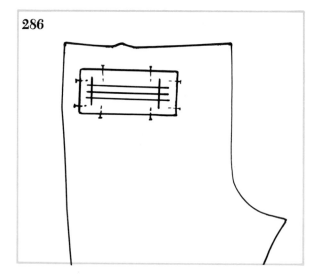

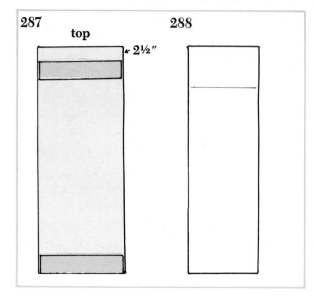

Measure distance from top edge of slacks to pocket location. Double this amount, and use the new figure to measure down from the top of the pocket fabric. Draw a horizontal line on the wrong side of the pocket fabric. (FIG. 288)

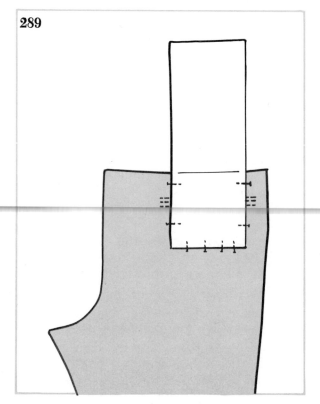

the diagram in FIG. 285 for a pattern, and trace it onto the stay fabric.

Place the stay fabric on the wrong side of the slacks back with line #1 on the tailor's tacks that mark the pocket location. Pin in place securely. (FIG. 286) Stitch along all the lines, using a basting stitch and a contrasting thread. Stitch parallel lines in the same direction so that fabric will not shift.

For each pocket, cut a piece of pocket fabric that measures 2″ wider than the pocket opening and 19″ long. Then cut two strips of slacks fabric that measure 1″ wider than the pocket opening and 3″ long.

Secure strips to the pocket piece by the machine or with one of the bonding products available in fabric stores. Position the wrong side of the strip against the right side of the pocket piece. Place one strip at the bottom edge of the pocket piece; place a second strip so that the top edge of the strip is 2½″ below the top of the pocket piece. (FIG. 287)

Place the pocket against the slacks back, right sides together, with the horizontal line running along the top edge of the slacks. The pocket fabric should be centered over the pocket marking on the slacks; most of the pocket piece extends above the waistline of the slacks. Pin securely in place. (FIG. 289)

Turn the slacks to the wrong side and stitch along line #1 between the vertical lines A and B. (FIG. 290) Use a matching thread and sew with 12 stitches per inch. Backstitch at the beginning and end of the stitching line.

Turn the slacks to the right side. Pin the small pocket extension up out of the way. Make a 1″ fold at the long end of the pocket

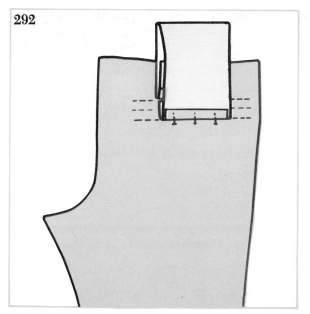

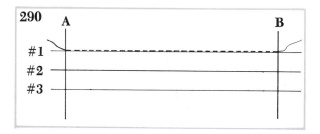

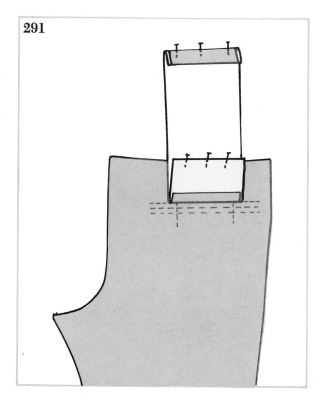

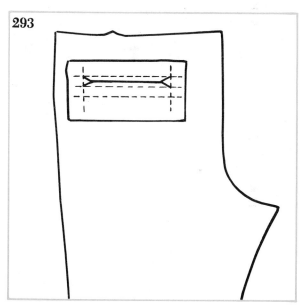

so that the strip of slacks fabric is to the outside. (FIG. 291)

Place the folded edge along line #3 and secure with transparent tape or pin in place. (FIG. 292)

Turn the slacks to the wrong side and stitch along line #2, starting and stopping at the vertical lines. Slash the pocket open between lines #1 and #2. Cut to within ½″ of each end, then make a large wedge by cutting into each corner. (FIG. 293) Cut only the stay fabric and the slacks fabric. Do not cut the pocket fabric.

Pull the pocket fabric through to the wrong side and arrange it in position. Baste the pocket closed so that the edge of the welt is held against the top of the pocket opening. (FIG. 294) Press from the wrong side.

Work from the right side of the slacks, and fold back one edge until you see the wedge.

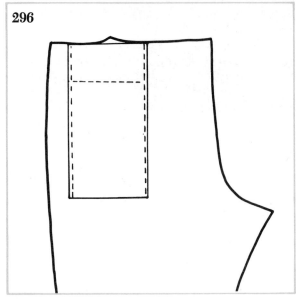

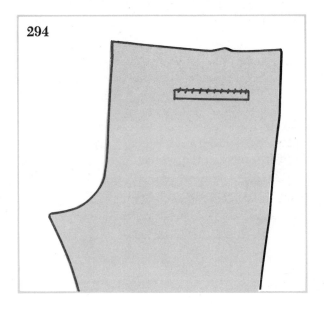

Straight stitch along the base of the wedge making it secure. (FIG. 295) Stitch through all layers of the pocket. Do the same on the other side of the pocket.

Fold in the raw edges of the pocket about ¼" and press. Stitch along the edge of the folds, closing the pocket. (FIG. 296) Do not catch the slacks in this stitching. Remove the basting stitches and trim the excess stay fabric.

To provide extra strength, finish each pocket end with a bar tack. (FIG. 297) Do this by hand or machine.

Stitch in the dart above the pocket. Run the stitching line from the waist to the top edge of the pocket. (FIG. 298) Cut the dart open along the fold and press open. Press the pocket carefully so there is no bulge at the end of the dart.

Pull the pocket extension up to the top of the slacks, and stitch along the waist edge. (FIG. 299) This will hold it in position for the waistband application.

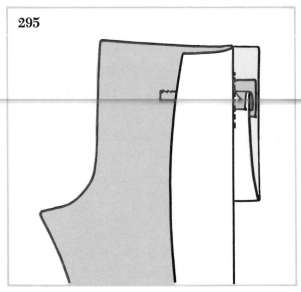

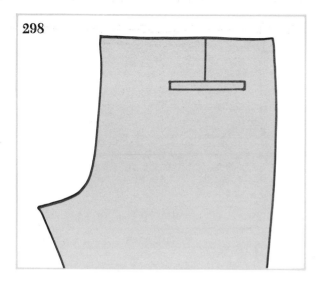

298

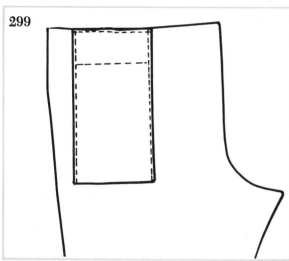

299

DOUBLE WELT POCKET: This pocket is similar to a bound buttonhole. A button tab sewn in the upper welt is optional.

For each pocket, cut a piece of pocket fabric that measures 2″ wider than the pocket opening and 19″ long. Then cut one strip of slacks fabric that measures 1″ wider than the pocket opening and 3″ long.

Place the strip 2½″ down from the top edge of the pocket fabric. Have wrong side of strip against right side of pocket fabric. (See illustration under "Single welt pocket" earlier in this chapter. For this application, use only the top strip of slacks fabric.) Secure strip

to the pocket piece by machine stitching or with one of the bonding products available in fabric stores.

For each pocket, cut a piece of stay fabric that measures 2″ longer than the pocket opening and about 3″ wide. Enlarge the diagram in **FIG. 300** and trace it onto the stay fabric. Pin stay fabric in place on the wrong side of the slacks fabric; have corners of the diagram directly on top of the pocket marking on the slacks. Stitch along all lines; use a basting stitch and a contrasting thread so the lines will be visible on the right side of the slacks fabric.

For each pocket, you need two welts. Cut two strips of slacks fabric lengthwise; make them 1″ wide and 1″ longer than the pocket opening. Press the strips in half lengthwise, wrong sides together. You can press a narrow strip of bonding material inside the strips to add firmness to the welts.

Draw or stitch a line down the exact middle of each folded welt strip. Use whatever method is most accurate for you. The strips should look like **FIG. 301**.

NOTE: A button tab is optional. If you want to include one, make the tab and pin it into position at this point. Directions are at the end of this section on double welt pocket.

To position the top welt strip, have slacks right side up. Place one welt strip so cut edges run along the horizontal stitching line; center it between the vertical basting stitches. (**FIG. 302**)

300   5½″

301

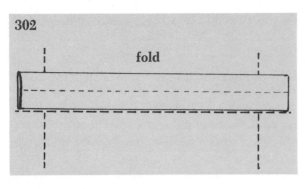

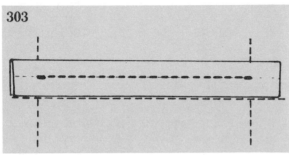

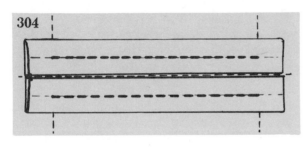

the stay fabric and the slacks fabric; do not cut the welts.

Push the welts through the opening and pull them into position on the wrong side. Baste the welts together across the opening (FIG. 306) and press from the wrong side.

Turn the slacks to the right side. Fold back one edge until you find the wedge on top of the welt strips. Stitch across the base of the wedge, catching it to the welts. (FIG. 307) Double stitch, then do the same on the other side of the pocket opening.

Turn the slacks to the wrong side again and position the pocket piece. Place the right side

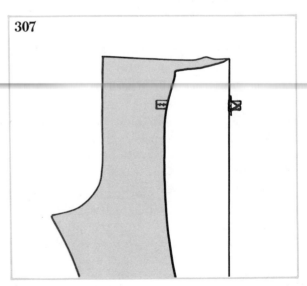

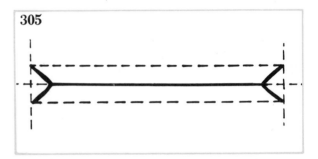

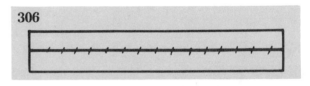

Secure the strip to the slacks by stitching down the middle of the strip; sew directly over the stitching line on the strip. Use a thread that matches the slacks fabric and 12 stitches to the inch. The stitching line should start and end at the vertical basting lines. (FIG. 303) Backstitch at the beginning and end, or tie the threads securely.

Place the other welt strip in position. Center it between the vertical basting stitches. Butt the *cut edges* of the two strips together (edges touch, but do not overlap). (FIG. 304) Sew the second welt as you did the first one.

Turn the slacks to the wrong side and carefully cut the pocket open. Cut along the horizontal basting to within ½" of the vertical lines; then cut into each corner, making a good-size wedge. (FIG. 305) Cut only through

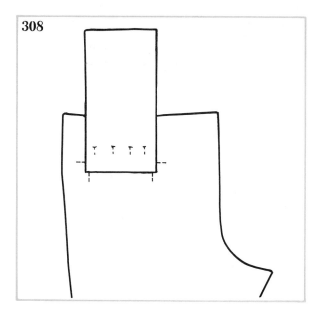

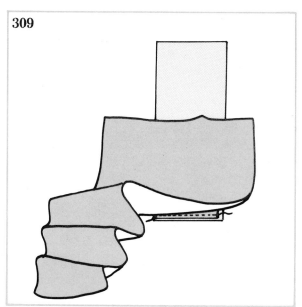

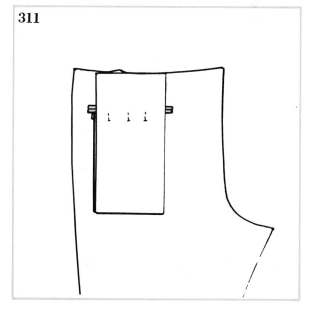

Turn the slacks to the wrong side. Unpin the pocket fabric and press it down against the slacks. (FIG. 310)

Pull the pocket fabric up into the final position with the edge of the pocket even with the top edge of the slacks. (FIG. 311) The patch of slacks fabric that you secured to the pocket fabric should be directly over the pocket opening. Pin pocket in place below the opening.

of the pocket against the wrong side of the slacks. Center the pocket piece over the opening, with the bottom edge of the pocket ½" below the bottom welt. Pin in place above the pocket opening. (FIG. 308)

With the slacks right side up, lift the leg until you see the pocket welt and the edge of the pocket fabric. Stitch along the welt seam allowance, catching the welt and pocket fabric together. (FIG. 309)

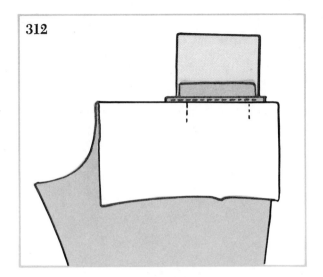

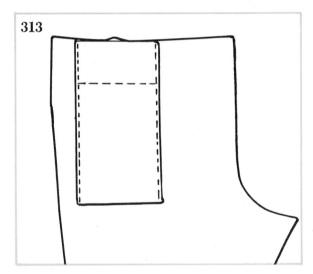

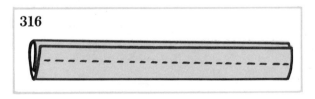

To add strength to the pocket opening, make a bar tack at each end. (FIG. 314)

Stitch in the dart above the pocket. (FIG. 315) Cut dart open along the fold and press open.

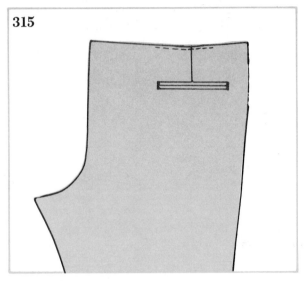

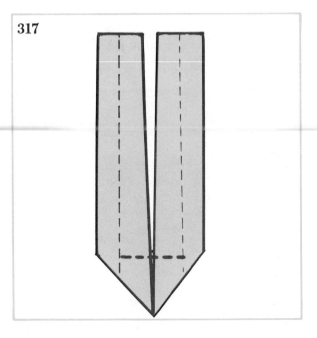

Turn the slacks to the right side. Fold down the top of the slacks until you see the top welt. Stitch along the welt seam allowance, catching it to the pocket fabric. (FIG. 312)

Fold in the raw edges of the pocket about ¼″ and press. Stitch along the folded edges, closing the pocket. (FIG. 313) Do not catch the slacks in this stitching. Remove the basting stitches and trim the excess stay fabric.

Pull the pocket extension up to the top of the slacks, and stitch along the waist edge. This will hold it in position for the waistband application.

Button tab (optional): Cut a lengthwise strip of slacks fabric that is 1″ wide and 2½″ long. Fold it in thirds and stitch down the middle with a straight or small zigzag stitch. (**FIG.** 316)

Fold the strip to make a point as illustrated in **FIG.** 317, and stitch across the point to hold it in place.

Pin the tab in position on the right side of the slacks. Point of the strip should extend 1″ above the horizontal basting line. (**FIG.** 318) The tab is held in place when the top welt is sewn to the slacks.

After you complete the pocket, press the tab area well to reduce bulk. Use lots of steam, and press only from the wrong side. Sew the button in position. (**FIG.** 319)

WAIST SEAM POCKET: This pocket opening is concealed in the waist seam. A similar pocket is found in the yoke seam of slacks and on the front of ski pants where only a small coin pocket is needed.

To locate the pocket opening on the pattern, measure along the waist seam 2⅝″ from the side seam. Begin the pocket width from here; it can be 5½″ to 6″ wide. (**FIG.** 320) Mark these points on your slacks fabric with tailor's tacks. Pocket crosses a dart; so, add the width of the dart to the pocket measurement.

For each pocket, cut a section of pocket fabric that is 16″ long and 2″ wider than the pocket opening. Cut two strips of slacks fabric that measure 1″ wider than the pocket

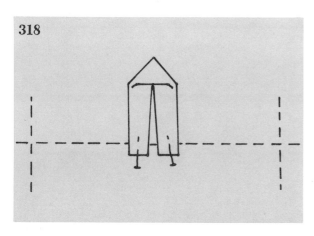

318

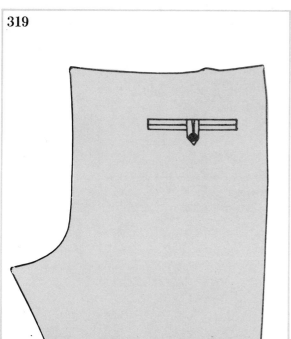

319

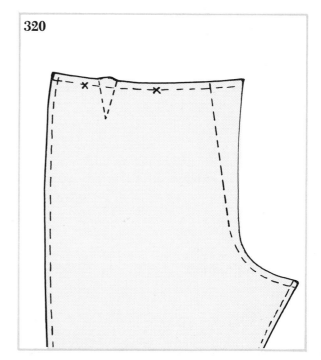

320

321

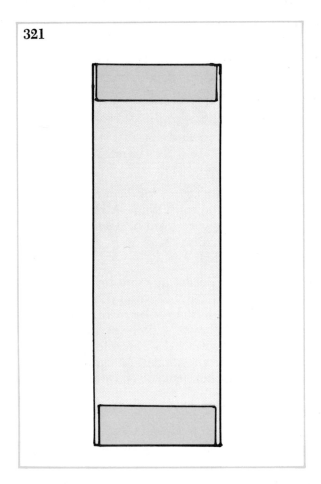

322

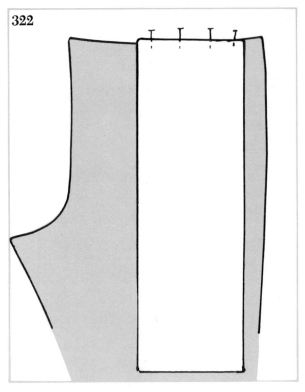

323

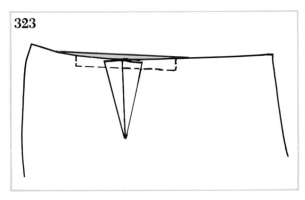

324

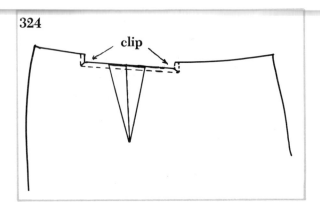

opening and 3″ long. Secure these strips to each end of the pocket fabric, wrong side of strip to right side of pocket fabric. (**FIG. 321**)

Sew dart in the slacks back. Cut the dart open along the fold, and press it flat.

Place the right side of the pocket against the right side of the slacks. Center the pocket piece over the tailor's tacks, with the edge of the pocket even with the top of the slacks. (**FIG. 322**)

Turn the slacks to the wrong side; stitch as indicated in **FIG. 323**. Stitching line is along the waistline seam and marks the width of the pocket.

Clip into the corners, and trim the seam allowances. (**FIG. 324**)

Turn the pocket fabric to the wrong side of the slacks and press carefully. (**FIG. 325**) Roll

325

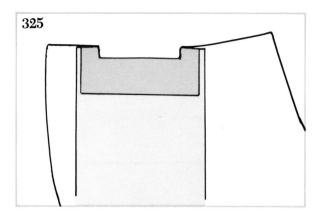

326

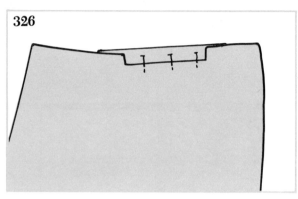

327

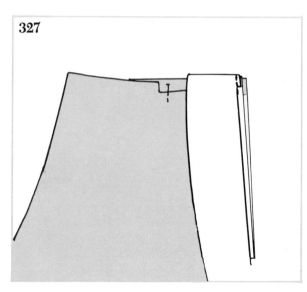

328

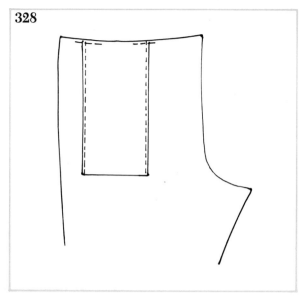

the seam so that it will not show on the right side.

Bring the free end of the pocket up to the top of the slacks and pin it in place along the pocket opening. (**FIG. 326**)

Fold back the side of the slacks until you see the stitching on the pocket facing. Stitch over the same seam allowance, catching it to the back of the pocket. (**FIG. 327**) Do this on both sides of the pocket.

Turn the slacks to the wrong side and fold in the raw edges of the pocket ¼" and press. Stitch along the edge of the fold, closing the pocket. (Do not catch the slacks in this stitching.) Sew along the top edge of the slacks to hold the pocket in place for the waistband application. (**FIG. 328**)

Front pockets

You have many choices of front pocket styles. The most popular probably is the pocket that opens from the top, with either a slanted "continental" line (**FIG. 329**) or a curved line (**FIG. 330**). Another favorite style is the pocket with a deep slant. (**FIG. 331**)

This chapter includes directions for making a continental pocket. You can vary the shape of the opening once you master the basic pocket construction; it's easy to create a jeans pocket or a notched pocket, for instance. Of course, you also can use the regular pocket that opens from the side seam. For this, you should buy a pattern with a side-seam pocket and follow the pattern instructions.

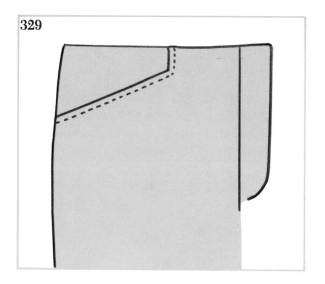

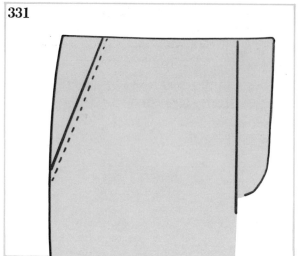

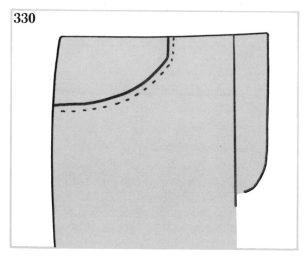

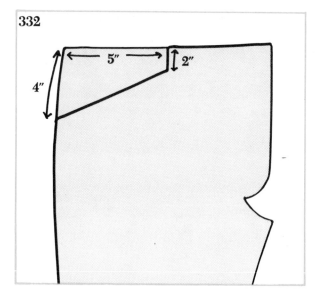

THE CONTINENTAL POCKET: You can find this slanted pocket on a pattern, or you can design your own by following FIG. 332.

For each pocket, cut an upper pocket section from the pocket lining fabric. Top edge follows the slant of the slacks pocket opening and will look like FIG. 333. This is called an upper pocket. If you are designing your own pocket, use the measurements given here to help you cut the correct size. With pattern in this position, cut right-hand upper pocket with wrong side of fabric up.

Using pocket lining fabric again, cut an under pocket section. Make this the same size as the upper pocket, but do not slant it at the waist.

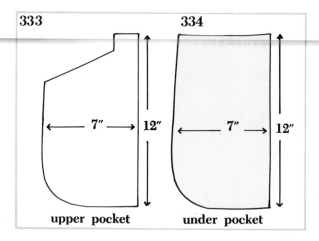

upper pocket   under pocket

Top edge follows the waistline curve of the slacks front. (FIG. 334) Cut right-hand under pocket with right side of fabric up.

From the slacks fabric, cut patches to cover the top portions of both upper and under pocket sections. If you do not have pattern pieces for these, you can use the pocket pieces as guides for cutting. Put the wrong side of fabric patches against the right side of the pocket sections. (FIGS. 335 and 336) Sew or bond together.

Now place the shaped pocket piece against the slacks front, right sides together. Stitch

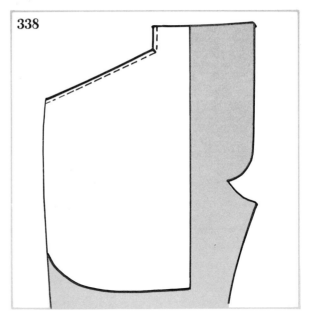

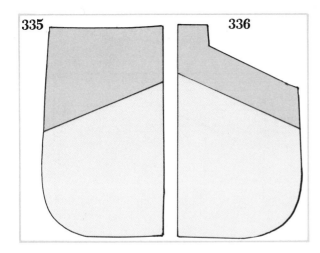

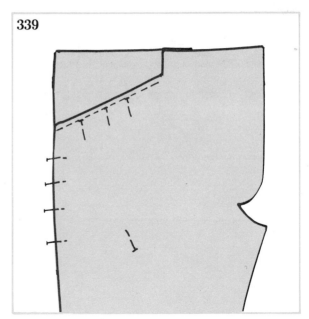

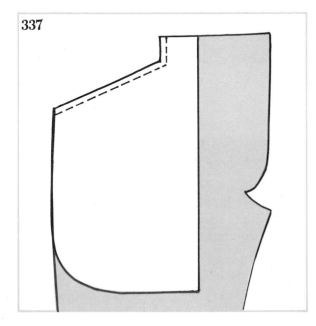

the two pieces together along the slanted edge and up to the waist, using a ⅝″ seam allowance. Stitch with pocket side up. (FIG. 337)

Clip to the stitching line at the corner and grade the seam allowance. (FIG. 338) Press the pocket fabric to the inside of the slacks, rolling the seam under so it does not show on the right side.

Topstitch ¼″ from the edge; stitch only from side to corner. Knot the thread at the back rather than backstitching.

Pin the under pocket into position underneath the slacks front, making sure all edges line up neatly. (FIG. 339)

Fold back the center front of the slacks until you see the pocket seam allowance. Stitch along the original seamline, catching the up-

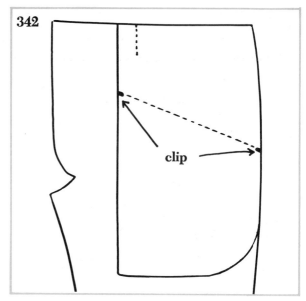

342

clip

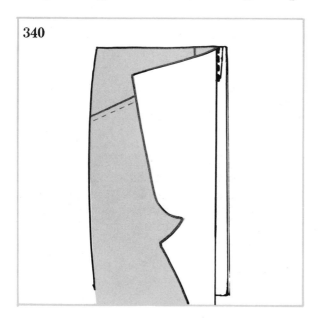

340

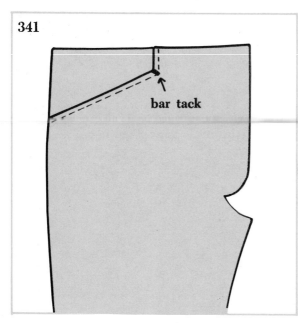

341

bar tack

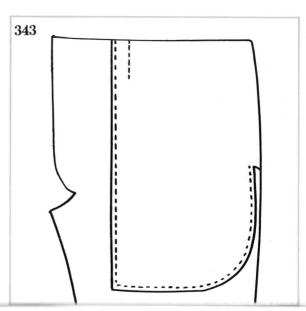

343

per pocket to the under pocket. (FIG. 340) Backstitch here to make the seam stronger.

You now can continue the topstitching up to the top of the pocket, or you can leave it as is. In either case you should add a bar tack at the corner of the pocket for extra strength. (FIG. 341)

Turn the slacks to the wrong side, and smooth the two pocket pieces into position. Locate the line where the patches of slacks fabric slant across the pocket. Make small clips through both layers of pocket fabric just below this line. (**FIG. 342**) These clips will act as notches when you sew the pocket sections together.

Turn the pocket inside out, and pin the edges of the pocket lining together. Match the clip marks. Stitch around the outer edge of the pocket with a ⅝″ seam allowance. Trim the seam to ⅛″, and clip the curves.

Push the pocket back down into the slacks as it should be. Press the pocket, then stitch around the outer edge with a ¼″ seam allowance. (**FIG. 343**)

THE JEANS POCKET: A western or jeans-style pocket (**FIG. 344**) can be made in a pair of casual slacks by using the same construction method indicated for the continental pocket. The only difference is the shape at the top opening.

Redraw the pocket opening to correspond to the shape you want, and cut the upper pocket lining in that shape. Follow the pocket construction steps given for "The continental pocket."

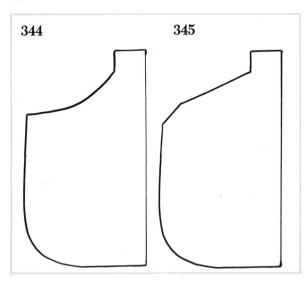

THE NOTCHED POCKET: Redraw the top of the pocket opening to a notched shape. (**FIG. 345**) Follow the construction steps for "The continental pocket."

The zipper fly

There are several ways to make a zipper fly; some methods are more complicated than others. The simplest way probably is the best for knits, and that is the method described here. You should cut the fly facing as part of the slacks front (see "The fly" under "Study the pattern pieces" earlier in this chapter). Before you remove the pattern piece from the fabric, mark the center front line with tailor's chalk or dressmaker's tracing paper.

Cut one piece of press-on, nonwoven interfacing to fit the fly extension and to extend ½″ beyond the center front line. You will bond this to the left front section; make sure the bonding surface will be against the wrong side of the fly extension.

Cut fabric (as described below) for the fly shield; this unit will be stitched in place after the zipper is installed. If your pattern does not have a special pattern piece for this, you can enlarge the diagram in **FIG. 346** and use it as a cutting guide.

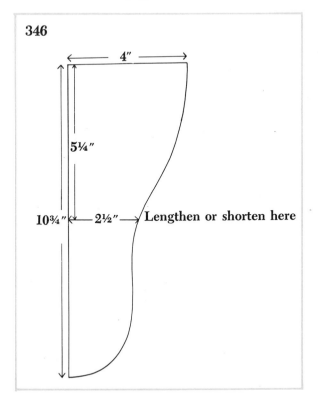

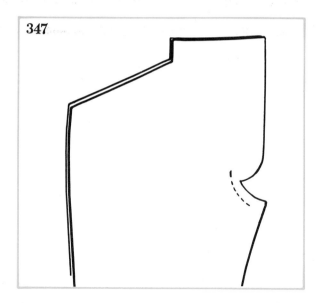

347

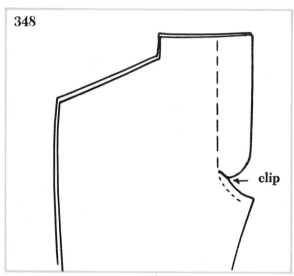

348

clip

curve, and go ⅝" up into the fly extension, along the center front marks. (**FIG. 347**) Double stitch this line to make a strong seam.

Close the rest of the center front line with a long basting stitch. Clip as indicated in **FIG. 348**, and press the fly extension open.

Pin the left fly extension against the front sections, and pull the right fly extension out to the side. (**FIG. 349**) The zipper will be stitched to the right fly extension.

Place the right side of the trouser zipper against the right side of the fly extension. The

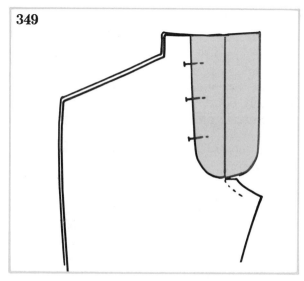

349

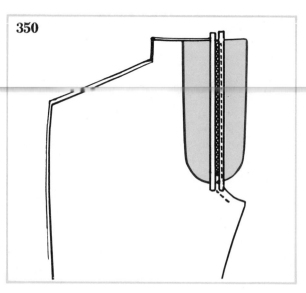

350

With the straight edge of your pattern to the left as illustrated, cut one each of slacks fabric (right side up), press-on interfacing (bonding side up), and pocket fabric (wrong side up). Trim ¼" off the curved edge of the interfacing so it will not be in the seam allowance; press interfacing to the wrong side of the slacks fabric piece. Put all fly shield pieces aside until later.

Pin the slacks front sections, right sides together. Stitch a small area of the crotch curve, and use a ⅝" seam allowance. Begin stitching 1" from the fabric edge; stitch along the

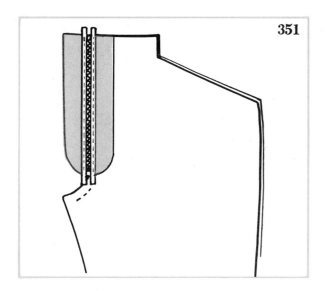

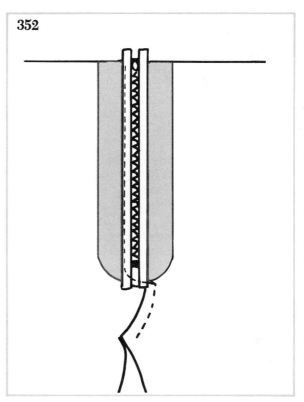

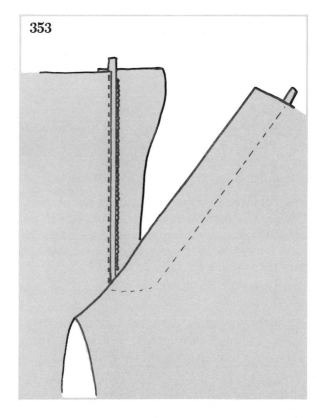

bottom of the zipper teeth should be about ¾″ above the bottom of the fly extension. (Later, you will cut the zipper at the top.) The left edge of the zipper tape is against the center front seam. Use a zipper foot on your machine. Stitch from the top down the right edge of the zipper tape, about ⅛″ from the teeth. (**FIG. 350**) Backstitch at the bottom.

Unpin the left fly extension and fold the slacks so that this extension goes out to the side. Pull the free edge of the zipper over as far as it will go, and place the right side of the zipper against the right side of this fly extension. Stitch along the left side of the zipper tape, about ⅛″ from the teeth. (**FIG. 351**) Stitch from the top; backstitch at the bottom.

Unfold the slacks, and pin the zipper to the left half of the slacks. Stitch along the very edge of the zipper tape; this line should be about 1⅛″ to the left of the center front. Curve the stitching below the zipper teeth and stitch to the center front seam. (**FIG. 352**) Remove the basting stitches.

NOTE: If you plan to use a lined waistband or a tailored waistband, do not stitch the top 2″ of this left side of the fly until later.

To add the fly shield, open the zipper. Work with both slacks and shield right side up.

Place the fly shield under the right half of the zipper; straight edge of the shield should be ⅝" past the zipper teeth. Catch the shield to the slacks by topstitching along the edge of the slacks fabric, close to the zipper teeth. (FIG. 353) Stitch from the top to the bottom as far as you can go; backstitch at the bottom.

Trim off the excess fly extension behind the shield, and overcast the edges with a zigzag stitch. You will add the fly shield lining later.

The side seams

Carefully pin the front and back legs together along the side seams. The legs should be the same length; no stretching should be required to make top and bottom meet.

Stitch together with a ⅝" seam allowance. Backstitch at the point where the front pocket joins the side seam. Press the seam open, using lots of moisture.

The waistband

There are several waistband finishes you can use. The choice will be partially determined by the man's preference and by the products available to you. If you can't find the supplies you want in fabric stores, try tailor supply houses.

The three waistbands discussed here include the elastic waistband (an easy one), the lined waistband, and the tailored waistband (a professional looking finish).

THE ELASTIC WAISTBAND: You use a piece of heavy 1½" to 2" elastic inside this waistband for stiffening. For length of elastic, use the man's waist measure plus 8". Wash the elastic before you use it.

Cut two waistband strips of slacks fabric. Make them 6" wide. For length, use one half the waist measurement, plus 6". Cut the strips along the lengthwise grain of the fabric.

Pin the right sides of the waistband strips to the right sides of the slacks. Line up the edge of the waistband with the back seam edge of

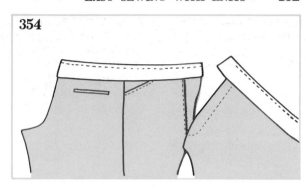

354

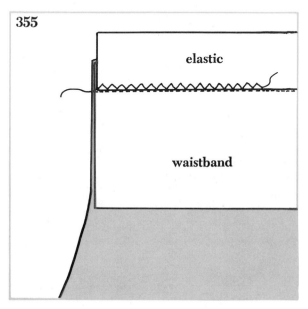

355

elastic

waistband

the slacks, and let the excess extend beyond the center front edge. (FIG. 354)

Sew the waistband to the slacks with a ⅝" seam. As you stitch across the zipper, run the machine by hand to make sure you don't strike the zipper teeth and break the needle. Cut off any excess zipper that extends above the seam allowance.

Cut one piece of elastic that is one half the waist measurement, plus 5½"; cut another piece that is one half the waist measure, plus 1½". You will sew the longer piece to the right half of the slacks and the shorter to the left half.

Sew elastic to the waist seam allowance only; place cut edge of the elastic at the back seam edge of the slacks. As you sew the elastic to the seam allowance, make sure that the bottom edge of the elastic is always slightly above the original seamline. (**FIG. 355**)

NOTE: Use a zigzag or an automatic stretch stitch for this. If you use a straight stitch, stretch both fabric and elastic slightly as you sew.

On the right half of the waistband, trim the elastic at the front edge so it is ¼″ behind the edge of the fly shield. (**FIG. 356**)

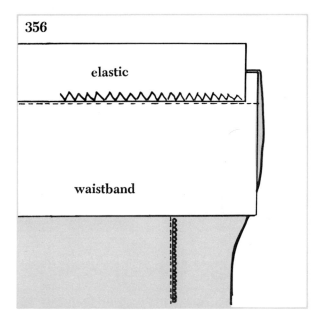

356

elastic

waistband

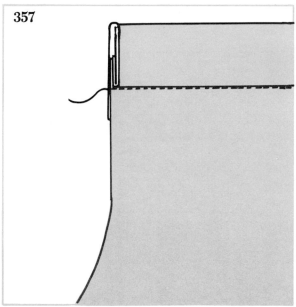

357

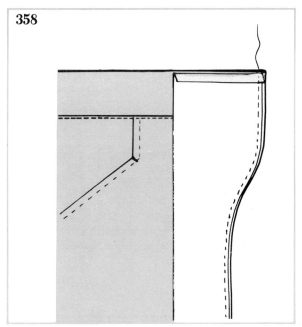

358

Pull the right half of the waistband up over the elastic and to the inside of the slacks. Pull it snugly; pin it in place on the right side of the slacks, just below the seamline. Catch the waistband to the slacks by stitching in the seam groove on the right side. (**FIG. 357**)

Place the right side of the fly shield lining against the right side of the fly shield. Turn down the top edge until it is slightly below the edge of the waistband; press. Stitch down the edges of the fly shield. (**FIG. 358**) Trim the seam, clip the curve, and press the lining to the inside of the slacks.

Fold under the straight edge of the shield lining about ½″. (**FIG. 359**) Hold it in place by stitching from the right side; sew on top of the stitching line that you made to join fly shield to slacks. (**FIG. 360**) Start the stitching at the top of the waistband.

On the left half of the waistband, trim away any elastic that extends beyond the fold of the fly opening. Pull the front edge of the waistband up to the top edge of the elastic; then, fold it back on itself, right sides together. Stitch next to the cut edge of the elastic through all layers of waistband fabric. (**FIG. 361**) Trim the seam allowance to ¼″.

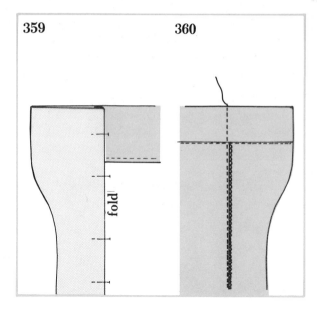

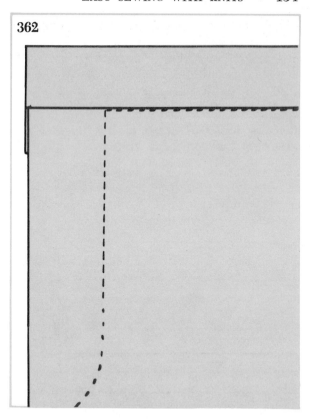

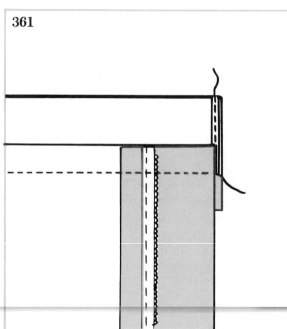

better if the seam allowance is turned under and closed by hand.

Sew two pants hooks to the waistband as indicated in FIG. 363.

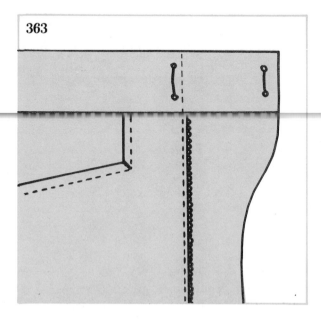

Turn the waistband corners right side out. Pull the waistband up over the elastic and to the inside of the slacks. Pull it snugly, and pin in place just below the seamline on the right side. Catch down the back of the waistband by stitching in the seam groove on the right side. Start the stitching line where the fly topstitching meets the waistband. (FIG. 362) The section in front of this line looks

Belt loops: If you want to make belt loops for slacks, follow a pair of ready-made slacks as a guide for positioning them. They can vary in number, width and placement.

An easy way to make a belt loop is to cut a lengthwise strip of fabric 2″ wide. Fold the strip in thirds, and stitch down the middle. (FIG. 364) The cut edge will not fray.

Place end of strip against waistband, right sides together. Position strip with ¼″ above the waistline seam. Stitch across the strip at the seamline. Turn strip up.

Fold under the unfinished end of the strip (about ½″), and topstitch it to the top of the waistband.

364

THE LINED WAISTBAND: This waistband has a 2″ tab extension at the waist opening and looks nice without a belt. (You can eliminate the extension and add belt loops, if the man prefers.) The waistband should have a finished width of 1½″ or 2″; width will depend upon the width of interfacing you can buy.

The lined waistband requires some type of waistband stiffening. Tailor supply houses and some knit fabric shops carry firm interfacings in 1″, 1½″ and 2″ widths. You will need two widths—the 1″, and either the 1½″ or 2″. Length for both widths will be the waist measurement, plus 8″. Be sure the stiffening is washable and dry-cleanable.

Cut two lengthwise strips of slacks fabric for the waistband. These should be 1¼″ wider than the waistband interfacing you are using. The right half of the waistband should measure one half the waist measurement, plus 5½″. The left half of the waistband should measure one half the waist measurement, plus 8½″. Be sure to match the two waistband pieces if you are using a striped or patterned fabric.

Use a strip of press-on interfacing for the tab extension if you are making this style. This piece should measure 1½″ or 2″ (to match the interfacing) by 8½″.

Cut two bias strips of lining fabric that are 1″ wider than the finished waistband and as long as each waistband piece. You can use the pocket lining fabric for the waistband lining.

Begin with the left side of the waistband, wrong side up. Position the strip of press-on interfacing at the front end. Center it inside the seam allowances (FIG. 365), and press in place.

At the top of both waistband fabric strips, press down a ⅝″ seam allowance. Pin the bottom edge of the waistband strips to the waist of the slacks, right sides together. Have waistband strips even with center back seam edges of slacks; sew with a ⅝″ seam. Do not catch the back part of the left fly in this stitching. (You topstitched the fly to within 2″ of the waist; and you can pull top edge of the fly extension out of the way as you stitch.) Press the seam allowances up into the waistband strips.

Place the 1″ interfacing on top of the wider interfacing. Then position the two strips under the seam allowance at the top of the waistband. (FIG. 366) The edges of the two interfacing pieces should be along the fold

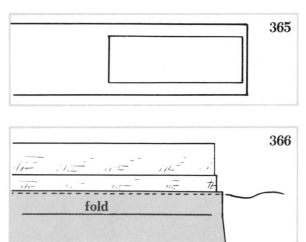

365

366

fold

line. The interfacing should stop ¼" behind the edge of the fly shield on the right waistband strip and go to the fold of the fly on the left waistband strip. Stitch along the edge of the waistband seam allowance, catching it to the two strips of interfacing.

On each bias strip of lining fabric, make a ¾" fold along the bottom edge; turn fold to wrong side and press. Place the right side of a bias strip against the right side of the waistband; have the top edge of the strip even with the top edge of the waistband. (FIG. 367)

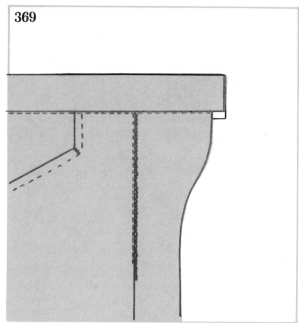

369

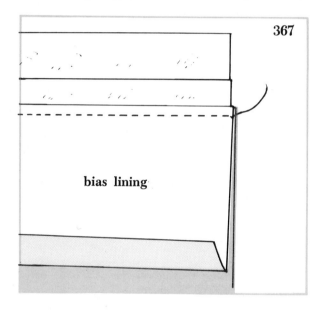

367

bias lining

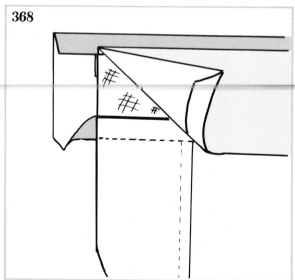

368

Stitch with a ¼" seam allowance—through lining fabric, waistband, and interfacings. Sew the lining only to the portion of the waistband to which you have already sewn interfacing. You will turn bias lining up against interfacings and press.

To finish the right half of the waistband, turn the lining and interfacing down into the slacks. Tuck the wide interfacing behind the waist seam allowance; this makes a smooth finish on the right side of the slacks. Pull the bias lining down over the waist seam allowances so the folded edge is slightly below the seamline. (FIG. 368) Pin in place from the right side.

From the right side, stitch along the waist seam groove, catching the lining on the wrong side. (FIG. 369) Be careful as you stitch over the zipper areas so that you don't break your needle.

Trim the end of the waistband so it is even with the fly shield. Place the right side of the shield lining against the right side of the fly shield. Press down the top edge of the shield lining, until it is slightly below the top of the waistband. Stitch down the curved edge of the shield with a ¼" seam. (FIG. 370)

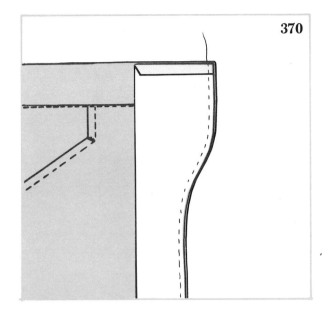

370

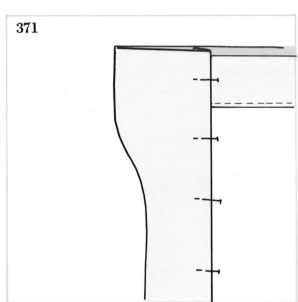

371

the front end of the waistband back on itself, right sides together. Fold it back far enough so the end of the waistband will be about ½″ beyond the topstitching line at the fly. Stitch along the seamline at the top edge of the waistband. (**FIG. 372**) This forms the tab for the button closure. Grade the seam allowance, and turn the tab right side out.

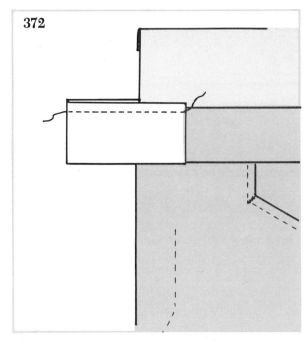

372

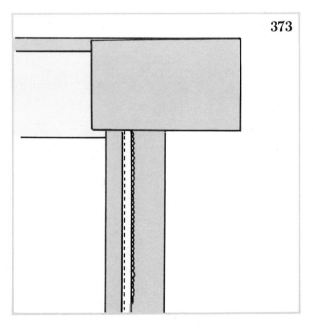

373

Trim the seam, clip the curve, and press the lining to the inside of the slacks. Fold under the straight edge of the shield lining. (**FIG. 371**)

Hold lining in place by stitching from the right side; sew on top of the stitching line that joined fly shield to slacks. Start the stitching line at the top of the waistband.

To finish the left side of the waistband, pull lining and interfacings out of the way. Fold

Turn the lining and interfacing down into the slacks, and tuck the wide interfacing behind the waist seam allowance.

Pull the lining down over the waist seam allowances so that the folded edge is slightly below the seamline. Pin in place from the right side. The back of the fly should now lap over the raw edges of the interfacing and lining. Turn in the bottom seam allowances of the tab area, and close by hand. (**FIG. 373**)

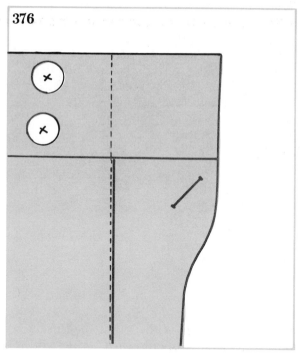

376

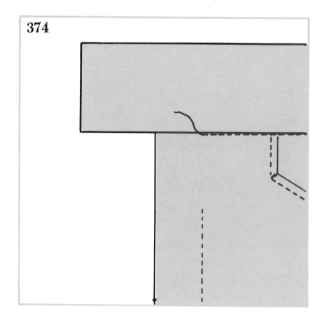

374

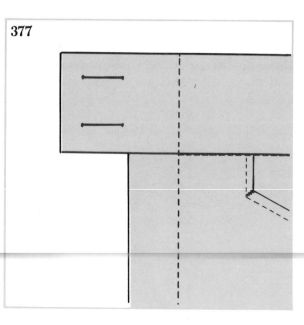

377

Turn the slacks to the right side. Stitch along the waist seam groove, catching the lining to the slacks. Start the stitching just behind the zipper teeth. (**FIG. 374**)

Complete the topstitching on the zipper and continue it up through the waistband. (**FIG. 375**)

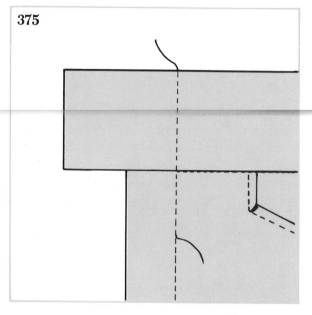

375

To finish the waistband, make two horizontal buttonholes in the tab, or apply heavy-duty gripper snaps. (If you have eliminated the tab, use pants hooks. To make belt loops, see directions under "The elastic waistband.") You also can make a buttonhole in the fly shield, just below the seamline; sew the button for this to the pocket or waistband lining. (FIGS. 376 and 377)

THE TAILORED WAISTBAND: This type of waistband is found in good quality slacks. It has a tab extension at the waist opening, which you can eliminate. You also can add belt loops. The finished waistband will be 1½" or 2" wide, depending upon the width of interfacing you can buy.

You will need two widths of waistband interfacing. (See explanation of interfacing under "The lined waistband" in this section.) Cut the strips as long as the waist measurement, plus 8". One strip should be 1" wide, and the other strip should be either 1½" or 2" wide.

Cut two strips of slacks fabric that measure 1¼" wider than the finished waistband. Cut them on the lengthwise grain of the fabric, and match fabric stripes or pattern if necessary. Make the right waistband strip one half the waist measurement, plus 5½". Cut the left waistband strip one half the waist measurement, plus 8½".

Use a strip of press-on interfacing for the tab extension if you are making this style. The

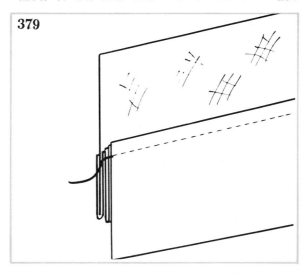

379

piece should measure 1½" or 2" wide by 8½"; width is the same as the interfacing.

Cut one strip of lining fabric, on the bias; it should be as long as the waist measure, plus 8". Make this 1½" wide if interfacing is 2" wide; make it 1¼" wide if interfacing is 1½" wide. Cut two other bias strips of the lining fabric the same length. Make one 2" wide and one 2½" wide. Press the 2" and 2½" strips in half lengthwise, with wrong sides together.

You assemble the interfacing and lining first, then sew the unit to the waistband. To assemble, slip one edge of the wide interfacing strip down inside the folded 2" lining piece. Place the other folded lining piece on top of the first one, making sure all cut edges are even. Stitch all three pieces together ¼" below the cut edges of the bias strips. (FIG. 378)

Position the remaining bias strip on top (wrong side up) and sew again, ¼" below the cut edges. (FIG. 379)

Press this last bias strip up to the top of the interfacing. Then turn under ¼" at the top edge of the bias and press. (FIG. 380) Now, set the lining section aside and apply waistband to slacks.

Take the left waistband strip, wrong side up. Position the 8½" strip of press-on interfacing

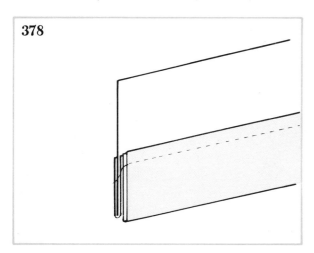

378

380

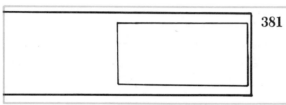

381

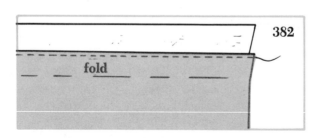

382

fold

Place the strip of 1″ interfacing under the seam allowance at the top of the waistband. Stitch along the edge of the seam allowance, catching it to the interfacing. (**FIG. 382**) The interfacing should stop at the edge of the fly opening on the left side and end ¼″ behind the edge of the fly shield on the right side.

Now apply the lining section. Place the slacks flat on a table and slip the stiff interfacing

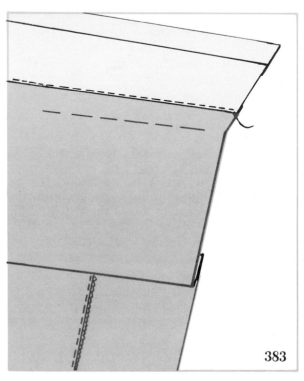

383

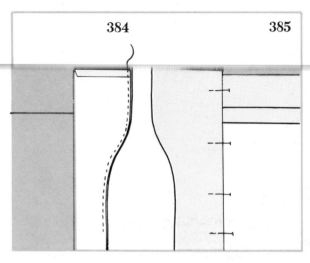

384   **385**

at the front end. Center it inside the seam allowances and press in place. (**FIG. 381**)

At the top of both left and right waistband strips, press down a ⅝″ seam allowance. Pin the bottom edge of the waistband strips to the slacks, right sides together. Have waistband strips even with center back seam edges of slacks; sew with a ⅝″ seam. Do not catch the back part of the left fly in this stitching. (You have topstitched the fly to within 2″ of the waist; pull the top edge of the fly extension out of the way as you stitch.) Press the seams up into the waistband strip.

part of the lining underneath the 1″ strip of interfacing already sewn to the top of the waistband. Pull the lining down to cover the raw edge of the waistband. Topstitch along the edge of the lining through all thicknesses. (**FIG. 383**)

To finish the right half of the waistband, trim the waistband strip so that it is even with the edge of the fly shield. Turn the waistband lining down into the slacks and pin in place.

Place the right side of the shield lining against the right side of the fly shield. Press down the top edge of the shield lining until it is slightly below the edge of the waistband. Stitch down around the shield. (**FIG. 384**)

Trim the seam, clip the curve, and press the shield lining to the inside of the slacks. Fold under and pin the straight edge of the shield lining. (**FIG. 385**)

Hold shield lining in place by stitching from the right side; sew on top of the stitching line that joined fly shield to slacks. Start the stitching line at the top edge of the waistband.

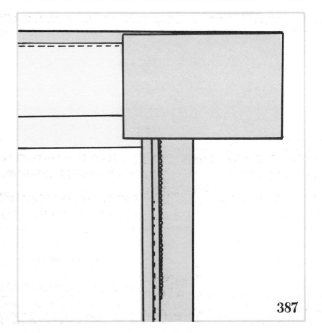

387

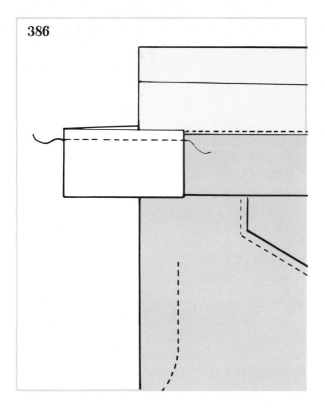

386

To finish the left half of the waistband, pull the lining section out of the way. Fold the excess waistband fabric back on itself, right sides together. Fold it back far enough so that the end of the waistband will be about ½″ beyond the topstitching line of the fly. Stitch along the seamline at the top edges of the waistband. (**FIG. 386**) This forms the tab for the button closure.

Grade the seam allowance, and turn the tab right side out.

Turn the lining down into the slacks, and tuck it behind the unsewn fly section. Fold in the seam allowances at the bottom of the tab extension. (**FIG. 387**) Sew these together by hand.

Continue the fly topstitching up through the waistband. (**FIG. 388**) Tie the threads on the wrong side where the stitching lines join.

To finish the tailored waistband, make two buttonholes in the tab extension. Use pants hooks if you have a straight finish with no tab extension at the waist opening. You will need an extra hook or buttonhole at the end of the right waistband. Adjust the position of hooks or buttons so there is no pulling on the right side.

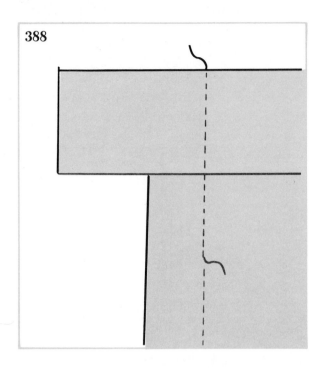

388

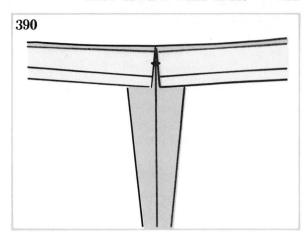

390

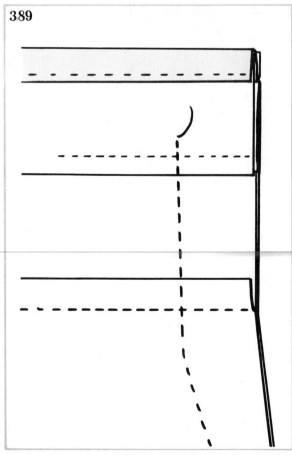

389

The inseam

Pin and sew the two inside leg seams. Press the seam allowances open.

The center back seam

Your slacks pattern allows a 1½″ center back seam. You can use this extra width to adjust the fit at the waist. Baste this seam to check the fit before you do any permanent stitching. Slip one slacks leg inside the other, right sides together. Sew the center back seam from the crotch, up through the waistband; stitch about ½″ into the waistband lining. (**FIG. 389**) Backstitch at the end of this line to make it strong. (Illustrations are for the tailored waistband.)

After you have adjusted the seam and made a final stitching, press the seam allowances open. Fold the waistband lining down into position. Whip the middle of the waistband lining together by hand. (**FIG. 390**) Tack the underside of the waistband to the pocket linings at 3″ intervals all around the waist.

The hems

Zigzag around the bottom of the slacks legs and turn up the hems. Make a knit hem by hand for the best results (see Chapter 3).

Back crease

Press the crease in the back of each leg to finish the slacks.

A. Vest with buttons
B. Vest with no closure

13

How to Sew Vests

A knit vest is a good-looking topper to wear with knit slacks or skirts, and it's a popular style with all ages. The vest can be long or short, with or without buttons and buttonholes; it can be belted or not. (FIG. 391) If you line the vest all the way to the edge, you'll have an attractive garment that goes together quickly. You won't need separate facing pieces and you won't have to use hand work on the hem.

Pick a pattern—cut the fabric

Select a conventional or special pattern for knits. For the vest, you can use a fabric that matches a pair of slacks or a skirt to make a coordinated outfit. For the lining, choose a lightweight knit rather than a woven fabric; this retains the stretch of the vest. Preshrink both vest and lining fabrics, and follow the cutting instructions included with your pattern. Cut the lining pieces exactly the same as the vest pieces.

Use interfacing

The neck and front edges of the vest need some light interfacing. An all-bias, nonwoven product works well in these areas. Cut the interfacing the same shape as the front and neck edges of your pattern, making it about 5″ wide in the front and tapering to 3″ wide around the neck. Pin the interfacing to the wrong side of the vest fabric pieces and stitch it to the seam allowance with a zigzag or straight stitch. Stitch with the interfacing side up to prevent the fabric from stretching.

Do you want pockets?

Some vest patterns have pockets, while others do not. If you use them, set pockets on the vest fronts after you stitch the interfacing in place and before you close any other seams. Make sure you mark the tops of all pocket locations with tailor's tacks; this helps you place the pockets evenly on the vest. Cut pockets so they will match the fabric pattern or grain when they are in position on the vest.

The pocket detail is up to you. Following, you will find some variations on the basic patch pocket.

SELF-LINED PATCH POCKET: Trim away the hem allowance at the top of the pocket pattern and place this new edge on a fold of fabric. The cut-out pocket will look like FIG. 392.

391

392

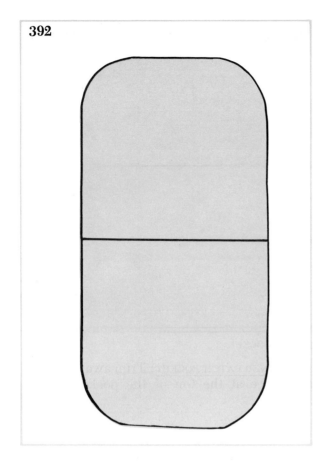

393

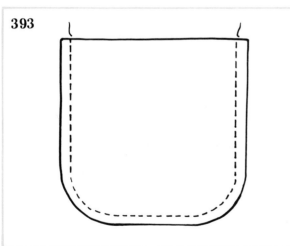

Fold the pocket in half, right sides together. Stitch as indicated. (FIG. 393) Trim the seam and clip the curves.

Cut a 1″ to 1½″ slash through one layer of pocket fabric. (FIG. 394)

394

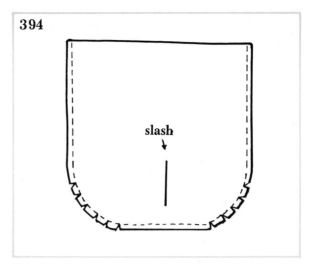

slash

Carefully turn the pocket right side out through the slash. Press the pocket, rolling the seam to the back of the pocket. The slash can be whipped closed or left as is. (Knit fabrics do not ravel.)

Sew the pocket on the vest using one of the following methods:

Method 1: Pin the pocket in place and top-stitch around the pocket ¼″ to ⅜″ from the edge. Backstitch at the top so the pocket will be secure.

Method 2: Topstitch around the pocket before it is pinned to the garment. Then pin the pocket in place, and catch it to the garment by hand. Work from the wrong side of the vest; use small stitches so they will not show on the right side.

INVERTED PLEAT POCKET: Fold the basic patch pocket pattern in half lengthwise. Place it on a folded piece of pattern paper with the folded edge of the pocket 2″ from the folded edge of the pattern paper. Trace around the pocket, extending the lines out to the folded edge. (FIG. 395) Mark along fold of original pocket pattern; this is the pleat line.

Cut out the pocket using this extra wide pattern piece. Mark the pleat line on the wrong side of the fabric. (FIG. 396)

With the pocket folded in half lengthwise, right sides together, stitch along the pleat

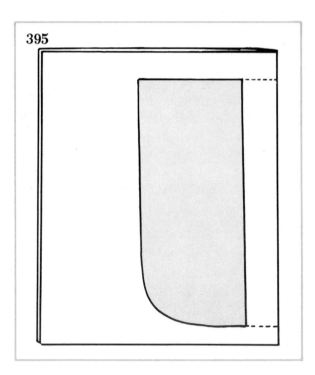

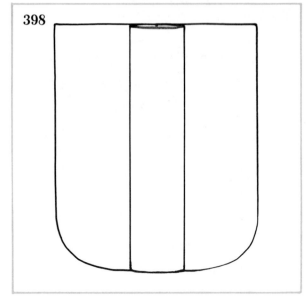

line. Stitch down 2½" from the top and up 1½" from the bottom. (FIG. 397)

Center the pleat on the wrong side, and press it flat. (FIG. 398)

Fold down the top of the pocket 1½" with the right sides together. Sew a ⅝" seam (FIG. 399); trim, turn and press.

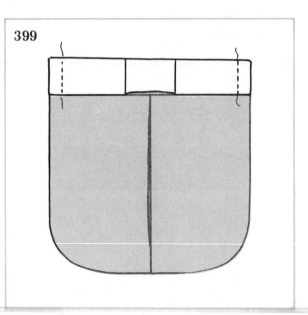

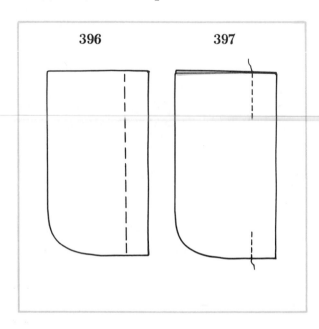

Turn under and baste a ⅝" seam allowance all around the edge of the pocket; press. Position the pocket on the vest and topstitch it in place. (FIG. 400)

SAFARI POCKET: Use the same pattern for a safari pocket as for the inverted pleat pocket. Cut out the pocket but, this time, mark the pleat line on the right side of the pocket.

Stitch along the pleat line down 2½" from the top and up 1½" from the bottom. Center the

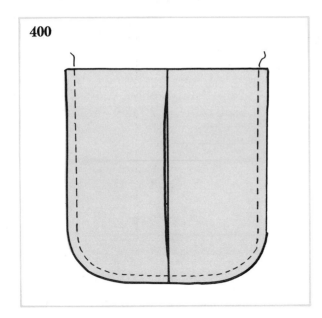

400

Finish this safari pocket according to preceding directions for the inverted pleat pocket.

POCKET FLAPS: You may want to put flaps above the pockets; these are very easy to add. Cut a pocket flap from vest fabric, lining fabric, and a lightweight, press-on interfacing.

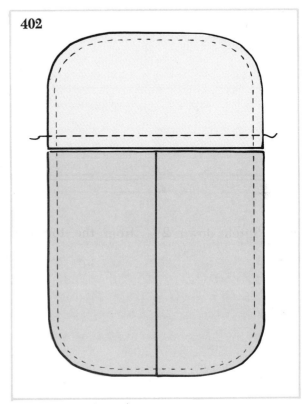

402

pleat and press it flat. The pleat is now on the right side of the pocket.

You can topstitch along both edges of the pleat, if you wish. Pull the edge of the pleat away from the pocket so that the stitching goes through the pleat edge only. (FIG. 401)

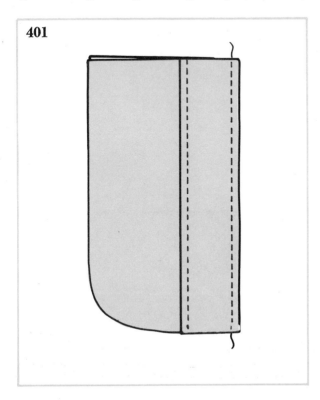

401

Secure the interfacing to the wrong side of the vest fabric. Place the right side of the lining against the right side of the flap and stitch around the curved edge. Trim the seam, clip the curve, and turn. Press the flap carefully from the wrong side and roll the seamline to the back so that it will not show on the right side of the flap. Topstitch around the edge of the flap, if you desire.

Place the right side of the flap against the right side of the vest. Center the flap over the pocket and put the raw edge of the flap against the top of the pocket. Stitch the flap with a ⅝" seam. (FIG. 402) Trim the seam allowance to about ⅜".

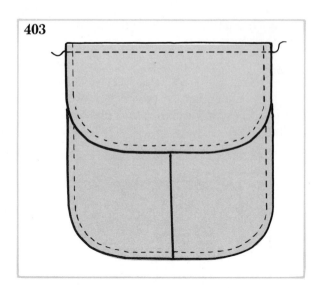

403

Press the flap down into position and top-stitch along the top edge. (FIG. 403) You can sew a button to the center of the flap, if you wish.

Assemble the vest

Sew the center back seams and shoulder seams of both the vest and the lining. Trim the seam allowances if fabric tends to curl; otherwise, press the seam allowances open.

If you want belt loops, it is best to stitch them in place before you line the vest; then the stitching will not show on the inside of the finished vest. To make, see "Belt loops" under "The waistband" in Chapter 12.

Place the right side of the lining against the right side of the vest. Smooth the lining, and pin the two layers together around all the edges except at the side seams. Sew as indi-cated in FIG. 404 with a ⅝" seam allowance. Trim the seams, clip the curves, and turn the vest to the right side. Press the edges so that the seams roll to the lining side.

Now pin one side seam together. Place the right sides of the vest together and the right sides of the lining together. Make sure that the seam in the underarm area and at the bottom of the vest match perfectly. As you pin these edges together, you will find that one side of the vest will slip down inside the

other; you can sew around the side seam in one continuous line.

Pin and sew the other side seam. This cannot be stitched all the way around. Leave an opening in the lining section. Close the opening with hand stitches. Make sure you carefully match the seams in the underarm area and at the bottom of the vest.

When the vest is completely lined, you may want to topstitch around all the edges. You'll find it easier to control the rolled edge if you work with the lining side up.

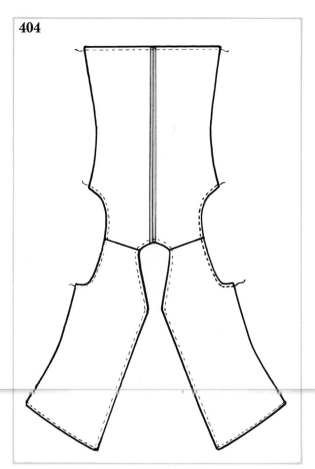

404

Finishing touches

Add buttonholes if you want them. Refer to "Machine buttonholes" in Chapter 8, and work them with lining side up. You can make a self-fabric belt, or buy one ready-made, to wear with the completed vest.

14

More Ways to Style a Man's Sport Shirt

Take the basic pattern for a pullover shirt and adjust it to make two more style variations—a golf shirt with a hidden placket, and the Wallace Beery shirt with placket and neck edge of ribbing. This chapter tells you how to do it. You'll also find some special finishing tips for shirts—making patch pockets, welt pockets and side vents.

GOLF SHIRT WITH HIDDEN PLACKET

Select a lightweight doubleknit or a single knit for this shirt. Many menswear knits are available; so, you should have no trouble finding something masculine. Preshrink the fabric before you cut it.

Use the high neckline (as for a turtleneck) on your pattern. Be sure the neck opening is large enough to fit comfortably around the man's neck. Measure and adjust the pattern if necessary. Trim the neck seam allowance to ¼" if your pattern allows more.

In this chapter, you'll find directions for making and inserting the hidden placket and for attaching the collar. Refer to "Placket with a collar" under "Plackets" in Chapter 7 for directions on cutting and making a collar; refer to "Casual top or shirt" in Chapter 4 for finishing the shirt.

Prepare the placket facing

Cut a lengthwise strip of shirt fabric; make it 3½" wide and twice the length of the opening. Suggested placket length is 9", which would make the placket strip 18" long.

Zigzag along one long side of the facing piece. Press it in half lengthwise, wrong sides together.

Draw the placket line on the wrong side of the shirt. This is 1" to the right of center front, and 9" long from the neck edge. Begin stitch-

ing ⅛" away from the line at the neck edge and taper to the line as you reach the bottom. Make one horizontal stitch at the bottom of the line; stitch up the other side, ending ⅛" to the side of the line. (FIG. 405) Slash the shirt front between the stitched lines, down to the bottom thread.

Spread the slash apart so that it almost forms a straight line. (FIG. 406)

Pin the right side of the facing strip against the right side of the shirt, with the edges of

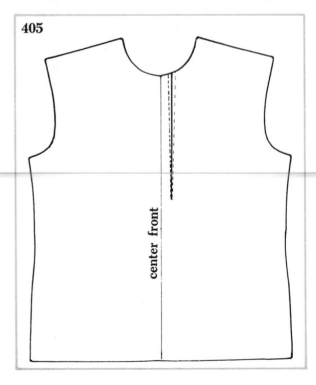

405

center front

406

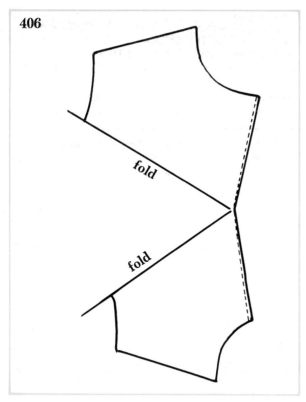

fold

fold

408

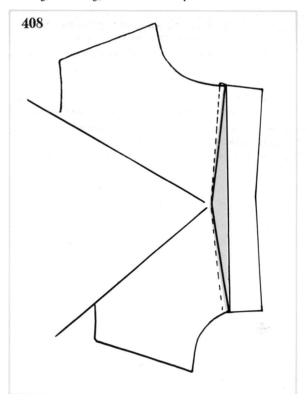

407

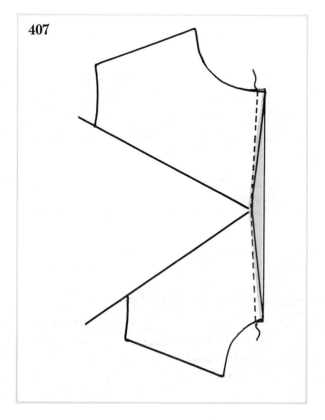

409

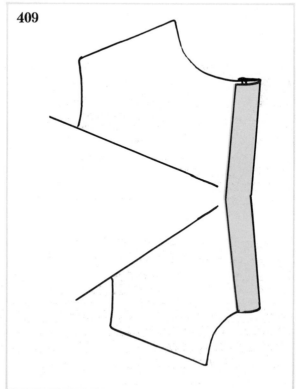

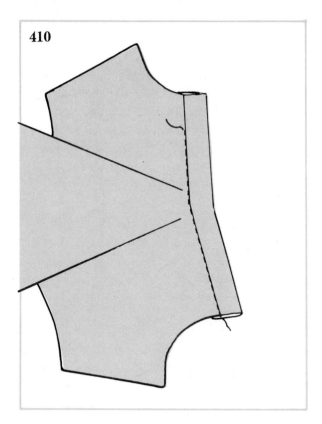

410

Divide the shirt neck edge into four equal sections, beginning and ending at center front. (**FIG. 411**) Remember that the center front is not on a seamline. As you look at the shirt front (right side out), center front is ¾″ to the right of the placket seamline on each side of the opening.

Pin the collar to the neck edge and stitch with a ¼″ seam. Do not catch the placket facings in this stitching. (**FIGS. 412 and 413**) You

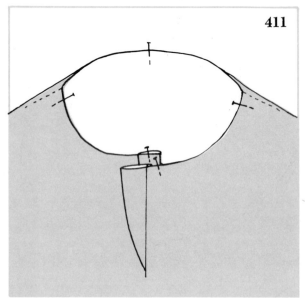

411

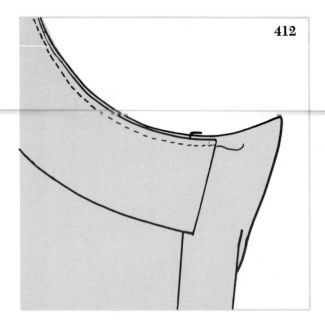

412

slash and facing even. The point of the slash will be about ¼″ away from the edge of the facing. Stitch down your original stitching line (**FIG. 407**); be careful not to form a tuck in the shirt fabric at the point of the slash.

Press the facing strip away from the shirt, and press the seam into the facing. (**FIG. 408**)

Fold the facing to the inside of the shirt. Pin it in place so that ¼″ extends beyond the stitched seamline. (**FIG. 409**)

Work from the right side, and catch the facing in place by stitching in the seam groove. Begin stitching on the right half of the shirt, 2″ below the neck edge. (**FIG. 410**) You'll close this 2″ later, after you apply the collar. Press the placket.

Apply the collar

Refer to Chapter 7 for cutting and preparing the collar. Divide finished collar into four equal sections at the neck edge; mark with pins.

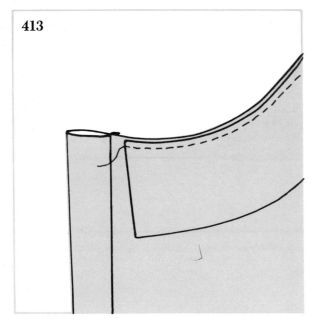

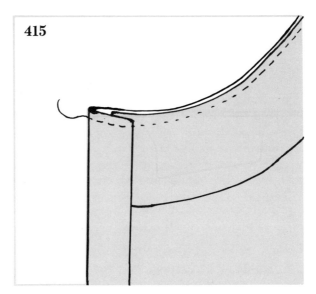

back—out of sight—on the left half of the shirt.)

To catch down the loose edge of the facing on the right shirt half, stitch in the placket seam groove from the right side. (FIG. 416)

Press the neck seam allowances down into the shirt; topstitch around the back, ⅛″ below the seamline, to hold seam allowances in place. Finish the placket with buttons and machine buttonholes (FIG. 417); refer to Chapter 8.

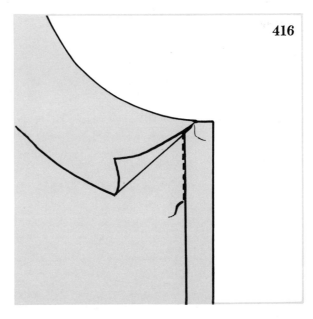

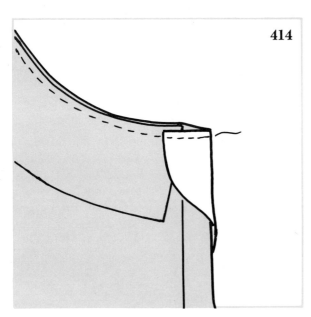

left 2″ of the placket open on the right half of the shirt; pull it out of the way as you stitch the collar in place.

Fold the facings back over the collar and complete the stitching lines, as illustrated in FIGS. 414 and 415.

Trim the seams, and turn the facings back to their finished position. (Facing will extend out on right half of shirt; facing will fold

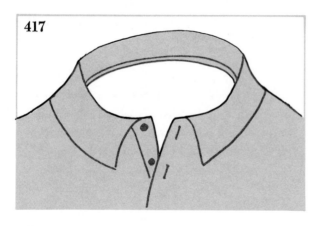

417

Complete sleeves, side seams and hem; refer to Chapter 4.

THE WALLACE BEERY SHIRT

This pullover shirt has a placket and neck edge of ribbing. Use a basic shirt pattern and follow the line for either a crew neck or turtleneck. Trim the neck seam allowance to ¼″ if it is wider. This shirt looks nice in lightweight doubleknit or single knit fabrics. You will need ¼ yard of matching or contrasting ribbing for the placket facings and the neck edge. Preshrink the fabric, but not the ribbing.

Stitch the shirt shoulder seams together and press. Divide the neck edge into four equal

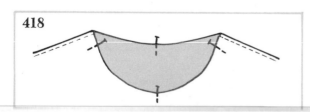

418

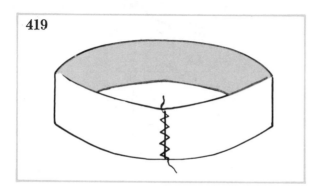

419

sections. (FIG. 418) Place pins at the center back and center front; bring these two pins together, and place pins in the folds that appear in the shoulder area. (The shoulder seams should not be one of your division marks.)

Cut a strip of ribbing that is 3″ wide and 1″ less in length than the man's neck circumference. Butt the two short ends together (ends touch, but do not overlap); zigzag over the edges, or whip them together by hand. (FIG. 419)

Fold the ribbing in half lengthwise, wrong sides together. Divide this circle of ribbing into four equal sections. Place one of the pins at the seam. (FIG. 420)

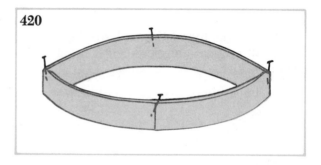

420

Have the shirt wrong side out. Pin the ribbing to the right side of the neck edge, cut edges together. Place the ribbing seam at the center front of the shirt, then match the other pins. Stitch around the neck edge with a ¼″ seam allowance, and press the seam allowance down into the shirt.

Turn the shirt to the right side, and press an 8″ crease down the center front.

Prepare the placket facings

Cut the two strips of ribbing that are 3″ by 9″. The grain of the ribbing should run the length of these two strips.

Fold each strip lengthwise, right sides together, and stitch across one end with a ¼″ seam. (FIG. 421) Strip will be 9″ by 1½″.

Turn the strip to the right side and press. Cut two strips of press-on bonding material

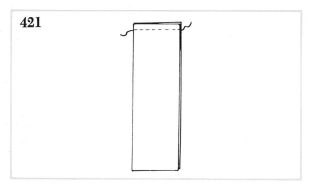

to the placket size, and slip them inside the prepared placket strips. Press with a steam iron to fuse the ribbing layers together.

Apply the placket facings

Place one facing strip on the right side of the shirt. Position it so the top of the strip is even with the top of the neck ribbing, and the long cut edge is along the center front crease. (**FIG. 422**)

Stitch the facing strip to the shirt with a ½" seam allowance. Begin the stitching line at the top and end it 1" above the bottom of the strip. (**FIG. 423**) Backstitch at this point.

Place the other strip on the shirt front, and butt the cut edge against the first strip. Sew

this strip just as you did the first (**FIG. 424**); backstitch at the end of the stitching line.

Turn the shirt to the wrong side, and cut a slash down the crease of the shirt. Stop the slash 1" above the end of the stitching line; then cut into the corners, forming a large wedge. (**FIG. 425**) Do not cut the placket facings.

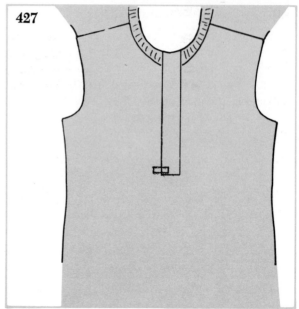

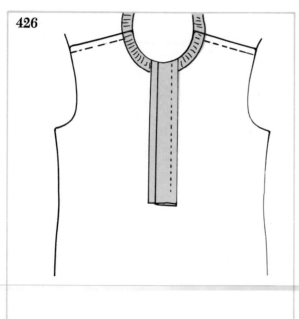

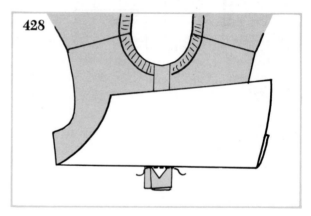

meets the seamline of the bottom piece. Secure this area with transparent tape or hand stitches (**FIG. 427**); this holds placket in place for the final stitching.

Lift the bottom of the shirt until you see the wedge on top of the two placket pieces. Carefully stitch across the base of the wedge through all layers (**FIG. 428**); trim to ¼".

Trim the placket seam allowances to ¼" and do a zigzag stitch along the edges.

Finish the placket with buttons and machine buttonholes (refer to Chapter 8).

Complete sleeves, side seams and hems (see Chapter 4).

Pull both placket strips to the wrong side of the shirt, and press them so that the seam allowances go out into the shirt. (**FIG. 426**)

Turn the shirt to the right side. Placket facings should lap left over right for a man's shirt. Tuck the wedge down into the opening at the bottom of the placket. Position the placket so the folded edge of the top piece

SHIRT FINISHING TIPS

There are many ways to add individual touches to a man's shirt. Use the suggestions here for a patch pocket, welt pocket or side vents. Refer to Chapters 4 and 8 for other finishing ideas.

Patch pocket

Follow the diagram for cutting a shirt pocket. (**FIG.** 429) Try to match the pocket section to the shirt fabric when you are cutting a striped or patterned fabric.

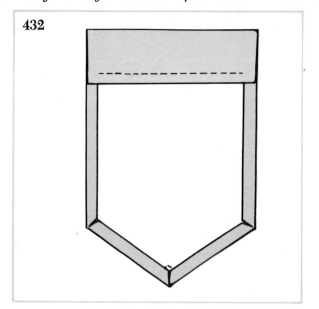

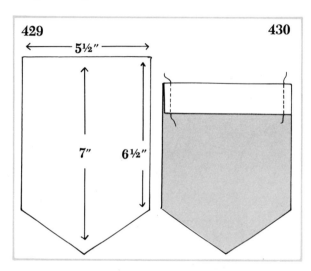

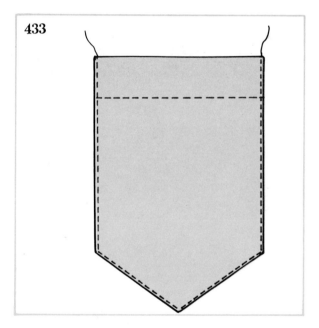

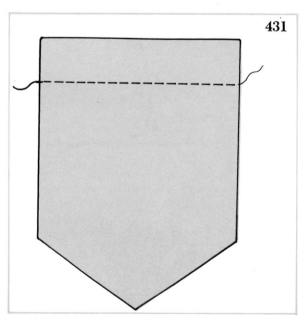

Fold down the top edge 1½", right sides together. Stitch along the edges as indicated in **FIG.** 430; use a ½" seam.

Trim, turn, and press. Topstitch along the top edge of the pocket 1" below the fold. (**FIG.** 431)

Turn the pocket to the wrong side; turn and press a ½" seam allowance along the remaining edges. (**FIG.** 432)

Pin the pocket in place on the shirt. Stitch along the pocket edge. (FIG. 433) Backstitch at the top to reinforce the corners.

Welt pocket

This welt pocket is quite easy to do and looks beautiful on a man's shirt. It is similar to the welt pocket used on slacks, and a variation of it can be used on sweaters.

Mark the pocket location on the shirt. The opening should be at least 4½″ wide. For the pocket, cut a strip of shirt fabric on the lengthwise grain; it should measure 2″ wider than the pocket opening and 10″ long. Cut a strip of stay fabric that measures 3″ by 7″.

To make the pocket, refer to "Make the welt pocket" under "Sweaters from alpaca" in Chapter 10. Enlarge the diagram, FIG. 228, to use as a pattern (you can alter the pocket width to 4½″ if you wish). Trace the enlarged diagram onto the stay fabric. Complete the pocket, following directions in Chapter 10.

Shirt with side vents

You must decide on vents before you cut the shirt fabric. Add an extra 1″ width to the lower 5″ of side seams, both front and back. (FIG. 434)

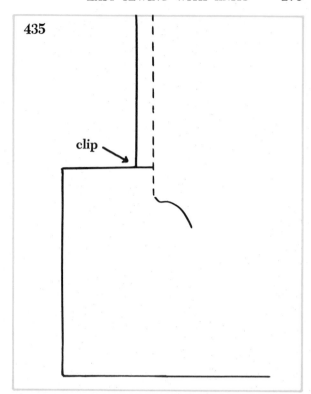

435

clip

434

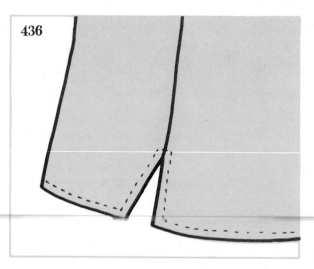

436

Leave the bottom 4″ open as you sew each side seam. (FIG. 435) Backstitch at the opening so that the seam is secure. Clip into the seam allowance at the top of the vent and press vent open.

Turn up the hem and secure it by topstitching. Continue the topstitching up around the vent. (FIG. 436)

A. Dress with princess lines
B. A-line skirt with pleats; top with yolk
Jacket with over-edge trim

15

How to Design Your Own Patterns

Designing patterns is not so difficult or complicated as you might think. Begin with a basic pattern that fits well, then learn a few design rules so that you can change the basic style. Soon you will be able to create new dress and suit styles without buying special patterns for them.

This chapter gives you guides for changing style lines on a top or dress pattern. It also shows you how to make patterns for a multiple-gore skirt, an A-line skirt and an A-line skirt with pleats.

NEW STYLE LINES FOR TOPS OR DRESSES

Start with a basic top or dress pattern that has an underarm dart. Then, create new style lines by shifting the dart. For instance, you can make a yoke, which is one of the easiest style changes. Or, you can change the dart into a princess line, an armhole dart or a French dart.

You must work from a basic pattern that has the underarm dart correctly located for your figure. (See directions for checking and correcting in "Bust dart location" under "Fit and ease guide," Chapter 2.) If the basic dart is not right for you, the new pattern will not fit properly.

Directions for making simple dart changes are given here. You will understand the principles more clearly if you work them out, step by step, with a pattern.

Designer's dart

In pattern design, you must work with a designer's dart. This is a long dart that goes all the way to the high point of the bust. In contrast, the dart you stitch in a garment usually ends 1″ or more short of the high point of the bust; this is called a dressmaker's dart.

Since your basic pattern usually has a dressmaker's dart, you must change it to the long designer's dart.

First, locate the high point of your bust on the paper pattern. (See "Bust dart location" under "Fit and ease guide," Chapter 2.)

Then, draw a long designer's dart, connecting the high point mark with the original dart lines at the side seam.

All style changes you find in this chapter involve closing this designer's dart and moving the dart opening to a new location. This is explained in detail under "The yoke," which follows.

The yoke

1. Draw the new style line. For this yoke, the new line goes straight across the pattern, through the high point of the bust. (FIG. 437)

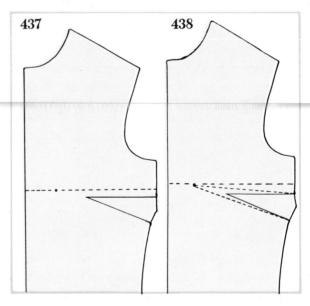

437   438

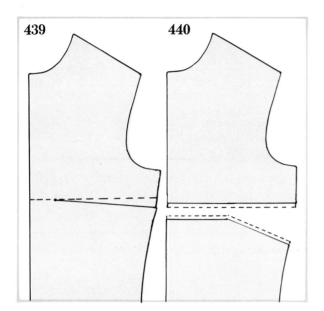

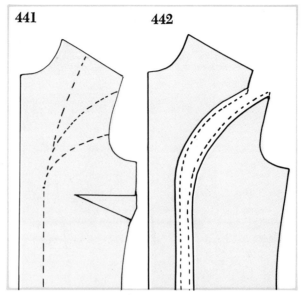

2. Change the dressmaker's dart into a designer's dart as shown in **FIG. 438.** (See preceding directions under "Designer's dart.")

3. Remove (or close) the designer's dart. Do this by cutting along the lower line of the designer's dart (from side seam to high point of bust). Overlap the pattern by moving the cut edge of the dart up to the top line of the designer's dart. (**FIG. 439**) Tape pattern in place. The pattern should have a bulge in it, just as fabric does when you stitch in a dart.

4. Cut along the new style line. The bulge will disappear as you cut, and the pattern will lie flat again. The dart is now part of the new style line.

5. Add ⅝″ seam allowances to the cut edges. (**FIG. 440**) The style line you cut becomes the new stitching line. When these two sections are sewn together, a bulge will appear again in the bust area.

Princess line

1. Draw the new style line (several variations are illustrated in **FIG. 441**). Take the new line through the high point of the bust.

2. Change the dressmaker's dart to a designer's dart. (See directions under "Designer's dart.")

3. Remove the designer's dart. (See directions under "The yoke.")

4. Cut along the new style line.

5. Add ⅝″ seam allowances to the cut edges. (**FIG. 442**)

Princess line with a dart

1. Draw the new style line. This line will be 1″ to 1½″ short of the high point of the bust. (**FIG. 443**)

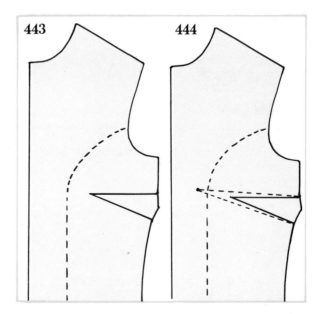

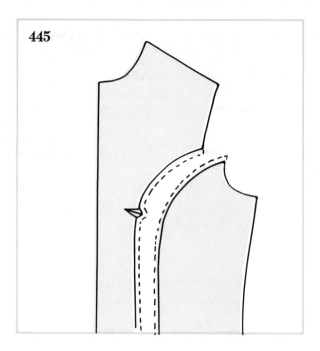

445

3. Remove the designer's dart. (See directions under "The yoke.")

4. Cut along the new style line. Smooth the pattern to make it flat—this creates a new dart.

5. Tape a piece of pattern paper under the new dart opening; leave some paper extending beyond the edge of the pattern piece.

6. Measure across the open end of the dart and mark the halfway point. Draw a line from

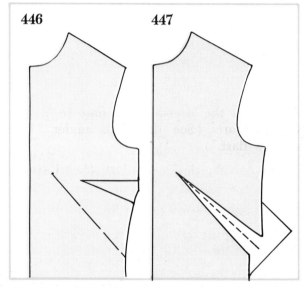

446   **447**

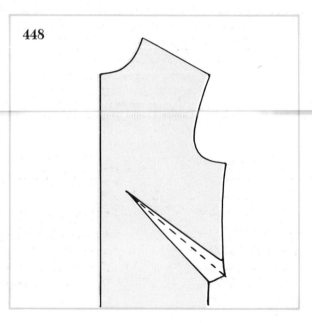

448

2. Change the dressmaker's dart to a designer's dart as shown in **FIG. 444**. (See directions under "Designer's dart.")

3. Remove the designer's dart. (See directions under "The yoke.")

4. Cut along the new style line.

5. You will have a small section of closed dart on the center front pattern piece. Remove the tape and open the dart. This dart will be stitched in the fabric before the princess line is sewn.

6. Add ⅝" seam allowances to the cut edges. (**FIG. 445**)

French dart

A French dart is flattering, but it does not work well in a striped fabric. The offset of the stripes is quite noticeable on this long dart line.

1. Draw the new style line. It goes from the waist or hip to the high point of the bust. (**FIG. 446**)

2. Change the dressmaker's dart to a designer's dart. (See directions under "Designer's dart.")

that point to the high point of the bust. (**FIG. 447**) This is the fold line of the French dart; the cut edges are the stitching lines. A French dart is sewn all the way to the high point of the bust.

7. Fold the dart into a closed position, as it will be when stitched in the garment. Folded edge should be down, against the lower part of the pattern. Trim off excess paper along the pattern edge. Open the dart, and you have the proper shape at the end of the dart. (**FIG. 448**)

Armhole dart

1. Draw the new style line. This begins about the middle of the armhole and extends to the high point of the bust. (**FIG. 449**)

2. Change the dressmaker's dart to a designer's dart. (See directions under "Designer's dart.")

3. Remove the designer's dart. (See instructions under "The yoke.")

4. Cut along the new style line.

5. Tape a piece of pattern paper under the dart opening; leave some paper extending beyond the edge of the pattern piece.

6. Measure across the open end of the dart and mark the halfway point. Draw a line

451

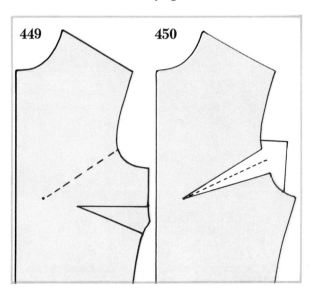

449   450

from that point to the high point of the bust. (**FIG. 450**) This is the fold line of the dart; the cut edges are the stitching lines. The armhole dart is sewn to within about 1″ of the high point of the bust. Draw the new stitching line on the pattern.

7. Fold the dart into a closed position, as it will be when stitched in the garment. Folded edge should be down, against lower part of the pattern. Trim off excess paper along the pattern edge. Open the dart, and you have the proper shape at the end of the dart. (**FIG. 451**)

DRAFTING SKIRT PATTERNS

Three styles that are popular in knits are the multiple-gore skirt, the A-line and the A-line with pleats. You can buy patterns for these styles; or you can make your own patterns, following the directions in this section.

Multiple-gore skirt

This style works up well in doubleknits. (**FIG. 452**) You can wear it with knit tops or as a suit skirt; it also makes an attractive skirt for a child.

MAKE YOUR OWN PATTERN: All gores in the skirt are alike; so, you will have to measure

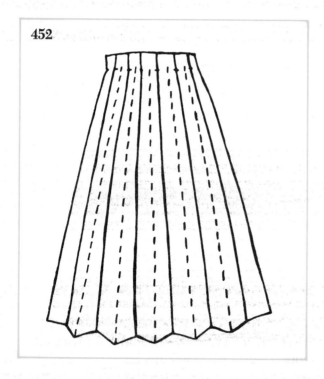

452

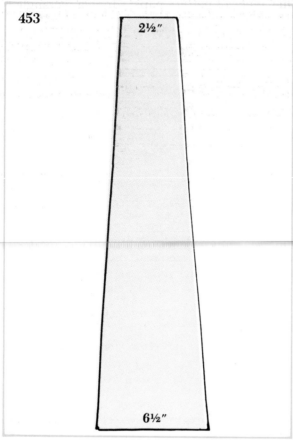

453

2½"

6½"

only one gore for your pattern. The number of gores depends on your waist measurement.

The width of the gore will be 2½" at the top and 6½" at the bottom. (FIG. 453) You can change the bottom width to 4½" for a child.

The length of the gore is determined by the finished length of the skirt, plus 3½" (for the hem and the fold-over waistband). Measure carefully, because you determine the final length of the skirt at this point.

Determine the number of gores you need by dividing the waist measure in half, then adding one extra gore. For example: A 26" waist divided in half is 13. Add one gore for a total of 14 gores. (If half the waist measure ends in a fraction, such as 13¾, use the nearest whole number, 14. Then add the extra gore for a total of 15 gores.)

You need two skirt lengths of 62" fabric for the skirt. This allows you to cut the pattern with all the gores running in the same direction and thus avoid any color change at the seamline.

ASSEMBLE THE SKIRT: Fold each gore in half lengthwise, wrong sides together, and press a crease along the fold.

Stitch the gores together, using ¼" seam allowances. These seams do not have to be double stitched; do not press them open.

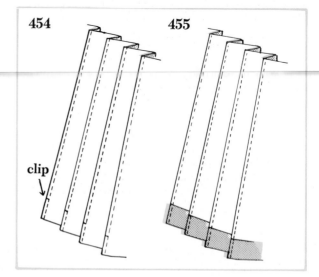

454   455

clip

Measure 4″ up from the skirt bottom and clip to the stitching line on all seams. (FIG. 454) The bottom 4″ of each seam should be pressed open; this is the hem section.

Fold a 2″ hem in place, and pin at the seamlines. Next, fold the skirt back on the seamlines with the right sides together. Stitch a welt along each seamline, through the hem area only. (FIG. 455) Make this a narrow welt, and taper the stitching line into the original seam at the top of the hem. This stitching keeps the inside folds of the skirt sharp.

Turn the skirt to the right side. Fold each gore along the crease that you pressed in. Stitch along the crease from top to bottom, keeping as close to the edge as you can. (FIG. 456) Make sure you catch the back of the hem in these seamlines when you reach the hem area.

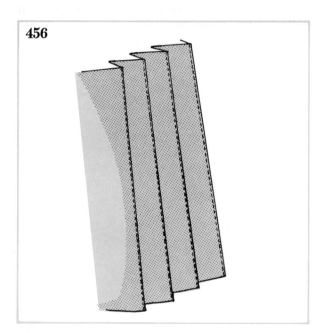

456

Turn the skirt to the wrong side. You will see that the hem is caught in the stitched creases about every 2″. This is all the hemming needed for this skirt unless you want to catch down the remainder by hand. It is best to close the hem completely on white or light-colored skirts; this prevents dark lint from

accumulating in the hem crease when you wash the skirt.

FINISH THE WAIST: Refer to "Finish the fold-over waistband" under "Simple knit pants" in Chapter 5 for directions on applying elastic and completing the waistband.

NOTE: The waist area will be less bulky if you measure down from the top edge about 1¾″ and clip to the stitching line. Press seam allowances open in that small section, just as you did for the hem.

A-line skirt

This style of skirt looks best when made from a doubleknit; the fabric has enough body to keep the A-shape. You can flare the pattern as much as you want.

MAKE YOUR OWN PATTERN: Draft one pattern piece, then use it for both front and back sections.

On a piece of pattern paper, draw a rectangle. To determine the width, take your waist measurement, add 4″ and divide the total by four. Find the rectangle length by adding 2⅝″ to the length of the finished skirt. See explanation below.

To determine pattern *width*, take your actual waist measurement. Then add 2″ for ease and 2″ for side seam allowances (four seam edges, ½″ each).

Example:	Waist measurement	26″
	Seam allowances, add	2″
	Ease, add	2″
	Total skirt width	30″

Divide this total by four; use the result to draw the width of the rectangle.

To determine pattern *length*, take the finished length of the skirt. Then, add 2″ for hem and ⅝″ for a seam allowance at the waist edge.

Example:	Finished skirt length	20″
	Hem, add	2″
	Seam allowance, add	⅝″
	Total length	22⅝″

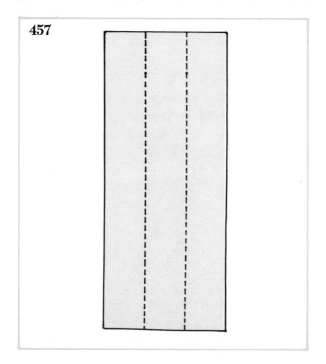

457

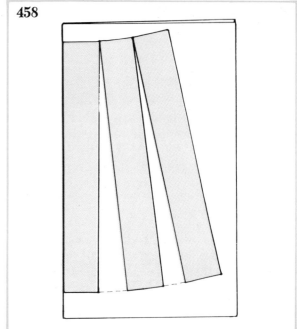

458

Use this total as the length of the rectangle; this is for a skirt with a separate waistband.

NOTE: If you want to make a fold-over waistband with elastic, add 1½″ (instead of ⅝″) at the waist edge.

After you have completed the rectangle, divide the width into three equal sections. Draw these division lines the length of the rectangle; your skirt pattern should look like **FIG. 457.**

Slash the pattern on the lengthwise lines up to, but not through, the top edge.

Place the slashed pattern on another folded piece of paper, with one edge directly over the fold. Spread the strips apart until you have the desired flare. An average A-line skirt is about 45″ around the bottom. You should have 1″ to 2″ of ease across the hipline of your skirt; flare the pattern until you achieve this ease.

Draw around the outside edge of the slashed pattern, making a new pattern piece. (**FIG. 458**) Notice that the waist and bottom edge are now curved lines. This is correct for an A-line skirt.

CUT AND ASSEMBLE THE SKIRT: Cut the fabric, and stitch the side seams. Refer to "The string fit" under "Simple knit skirt" in Chapter 6 to check side seams and waistline curve.

If you designed the pattern for a separate waistband, refer to "Apply the closed waistband" under "Skirt with separate waistband" in Chapter 6.

If you designed the pattern for a fold-over waistband, refer to "Finish the fold-over waistband" under "Simple knit pants" in Chapter 5.

Finish the skirt with a knit hem (see Chapter 3).

A-line skirt with pleats

This is a graceful, attractive skirt that adapts well to doubleknits. However, because of the wide flare, it does not work well with a striped or regularly patterned fabric.

ADJUST THE PATTERN: Work with the basic A-line pattern discussed in the preceding section. Divide the pattern piece into thirds at the top and bottom edges; do not include the seam allowance when you make these di-

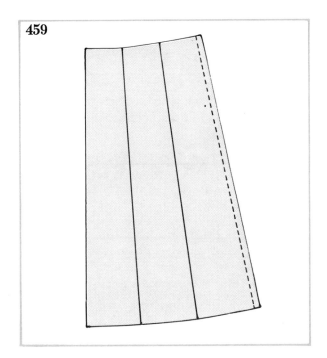

459

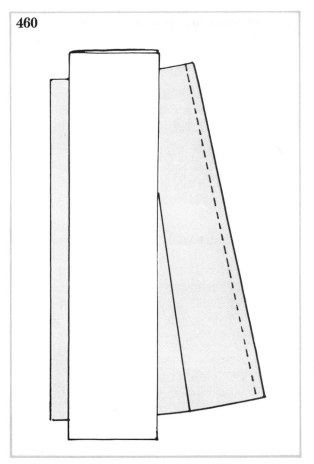

460

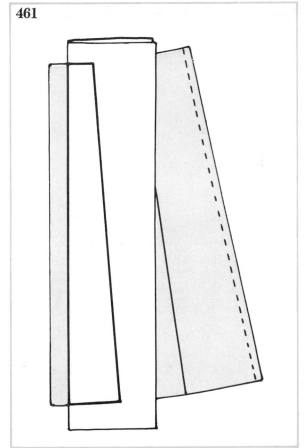

461

visions. (**FIG. 459**) Draw lines connecting the top and bottom divisions; these lines indicate pleat locations.

Since the skirt has flare at the bottom, the pleats also must flare. Fold a piece of pattern paper in half; lay it on top of the skirt pattern, with the folded edge 1″ away from the center front line. (**FIG. 460**)

On this folded paper, trace the top and bottom edge of the skirt pattern. Also, trace along the first pleat line. (**FIG. 461**) Cut along the traced lines; this gives a pleat pattern. Make another pleat pattern exactly the same way.

To insert these pleat patterns, cut apart the skirt pattern, slashing along the pleat lines. Position the pleat patterns by lining up the top and bottom of the skirt with the top and bottom of each pleat section. Butt the cut

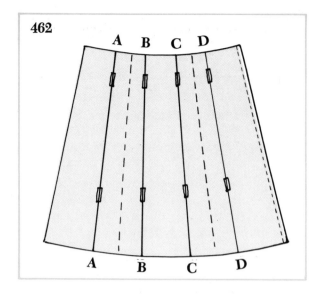

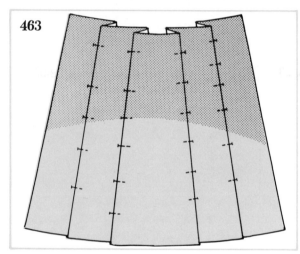

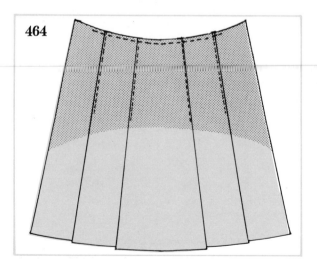

edges together (edges will meet, but not overlap). Tape securely in place; mark fold lines for pleats. (FIG. 462)

CUT THE FABRIC: Use the completed pattern to cut a skirt back and a skirt front. Place the pattern on a fold each time; cut two identical fabric pieces.

You will need two skirt lengths, plus ⅓ yard to cut the skirt; this yardage is for any fabric at least 52″ wide. Remember to allow extra inches for shrinkage (see Chapter 1).

ASSEMBLE THE SKIRT: Mark the top and bottom of the skirt fabric pieces at lines A, B, C and D, as shown in FIG. 462. You can use a small clip, a notch or tailor's chalk.

Form the pleats before you stitch the side seams. Fold line A over to meet line B; pin in place. Fold line C over to meet line D; pin in place.

Fold and pin pleats on the opposite side of this skirt piece. (FIG. 463) Use the same procedure to arrange pleats on the other skirt section.

On the right side of the skirt, topstitch along the edge of each pleat. Start at the waist edge and stitch down for about 6″.

Press the pleats with a moist press cloth, then stitch across the top of each pleat ¼″ down from the waist edge. (FIG. 464) This will hold the pleats in place as you apply the waistband.

Sew the side seams, and press them open. Try on the skirt. Refer to "The string fit" under "Simple knit skirt" in Chapter 6. You may need to trim the waist at the center front and center back to give a smooth fit. Also, check the side seams to be sure they are perpendicular to the floor.

Cut and apply a separate waistband; see "Apply the closed waistband" under "Skirt with separate waistband" in Chapter 6 on skirts.

Finish the skirt with a knit hem (see Chapter 3).

Index